THE SIDE AND BACK PANEL COOKBOOK

THE SIDE AND BACK PANEL COOKBOOK

RECIPES FROM THE BOXES, PACKAGES, CANS, AND BOTTLES OF YOUR FAVORITE FOODS

EDITED BY

CRAIG T. NORBACK

A DELL/NORBACK TRADE PAPERBACK

Managing Editor: Roy Winnick
Research Director: Leslie R. Goldwater
Research Editor: Sarah W. Masters
Editor: Roy A. Grisham

Cover design by Moonlight

Note: Variations in style, usage, and spelling from one recipe to another reflect manufacturers' preferences. Abbreviations and format have generally been standardized throughout.

A DELL/NORBACK BOOK
Published by
Dell Publishing Co., Inc.
1 Dag Hammarskjold Plaza
New York, New York 10017

ISBN: 0-440-57846-9

Printed in the United States of America
First printing — June 1981

Contents

Acknowledgments

We wish to express our gratitude to the following organizations for granting permission to publish the recipes and artwork that appear in *The Side and Back Panel Cookbook:*

Almadén Vineyards
American Kitchen Products Inc.
Amstar Corporation, American Sugar Division
Anderson Clayton Foods
Anheuser-Busch, Inc.
Argo Corn Starch
Arm & Hammer Division, Church & Dwight Co., Inc.
Armour and Company
Arnold Bakers, Inc./Oroweat Foods Company
Berio Importing Corp.
Best Foods, a unit of CPC North America
Booth Fisheries Corporation
Borden Kitchens
Bordo Products Company
Buitoni Foods Corp.
Calavo Growers of California
California Almond Growers Exchange
California Avocado Commission
California Dried Fig Advisory Board
Campbell Soup Company
Canada Dry Corporation
Carnation Company
Castle & Cooke Foods (Bumble Bee® and Dole®)
Celestial Seasonings Herb Teas
The Christian Brothers of Napa Valley
D. L. Clark Company, a division of Beatrice Foods
Coca-Cola Company Foods Division
Colombo, Inc.
Colonna Brothers
Comstock Foods, a division of Curtice-Burns, Inc.
The Creamette Company
Crush International Inc.
The Dannon Company
Del Monte Kitchens, Del Monte Corporation
Diamond Walnut Growers, Inc.
Dorman Cheese Co.
Doxsee Kitchens
Duffy-Mott Company, Inc.
Durkee Famous Foods, a division of SCM Corporation
Durkee-Mower, Inc.
Elam's
Faygo Beverages Inc.
Fisher Cheese, an Amfac Company
Food and Beverage Products Group of Del Monte Corporation
R. T. French Company
Friendship Food Products, Inc.
Frito-Lay, Inc.
E. & J. Gallo Winery
The Jos. Garneau Co.
Gebhardt Mexican Foods
General Foods Corp.
General Mills, Inc.
Gerber Products Company
Gold Pure Food Products
Golden Grain Macaroni Co.
Gorton's of Gloucester
The Green Giant Company
L. S. Heath & Sons, Inc.
Heinz U.S.A., a division of H. J. Heinz Company
Hellmann's Real Mayonnaise
Hershey Foods Corporation
Heublein Grocery Products Group
Heublein Spirits Group
Hiram Walker Incorporated
H. & J. Foods

Holland House Brands Co.
Geo. A. Hormel & Co.
Hulman & Company
Hunt-Wesson Foods, Inc.
IGA, Inc.
International Co-Op (Okray's)
Jack Frost Sugar
Johnston's Ready-Crust Company
Jolly Time Pop Corn
Karo Corn Syrup
Keebler Company
Kellogg Company
Kikkoman International Inc.
King Oscar Sardines
Knouse Foods
Knox Gelatine, Inc.
Kraft, Inc.
Kretschmer Wheat Germ, a product of International Multifoods
La Choy Food Products
Land O'Lakes Kitchens
V. La Rosa & Sons, Inc.
The Larsen Company
Lawry's Foods, Inc.
Lea & Perrins, Inc.
Lever Brothers Company
Libby's
Lindsay International, Inc.
Lipton Kitchens
Luzianne Blue Plate Foods
The Maillard Corporation
Marion-Kay Co., Inc.
Mazola Corn Oil
McCormick & Company, Inc.
McIlhenny Company
MCP Foods, Inc.
Medaglia d'Oro, S.A. Schonbrunn & Co., Inc.
Miller Brewing Company
M&M/Mars
Mogen David Wine Corporation
Mrs. Cubbison's Foods, Inc.
Mrs. Smith's Frozen Foods Co.
C. F. Mueller Company
Nabisco, Inc.
The Nestlé Company, Inc.
No-Cal, Inc.
Ocean Spray Cranberries, Inc.
Oconomowoc Canning Co.
Ore-Ida
Oscar Mayer & Co.
Ovaltine Products, Inc.
Pacific Pearl Seafoods
Pepperidge Farm, Inc.
Pet, an IC Industries Company
The Pillsbury Company
Pompeian Olive Oil
Premier Malt Products
The Prince Company, Inc.
Princeton Farms
Procter & Gamble Company
Progresso Quality Foods
The Pure Food Company, Inc.
The Quaker Oats Company
Ragú Foods, Inc.
Ralston Purina Company
Rath Packing Company
Rich-SeaPak Corporation
Riviana Foods Inc.
Robinson Canning Co., Inc.
I. Rokeach & Sons, Inc.
Roman Meal Company
Ronzoni Macaroni Co., Inc.
San Giorgio-Skinner, Inc.
Sanna Division, Beatrice Foods Company
Jos. Schlitz Brewing Co.
Shasta Beverages Inc.
Skippy Peanut Butter
The J. M. Smucker Company
A. E. Staley Manufacturing Company, Consumer Products Group
Standard Brands Incorporated
Standard Milling Company
Stokely-Van Camp, Inc.
Sunkist Growers, Inc.
Sun-Maid Growers of California
Swift & Company
Taylor Wine Company, Inc.
S. B. Thomas, Inc.
Tootsie Roll Industries, Inc.
Uncle Ben's Foods
Wm. Underwood Co.
Universal Foods Corporation
Van Camp Sea Food Company, a division of Ralston Purina Company
Ventre Packing Company, Inc.
Welch Foods, Inc.
Widmer's Wine Cellars, Inc.
Wilderness Foods

We would also like to thank the following people for their help in researching, compiling, editing, and producing *The Side and Back Panel Cookbook:* Betty J. Junna, Dena Rogin, Margaret E. Masters, Claire Bien, Evie Righter, and Robert M. Faustini.

Introduction

The Side and Back Panel Cookbook is an exciting new cookbook that is both practical and fun to use. It is filled with the recipes that are found on your favorite cereal boxes, vegetable or soup cans, bottles, brochures, bread wrappers, sugar and flour packages, and anywhere else a manufacturer's recipes are likely to appear. These are the recipes—many of them classics, some of them brand new—that you clip and tuck away in your kitchen drawer for that special occasion when you want to prepare something different and delicious. Unfortunately, the recipes sometimes get misplaced, or worn out—or, more likely, you simply forget to clip and save them when the box, can, bottle, or package is empty.

With the help of participating companies—and they were very helpful indeed—we have tried to include the most popular and the most interesting recipes available, past and present, in *The Side and Back Panel Cookbook.* Here you will find dozens of delectable recipes for every taste, from the simplest to the most sophisticated. Never again will you be at a loss for that terrific name-brand recipe you meant to save.

The Side and Back Panel Cookbook includes well over 500 recipes from more than 160 major food manufacturers. The recipes are arranged within the following categories: appetizers, soups and sandwiches, salads, breads, main dishes (including meats, poultry, seafood, and eggs and cheese), pasta, side dishes (including vegetables, and rice and others), sauces, beverages and desserts (including pies and pastries, cakes and frostings, custards, cookies, and candies). The book has been designed to stay open so that you can read it while you prepare meals, and the large type allows you to read at a distance. There are product logos or package illustrations on nearly every page for easy product recognition, and the easy-to-use index at the back of the book lets you find the recipe you want either by product name, recipe name, or type of food. Easy to read, easy and fun to use. brimming with hundreds of recipes to suit every palate, *The Side and Back Panel Cookbook* is a must for every kitchen library.

Appetizers

Hors d'oeuvres, snacks, canapés, munchies—whatever you call them, the little extras that begin a party can go a long way toward making an ordinary gathering into a very special event.

The most tempting appetizers are not necessarily the most expensive, the highest in calories, or the hardest to prepare. In fact, the ingredients for many festive party foods are probably already in your kitchen cabinet. For example, breakfast cereals can be transformed into savory snacks, prepared soups can be used to spice up dips, and canned vegetables can be featured as marinated hors d'oeuvres.

All that is needed to turn ordinary foods into extraordinary appetizers is a little imagination and a little help from the recipe suggestions in this chapter. Traditional favorites are now made easy by the use of prepared foods and food manufacturers' suggested shortcuts. Some of the classic combinations are almost unbeatable: spicy guacamole and corn chips as openers for a Mexican dinner, classic Italian antipasto before spaghetti and meatballs, or crisp shrimp rolls at the start of a Chinese feast.

Whatever appetizers you serve, remember to make it easy for your guests to socialize as they snack. Finger foods should be about finger size—or at least small enough to be eaten in two bites. Hot foods should be served with toothpicks or small forks, and no dip should be so thin that crackers drip after being dunked. Remember, too, that your weight-watching guests will enjoy the party even more if you offer a low-calorie snack, such as fresh vegetables with a yogurt dip, along with the usual party fare.

To be sure that you have time to enjoy your guests, prepare and decorate your appetizers beforehand. Apple slices dipped in lemon juice, colorful radishes, bright green lettuce leaves, and even the old stand-by parsley all can be used to quickly turn a plain plate of food into a party platter. No need to limit yourself, though, to a single large platter. Your appetizers will be easier to serve (and replenish) if you arrange them on several small platters instead of one large dish.

Pepperidge Farm Cocktail Franks Deluxe

¼ lb liverwurst
2 Tbsp grated Parmesan cheese
2 Tbsp minced green onion
½ tsp dry mustard
1 sheet PEPPERIDGE FARM Frozen Puff Pastry
16 (about ½ lb) cocktail frankfurters

In a small bowl, blend liverwurst, Parmesan cheese, onion, and mustard. Thaw pastry slightly, about 20 minutes, and cut sheet into 16 2½-inch squares. Spread about 1 tsp liverwurst mixture in center of each square. Place frankfurter on pastry diagonally and wrap 1 corner of pastry over frank; repeat with opposite corner. Moisten with water to seal. Bake on ungreased baking sheet in preheated 400°F oven for 10 minutes or until puffy and golden brown. Makes 16 hors d'oeuvres.

COURTESY PEPPERIDGE FARM, INC.

Minute Maid®

Lemon Marinated Mushrooms

¾ cup salad oil
¼ cup olive oil
½ cup MINUTE MAID® 100% Pure Lemon Juice
1 medium onion (chopped fine)
1 tsp salt
¼ tsp pepper
3 bay leaves
1 tsp chopped parsley
1½ cups small fresh tiny mushrooms or 3 cans (4 oz) button mushrooms

Mix all ingredients except mushrooms in a jar with screw top. Shake well. Add mushrooms. Let stand 12 hours or more.

 COURTESY THE COCA-COLA COMPANY FOODS DIVISION.

Oscar Mayer Pork Sausage Wontons

1 pkg (1 lb) OSCAR MAYER Ground Pork Sausage
1 can (8 oz) water chestnuts, drained, finely chopped
2 green onions, finely chopped
30 wonton skins 3½ inches square
Peanut or vegetable oil for frying

In skillet, cook sausage over medium heat about 12 minutes, stirring and separating sausage as it cooks; drain on absorbent paper. Combine sausage, water chestnuts, and onion. Place 1 Tbsp sausage mixture on center of wonton skin. Moisten corners of wonton skin with water and fold up over sausage mixture like an envelope. Pinch to seal. (Wontons and skins should be covered with moist towel when they are not being handled; they have a tendency to dry out and become brittle.) Heat at least 1 inch of oil in heavy skillet, wok, or deep-fat fryer to 375°F. Fry wontons until golden brown, turning once. Drain on absorbent paper. Makes 30.

COURTESY OSCAR MAYER & CO.

Widmer Savory Cheddar Puffs

1 cup mayonnaise
½ cup New York State sharp Cheddar cheese, grated
2 tsp Worcestershire sauce
¼ tsp French's Garlic Salt
1 Tbsp WIDMER New York State Port

Combine all ingredients; mix thoroughly. Spoon mixture onto round crackers. Broil 4–5 inches from heat until topping is bubbling and lightly browned. Serve immediately. Makes about 24 hors d'oeuvres.

COMPLIMENTS OF WIDMER'S WINE CELLARS, INC., NAPLES, NEW YORK. RECIPES DEVELOPED AND COMPILED BY SUE BARRA AND PAT CALLAHAN, HOME ECONOMISTS.

Arnold Melba Thin Shrimp Rolls

20 slices ARNOLD Melba Thin Dietslice White Bread
4 tsp instant powdered beef broth mix
8 Tbsp water
8 Tbsp finely chopped celery
4 Tbsp finely chopped canned mushrooms
8 Tbsp finely chopped Chinese vegetables
1 cup finely chopped defrosted frozen shrimp
2 Tbsp soya sauce
2 Tbsp sherry wine
2 Tbsp cornstarch
1 beaten egg

In a small skillet, combine celery, broth mix, and water. Cook over low heat for 5 minutes or until celery is tender. Drain well. Combine mushrooms, Chinese vegetables, shrimp, and cooked celery. Blend well and drain off any excess liquid. Blend soya sauce, sherry wine, and cornstarch together. Stir until mixture is smooth, and add to other ingredients. Remove crusts from slices of ARNOLD Melba Thin Bread. Roll out slices. Place

1 Tbsp of filling along one end of slice and roll carefully. Pin with food picks, one at each end. Brush entire roll lightly with beaten egg. Place on lightly greased baking sheet and bake in 350°F oven for 20 minutes. (Can be made ahead of time and frozen unbaked.) Yield: 20.

FROM ARNOLD, "ONE OF THE WORLD'S MOST RESPECTED BAKERS".

Dole® Piroshki

- ½ *lb ground chuck*
- ⅔ *cup minced onion*
- ½ *cup finely chopped DOLE® Fresh Mushrooms*
- 2 *Tbsp lemon juice*
- 1¼ *tsp mint flakes*
- 1 *tsp salt*
- 1 *tsp cinnamon*
- ¼ *tsp pepper*
- 1 *pkg (7½ oz) refrigerated buttermilk biscuits*
- 1 *Tbsp butter, melted*

Mix first 8 ingredients together. Separate biscuits, cut in halves, and shape into balls. Roll each on floured board to a 3-inch circle. Place 1 Tbsp of meat mixture on center of each. Moisten edges and pinch together over filling, shaping into half-moons. Arrange on ungreased baking sheet and brush with butter. Bake at 400°F 10–12 minutes until golden brown. Makes 20 piroshkis.

COURTESY OF CASTLE & COOKE FOODS (DOLE®).

McCormick/Schilling Turkey Nibblers

- 1 *cup minced turkey*
- ½ *cup mayonnaise*
- ¼ *cup grated Parmesan cheese*
- ½ *tsp MCCORMICK/ SCHILLING Poultry Seasoning*
- 1 *loaf cocktail bread*
- *Parsley*

Mix first 4 ingredients. Spread on bread slices. Broil 45–60 seconds. Garnish with sprigs of parsley. Serve hot. Makes 24 hors d'oeuvres.

Fritos® Brand Corn Chips Cream Cheese Salami Wedges

5 slices salami (approx. 4 inches in diameter)
1 3-oz pkg cream cheese, softened
2 Tbsp milk
1 tsp lemon juice
½ tsp monosodium glutamate
½ tsp prepared mustard
¼ tsp salt
1 tsp horseradish
2 Tbsp finely crushed FRITOS® Brand Corn Chips

Blend cheese with milk. Add remaining ingredients. Spread on slices of salami, placing one on top of the other to form a stack. Chill. Slice in wedges. Makes 12 wedges.

COURTESY FRITO-LAY, INC. FRITOS® IS A REGISTERED TRADEMARK OF FRITO-LAY, INC.

SeaPak Appetizer Shrimp

2 lb SEAPAK Frozen, Peeled and Deveined Shrimp
2 medium onions, sliced
1½ cups vegetable oil
1½ cups white vinegar
½ cup sugar
1½ tsp celery seed
1½ tsp salt
4 Tbsp capers with juice

Cook shrimp according to package instructions. Drain. Combine remaining ingredients. Marinate at least 6 hours.

COURTESY RICH-SEAPAK CORPORATION.

Widmer Tiny Meatballs with Three Wine Sauces

Meatballs

2 eggs, beaten
½ cup water
1 envelope (4 servings) French's "Big Tate" Potato Pancake Mix
1½ lb ground beef

Combine eggs, water, and contents of potato pancake mix envelope; let stand 10 minutes. Add ground beef; mix lightly. Shape mixture into bite-sized balls. Arrange meatballs in single layer on lightly greased baking sheet. Bake at 400°F for

10 minutes. Then drop meatballs into one of the three wine sauces (recipes follow) and simmer 10 minutes.

Barbecue Sauce

- *1 medium onion, chopped*
- *¼ cup salad oil*
- *1 tsp French's Prepared Mustard*
- *¾ cup tomato catsup*
- *1 Tbsp Worcestershire sauce*
- *1 tsp French's Paprika*
- *Dash French's Ground Black Pepper*
- *Salt to taste*
- *¾ cup WIDMER Sauterne*

Brown onion lightly in salad oil. Stir in all remaining ingredients and simmer 10 minutes. Add meatballs and simmer an additional 10 minutes. Serve meatballs hot, in chafing dish or slow cooker.

Sauterne Sauce

- *3 Tbsp butter or margarine*
- *5 Tbsp flour*
- *1 10½-oz can condensed beef broth, undiluted*
- *½ cup evaporated milk, undiluted*
- *¼ tsp French's Mace*
- *2 Tbsp chopped fresh parsley*
- *1 cup WIDMER Sauterne*

Melt butter or margarine over low heat. Stir in flour to make a thick paste. Add beef broth, milk, wine, parsley, and mace and salt and pepper to taste. Cook, stirring constantly, until smooth and thickened. Add meatballs and simmer 10 minutes. Serve meatballs in hot sauce in chafing dish or slow cooker.

Burgundy Sauce

Follow instructions for sauterne sauce, but substitute 1 cup WIDMER Select American Burgundy for the sauterne and omit mace and parsley.

COMPLIMENTS OF WIDMER'S WINE CELLARS, INC., NAPLES, NEW YORK. RECIPES DEVELOPED AND COMPILED BY SUE BARRA AND PAT CALLAHAN, HOME ECONOMISTS.

Arnold Brick Oven Turnovers

- *2 1-lb loaves ARNOLD Brick Oven White Bread*
- *4 Tbsp butter*
- *1 4½-oz can liver pate or mushroom filling (see below)*

Roll out slices of ARNOLD Brick Oven White Bread, from which the crusts have been removed. Punch 1 round out of each slice with a 2½-inch cookie cutter. Cut three little slits in each round.

Put ½ tsp of the pate or the mushroom filling in the center and fold the bread over so that the slits are on top. Pinch the sides together and brush the tops generously with melted butter. Bake in a preheated 425°F oven for approximately 10 minutes until brown. Serve hot. Can be frozen before baking. Yield: 36 turnovers.

Mushroom Filling

2 cans (4 oz each) mushrooms
1 small onion
3 Tbsp butter
2 Tbsp chopped parsley
Salt to taste

Drain and chop mushrooms. Mix with finely chopped onion. Saute in butter and cook until moisture has evaporated. Add parsley and salt to taste. Cool. Yield: filling for 36 turnovers.

FROM ARNOLD, "AMERICA'S BRICK OVEN BAKER".

Minute Maid®

Zippy Lemon Marinated Vegetable Hors d'Oeuvres

1 small cauliflower, broken into flowerets
2 green peppers, cut into ½-inch strips
½ lb small mushroom caps
1 5¼-oz can black pitted olives, drained
1 4½-oz jar white cocktail onions, drained
¾ cup olive oil
¼ cup salad oil
¼ cup MINUTE MAID® 100% Pure Lemon Juice
1¼ cup white wine vinegar
¼ cup sugar
2 tsp salt
¾ tsp ground pepper
1 clove garlic, minced

Mix vegetables together in a shallow dish. Bring remaining ingredients to a boil, cook 5 minutes and pour over vegetables. Cover and marinate for 24 hours in the refrigerator. Drain and serve with toothpicks.

MINUTE MAID IS A REGISTERED TRADEMARK OF THE COCA-COLA COMPANY. COURTESY THE COCA-COLA COMPANY FOODS DIVISION.

BUMBLE BEE®

Bumble Bee® Spring Garden Antipasto

- *1 pkg (10 oz) frozen asparagus spears*
- *½ cup water*
- *2 cups sliced cucumbers*
- *2 cups sliced DOLE® Fresh Mushrooms*
- *¾ cup olive oil*
- *¼ cup red wine vinegar*
- *1 tsp salt*
- *¾ tsp oregano*
- *1 can (6½ oz) BUMBLE BEE® Chunk Light Tuna*
- *Crisp salad greens*
- *2 cups cherry tomatoes*

Cook asparagus in water in a small saucepan until crisp-tender. Drain. Arrange cooked asparagus, cucumber, and mushrooms in a 3-qt shallow baking dish. Combine olive oil, vinegar, salt, and oregano in a screw-top jar. Shake well to combine. Pour dressing over vegetables. Cover and refrigerate 1 hour. Drain tuna and remove bottom lid. Push tuna out gently so it retains its shape and place in center of large platter lined with crisp salad greens. Arrange marinated vegetables and cherry tomatoes around tuna. Pour dressing over all. Makes 8 servings.

COURTESY OF CASTLE & COOKE FOODS (BUMBLE BEE® AND DOLE®).

Green Giant® Party Pinwheels

- *2 6-oz pkg thinly sliced cooked ham*
- *2 3-oz pkg cream cheese, softened*
- *1 15-oz can GREEN GIANT® Extra-Long Green Asparagus Spears, drained*

Spread each ham slice with approximately 2 tsp cream cheese. Place 1 large or 2 small asparagus spears along the lengthwise edge of each ham slice. For short spears, add part of an additional spear; roll-up jelly-roll fashion. Chill. Cut each roll in fourths. Makes 4 dozen.

COURTESY THE GREEN GIANT COMPANY.

Lea & Perrins Egg and Caviar Stuffed Celery

3 hard-cooked eggs, finely chopped
2 Tbsp mayonnaise
2 Tbsp red caviar
4 tsp chopped chives
1 tsp LEA & PERRINS Worcestershire Sauce
1/8 tsp Tabasco
8 celery ribs

In a small bowl, combine all ingredients except celery; mix well. Cut celery ribs into 3-inch pieces. Spoon approximately 1 Tbsp filling into each piece. Garnish with paprika, if desired. Yield: 24 hors d'oeuvres.
COURTESY LEA & PERRINS WORCESTERSHIRE SAUCE, A PRODUCT OF LEA & PERRINS, INC.

Dannon Yogurt Stuffed Celery

1 bunch celery
2 cups DANNON Plain Yogurt
1/2 cup mashed blue cheese
1/2 cup finely chopped chives
1 Tbsp brandy
Salt to taste

Wash celery and cut into 2-inch pieces. Combine yogurt, blue cheese, chives, and brandy. Chill until hardened to spreading consistency. Fill celery pieces and serve cold. Makes filling for approximately 20 pieces.

Variation

Put 2 cups of DANNON Plain Yogurt through cheesecloth. Drain for 24 hours. Mix "yogurt cheese" remaining in cloth with blue cheese, chives, brandy, and salt. Fill celery pieces and serve cold. Makes filling for approximately 12 pieces.
COURTESY THE DANNON COMPANY.

Traditional Chex Party Mix

½ cup butter or margarine
1¼ tsp seasoned salt
4½ tsp Worcestershire sauce
2 cups CORN CHEX® cereal
2 cups RICE CHEX® cereal
2 cups BRAN CHEX® cereal
2 cups WHEAT CHEX® cereal
1 cup salted mixed nuts

Preheat oven to 250°F. Heat butter in large shallow roasting pan (about 15 X 10 X 2 inches) in oven until melted. Remove. Stir in seasoned salt and Worcestershire sauce. Add Chex and nuts. Mix until all pieces are coated. Heat in oven 1 hour. Stir every 15 minutes. Spread on absorbent paper to cool. Makes about 9 cups.

CREATED AND TESTED AT CHECKERBOARD KITCHENS. REPRINTED COURTESY OF RALSTON PURINA COMPANY.

Quaker® Granola

4 cups QUAKER® Oats (quick or old fashioned, uncooked)
⅓ cup firmly packed brown sugar
½ cup wheat germ
½ cup flaked or shredded coconut
¼ cup sesame seed
⅓ cup vegetable oil
¼ cup honey
1 tsp vanilla

Heat oats in an ungreased 13 X 9-inch baking pan in a preheated moderate oven (350°F) 10 minutes. Combine oats, brown sugar, wheat germ, coconut, and sesame seed. Add oil, honey, and vanilla; mix until dry ingredients are well coated. Bake in ungreased 13 X 9-inch baking pan in preheated oven (350°F) 20–25 minutes, stirring often to brown evenly. Cool. Stir until crumbly. Serve with cold milk or cream. Store in a tightly covered container in refrigerator. Makes about 6 cups cereal.

For variety, add 1 cup slivered almonds or chopped soybeans with dry ingredients; or add 1 cup raisins or chopped dried fruit after the cereal has cooled.

RECIPE REPRODUCED WITH THE PERMISSION OF THE QUAKER OATS COMPANY.

Golden Grahams

Golden Grahams® Backpack Snack

5 cups GOLDEN GRAHAMS® Cereal
1 cup salted peanuts
¼ cup creamy peanut butter
2 Tbsp margarine or butter
1 tsp ground cinnamon
1 cup raisins

Heat oven to 350°F. Mix cereal and peanuts in large bowl. Heat peanut butter, margarine, and cinnamon in 1-qt saucepan over low heat, stirring occasionally, just until blended. Pour over cereal and peanuts, stirring until thoroughly coated. Spread in ungreased baking pan, 13 X 9 X 2 inches. Bake 15 minutes, stirring occasionally. Stir in raisins; spread on waxed paper. Let stand 2 hours. Yield: about 6 cups snack.

COURTESY BETTY CROCKER FOOD & NUTRITION CENTER, GENERAL MILLS, INC. REGISTERED® TRADEMARK OF GENERAL MILLS, INC.

Jolly Time® Party Mix

2 qt popped JOLLY TIME® Pop Corn
2 cups slim pretzel sticks
2 cups cheese curls
¼ cup butter or margarine
1 Tbsp Worcestershire sauce
½ tsp garlic
½ tsp seasoned salt

In a shallow baking pan, mix popped corn, pretzel sticks, and cheese curls. Melt butter or margarine in small saucepan and stir in seasonings. Pour over dry mixture and mix well. Bake at 250°F for about 45 minutes, stirring several times. Note: 1 cup dry roasted peanuts may be added. Makes about 2½ qt.

COURTESY JOLLY TIME POP CORN.

Nabisco Shredded Wheat Snacks

4 cups SPOON SIZE Shredded Wheat
⅓ cup melted butter or margarine
1½ tsp seasoned salt

Spread cereal in a single layer on a large, shallow baking pan. Drizzle butter or margarine over cereal. Sprinkle with seasoned salt. Bake in preheated moderate oven (350°F) for 15 minutes. Serve warm or cold. Makes 4 cups.

Variations

In place of seasoned salt, use 1½ tsp onion salt or garlic salt. For added zestiness, shake on 3 Tbsp of your favorite grated cheese as you take the snacks out of the oven.
COURTESY NABISCO, INC.

Lipton California Dip

1 envelope LIPTON Onion Soup Mix
2 cups (16 oz) sour cream

In a small bowl, blend LIPTON Onion Soup Mix with sour cream; chill. Makes about 2 cups.

Variations

California Vegetable Dip: Add 1 cup each finely chopped green pepper and tomato and 2 tsp chili powder.

California Blue Cheese Dip: Add ¼ lb crumbled blue cheese and ¼ cup finely chopped walnuts.

California Seafood Dip: Add 1 cup finely chopped cooked shrimp, clams, or crabmeat, ¼ cup chili sauce, and 1 Tbsp horseradish.
COURTESY OF THE LIPTON KITCHENS.

California Avocado Guacamoles with Green Chili Peppers

4 soft CALIFORNIA Avocados, peeled, seeded, and mashed
½ cup finely chopped canned green chili peppers
¼ cup minced onion
1 Tbsp salt
¼ cup lemon juice

Combine all ingredients. Cover and chill. Makes about 3 cups. Serve with chips, crackers, or vegetable dippers.
COURTESY CALIFORNIA AVOCADO COMMISSION.

Nabisco Zippy Vegetable Dip

½ cup chopped tomato
½ cup chopped cucumber
1 cup dairy sour cream
2 Tbsp chopped parsley
1 Tbsp prepared white horseradish
1 tsp grated onion
¼ tsp salt
Ground black pepper
CHIPPERS Potato 'n Cheese Snack Crackers

Press chopped tomato and cucumber between paper towels to extract as much liquid as possible. Combine with next 6 ingredients. Cover and chill until ½ hour before serving. Serve with CHIPPERS Potato 'n Cheese Snack Crackers. Makes about 1½ cups dip.

COURTESY NABISCO, INC.

Green Giant® Shrimp Spread

1 8-oz pkg cream cheese, softened
½ cup dairy sour cream
½ tsp curry powder*
2 Tbsp finely chopped onion
1 Tbsp lemon juice
1 2½-oz jar GREEN GIANT® Sliced Mushrooms, drained and chopped
1 4-oz can tiny shrimp, drained
Assorted crackers

In small bowl, blend together cream cheese, sour cream, curry, onion, lemon juice, and mushrooms. Stir in shrimp. Cover; chill thoroughly. Serve with crackers. Makes about 2 cups.

*Note: Dill weed or garlic powder may be substituted for the curry powder.
COURTESY THE GREEN GIANT COMPANY.

Velveeta Mexicali Dip

1 lb VELVEETA Pasteurized Process Cheese Spread, cubed
1 16-oz can tomatoes, drained, chopped
1 4-oz can green chilies, drained, chopped
1 Tbsp instant minced onion
Corn or tortilla chips

Combine process cheese spread, tomatoes, chilies and onion in saucepan; cook over low heat until process cheese spread melts. Serve hot with corn chips. Yield: 3 cups.
COURTESY OF KRAFT, INC.

Armour Hot Chili-Cheese Dip

1 15-oz can ARMOUR Star Chili—No Beans
1 4-oz can chopped green chiles
1 lb process American cheese, shredded
1 Tbsp Worcestershire sauce
Corn chips

Combine all ingredients except chips; heat, stirring occasionally, over low heat until cheese melts. Serve as a dip with corn chips. Yield: 4 cups.
COURTESY ARMOUR AND COMPANY.

Green Giant® Cheesy Corn Spread

¾ lb sharp Cheddar cheese, shredded
½ cup dairy sour cream
½ cup mayonnaise or salad dressing
¼ cup finely chopped onion
½ tsp salt
1 12-oz can GREEN GIANT® Mexicorn® Golden Whole Kernel Corn with Sweet Peppers, drained
Assorted fresh vegetables or crackers

Bring cheese to room temperature. In large mixing bowl, mash cheese with fork or spoon until smooth. Blend in sour cream, mayonnaise, onion, and salt. Stir in corn. Cover; chill several hours or overnight. Serve with fresh raw vegetables or crackers. Makes about 2½ cups.
COURTESY THE GREEN GIANT COMPANY.

Friendship Anchovy Dip

1½ cups FRIENDSHIP Cottage Cheese
5 anchovy fillets, drained
2 tsp grated onion
¼ cup finely chopped green pepper
1 Tbsp chopped pimento

In small mixing bowl, beat together cottage cheese, anchovies, and onion at highest speed of mixer, until fairly smooth. Stir in green pepper and pimento. Cover and chill. Serve with crackers or raw vegetables. Makes 1¾ cups.

RECIPE COURTESY OF FRIENDSHIP FOODS' HOME ECONOMIST, HELEN SCHWARTZ.

Gold's Zippy Dip

1 large pkg cream cheese
1 Tbsp prepared GOLD'S Horseradish
½ tsp prepared mustard
1 tsp Worcestershire sauce
10 drops Tabasco sauce
2 Tbsp pickle relish
3 Tbsp chili sauce
1 Tbsp lemon juice

Blend all ingredients at room temperature and add additional seasoning to taste. Add enough milk to bring to desired consistency.

COURTESY GOLD PURE FOOD PRODUCTS, BROOKLYN, NY.

MICHELOB®

Michelob Swiss Cheese Dip

1 egg white, beaten stiff
1 lb Swiss cheese, grated
1 Tbsp vegetable oil
1½ tsp mustard
½ tsp salt
2 cloves garlic, mashed
1 Tbsp Worcestershire sauce
8 oz MICHELOB

Beat egg white until stiff, add remaining ingredients except MICHELOB. Blend ingredients, then add MICHELOB gradually while stirring until mixture is the consistency of whipped cream. Chill. Serves 12.

REPRINTED BY PERMISSION, ANHEUSER-BUSCH, INC., ST. LOUIS, MO.

Colombo Skinny Raw Vegetable Dip

- 2 cups plain COLOMBO Whole-Milk Yogurt
- ½ tsp onion powder
- ½ tsp garlic powder
- ½ Tabasco sauce
- ½ tsp prepared horseradish
- 1 Tbsp minced parsley
- 1 Tbsp Worcestershire sauce
- 1 Tbsp sugar or equivalent sugar substitute

Blend all ingredients until smooth. Chill thoroughly. Cut bite-sized pieces of raw turnip, carrots, fennel, celery, green pepper, cauliflower, broccoli, yellow squash, zucchini, cucumber, scallions, radishes, and whole mushrooms. Arrange attractively on a platter. Makes approximately 2 cups dip.

PERMISSION TO REPRODUCE GRANTED BY AMERICA'S ORIGINAL YOGURT COMPANY, COLOMBO, INC.

Friendship "Easy on the Waistline" Party Spread

- 1 bar (7½ oz) FRIENDSHIP Farmer Cheese
- 1 Tbsp chopped chives
- 2 Tbsp skimmed milk
- ⅛ tsp garlic powder
- Dash of salt
- Dash of pepper

Place FRIENDSHIP Farmer Cheese in bowl. Add remaining ingredients and mix with spoon until blended. Chill.

RECIPE COURTESY OF FRIENDSHIP FOODS' HOME ECONOMIST, HELEN SCHWARTZ.

Campbell's Zippy Clam Dip

- 1 can (10¾ oz) CAMPBELL'S Condensed Cream of Celery Soup
- 1 pkg (8 oz) cream cheese, softened
- 1 can (8 oz) minced clams, well drained
- 1 Tbsp chopped parsley
- 2 tsp prepared horseradish

With electric mixer or rotary beater, gradually blend soup into cream cheese. Beat *just* until smooth (overbeating makes dip thin). Stir in remaining ingredients. Chill. Serve as a dip with crackers or chips. Makes about 2½ cups.

COURTESY CAMPBELL SOUP COMPANY.

Kellogg's®

Kellogg's® Cracklin' Bran® Cheese Ball

1 cup KELLOGG'S® CRACKLIN' BRAN cereal
2 pkg (3 oz each) cream cheese, softened
¼ cup (2 oz) blue cheese
⅓ cup (3 oz) process cheese spread
1 Tbsp grated onion
½ tsp Worcestershire sauce
¼ cup finely chopped pecans
3 Tbsp dried parsley flakes
Assorted crackers

Measure cereal and crush to ¾ cup. Set aside. In small bowl of electric mixer, combine cream cheese, blue cheese, cheese spread, onion, and Worcestershire sauce. Beat until well blended. Stir in ½ cup of the crushed cereal, the pecans, and 2 Tbsp of the parsley flakes. Cover and refrigerate 3–4 hours or overnight. Stir together remaining ¼ cup crushed cereal and 1 Tbsp parsley flakes. Store in tightly covered container. One hour before serving, form cheese mixture into ball and roll in the remaining cereal mixture. Serve with assorted crackers. Note: Unused portion may be stored in refrigerator. Yield: 1 cheese ball.

COURTESY OF KELLOGG COMPANY.

Ritz Crackers Fancy Chicken Log

2 (8-oz) pkg cream cheese, softened
1 Tbsp bottled steak sauce
½ tsp curry powder
1½ cups minced cooked chicken
⅓ cup minced celery
¼ cup chopped parsley
¼ cup chopped toasted almonds
RITZ Crackers

Beat together first 3 ingredients. Blend in next 2 ingredients and 2 Tbsp parsley; refrigerate remaining parsley. Shape mixture into a 9-inch log. Wrap in plastic wrap and chill 4 hours or overnight. Toss together remaining parsley and almonds; use to coat log. Serve with RITZ Crackers. Makes about 3 cups spread.

COURTESY NABISCO, INC.

"Philly" Cheese Bells

- *1 8-oz pkg CRACKER BARREL Brand Sharp Cheddar Cold Pack Cheese Food*
- *1 8-oz pkg PHILADELPHIA BRAND Cream Cheese*
- *PARKAY Margarine*
- *2 tsp chopped pimiento*
- *2 tsp chopped green pepper*
- *2 tsp chopped onion*
- *1 tsp Worcestershire sauce*
- *½ tsp lemon juice*

Combine cold pack cheese food, softened cream cheese and 2 Tbsp margarine; mix until well blended. Add remaining ingredients; mix well. Mold into bell shapes, using the cold pack container coated with margarine or lined with plastic wrap. Chill until firm; unmold. Garnish with chopped parsley and pimiento strips, if desired. Yield: 2 bells.

COURTESY OF KRAFT, INC.

Lea & Perrins Apple Snackle

- *4 large apples*
- *2 pkg (4 oz each) shredded Cheddar cheese*
- *3 Tbsp LEA & PERRINS Worcestershire Sauce*

Preheat broiler. Core apples. Cut each apple into 4 slices crosswise. Place on a rack in a broiler pan. Combine cheese and LEA & PERRINS; mix well. Spoon a thin layer on each apple slice. Broil about 4 inches from heat source, until cheese melts, 3–4 minutes. Served hot as a snack, appetizer, salad-go-along, etc. Yield: 16 slices.

COURTESY LEA & PERRINS WORCESTERSHIRE SAUCE, A PRODUCT OF LEA & PERRINS, INC.

Soups and Sandwiches

A soup can take hours to prepare—or just minutes. It can be an elegant first course, a hearty main meal, or a refreshing fruit dessert. Perhaps best of all, even at current inflationary prices, a delicious soup can cost just pennies a serving.

Soup's versatility may explain why prepared soups have always been favorites with people who do not have time to cook. Canned soups have been in existence for more than one hundred years, and some of the best-known chefs recommend them as substitutes for homemade stocks. The origin of dried soups and bouillon cubes can be traced back to the eighteenth century. In those days, travelers carried "portable" soups made from highly concentrated meat stocks. The gluelike concentrates kept for years and could be mixed with boiling water to make a truly old-fashioned instant soup.

Prepared foods have come a long way in the past century, and resourceful cooks can take advantage of all the work that food manufacturers do for them. With the help of canned and frozen convenience foods, a hearty chowder can be whipped up in half the time it would take to make it from "scratch."

Besides being good by themselves, canned and packaged soups can also be the base for soups you make yourself. Good beef or chicken broth can be the start of a great soup. Cream of mushroom, cream of celery, and cream of chicken soups all blend well with vegetables or seafood to make fresh-tasting bisques.

The trick in making commercial soups seem homemade is to add to them your own personal touch. The list of nice things to do to soups is endless, but you might begin by adding a pinch of your favorite herbs to a clear soup or a dash of sherry to a cream soup. Also try serving soups in special dishes, such as rice bowls or individual oven-proof casseroles.

A great-tasting sandwich makes a perfect companion for almost any soup. Mix and match the soup and sandwich recipe ideas on the following pages, but do not limit them to lunch. Try soups and sandwiches together whenever you want a delicious, economical, and easy-to-prepare meal.

Soups

Campbell's Petite Marmite

½ lb boneless round steak (1 inch thick)
1 lb chicken parts
5 small turnips (about ½ lb), quartered
1 cup chopped celery
1 medium bay leaf
2½ cups water
2 cans (10½ oz each) CAMPBELL'S Condensed Chicken with Rice Soup
½ cup sliced green onions
1 cup diagonally sliced carrots

Cut meat in 1-inch cubes. In large saucepan, combine beef, chicken, turnips, celery, bay, and water. Bring to boil; cover. Reduce heat; simmer 30 minutes. Add soup, onions and carrots; cook 15 minutes more or until done. Stir occasionally. Skim off fat. Makes about 9½ cups.
COURTESY CAMPBELL SOUP COMPANY.

Stokely's Chicken Corn Chowder

½ cup chopped onion
¼ cup butter or margarine
3 Tbsp flour
2 cans (1 lb 1 oz each) STOKELY'S Finest® Whole Kernel Golden Corn
Milk
1½ cups pasteurized process cheese spread, cubed
1 tsp instant chicken bouillon

¼ tsp poultry seasoning
1½ cups chopped cooked chicken

Saute onion in butter until tender; remove pan from heat. Blend flour into butter. Drain corn, reserving liquid. Add milk to reserved corn liquid, to equal 3 cups; add to flour. Cook and stir over medium heat until mixture boils. Add cheese, bouillon, and poultry seasoning; stir until cheese is melted. Add STOKELY'S Corn and chicken and simmer slowly for 20 minutes. Makes 6 servings.
COURTESY STOKELY-VAN CAMP, INC.

Prince®

Prince Chicken Noodle Soup Parmesan

1 stewing chicken (4 lb)
1 carrot
3 stalks celery, chopped
1 tomato, halved
1 small onion, halved
1 sprig of parsley
1 tsp salt
1/8 tsp pepper
1/2 lb PRINCE Fine Egg Noodles
PRINCE Parmesan Grated Cheese

Cut chicken into 4 or 6 pieces. Place in 2 qt cold water and add vegetables and seasonings. Boil until chicken is tender, occasionally skimming fat from stock. Remove chicken from pot, strain broth. Return strained liquid to pot and add PRINCE Noodles. Cook until noodles are tender. Serve with PRINCE Grated Cheese, with chicken as a side dish. Serves 4–6.

COURTESY THE PRINCE COMPANY, INC.

Campbell's

Campbell's Kentucky Chicken Chowder

1 cup chopped onion
1/4 tsp basil leaves, crushed
1/4 tsp thyme leaves, crushed
2 Tbsp butter or margarine
2 cans (10 3/4 oz each) CAMPBELL'S Condensed Chicken Broth
2 cups shredded raw potato
1 1/2 cups cubed cooked chicken
1 pkg (10 oz) frozen succotash
1 can (about 8 oz) tomatoes, cut up
1 soup can water
1/8 tsp pepper

In large saucepan, cook onion with basil and thyme in butter until tender. Add remaining ingredients. Bring to boil; reduce heat. Cover; simmer 20 minutes or until vegetables are done. Stir often. Makes about 8 cups.

COURTESY CAMPBELL SOUP COMPANY.

Christian Brothers

Christian Brothers Fresh Mushroom Soup

- *½ lb fresh mushrooms, thinly sliced*
- *¼ cup butter*
- *3 Tbsp chopped parsley*
- *¼ tsp salt*
- *Dash of pepper*
- *1¼ cups CHRISTIAN BROTHERS Chablis*
- *1 cup heavy cream*
- *3 egg yolks*
- *2 cups sour cream*

Sauté mushrooms in butter for 5 minutes, or until lightly browned. Stir in parsley and seasonings. Add chablis and ¾ cup heavy cream; stir and simmer about 5 minutes. Beat egg yolks with 1¾ cups sour cream, stir in some of the hot soup. Return all to pan; keep hot. Whip remaining ¼ cup heavy cream; stir in ¼ cup sour cream. Pour soup into individual heat-proof bowls. Spoon whipped cream mixture onto soup. Place under broiler until topping browns. Serve at once. Serves 6.

FROM THE CHRISTIAN BROTHERS OF NAPA VALLEY, CALIFORNIA.

Shrimp Bisque

- *1 4½-oz can cold shrimp*
- *1 can cream of celery soup*
- *1 can cream of mushroom soup*
- *1 cup milk*
- *½ tsp TABASCO Pepper Sauce*
- *2 Tbsp butter or margarine*

Cover drained shrimp with ice water and let stand 5 minutes. Redrain. Combine soups in a saucepan. Add milk and blend until rich and creamy. Add TABASCO Pepper Sauce. Mince shrimp and add to soup mixture. Simmer for 10 minutes. Add butter or margarine, allow it to melt, and serve immediately. Yield: 6 servings.

RECIPE COURTESY MCILHENNY COMPANY, AVERY ISLAND, LOUISIANA, 70513.

Wakefield Bisque Alaska

1 (6 oz) pkg WAKEFIELD Alaska King Crabmeat
¼ cup butter or margarine
2 tsp flour
1½ cups milk
1½ cups half-and-half
¼ tsp Worcestershire sauce
½ tsp grated lemon rind
⅛ tsp ground mace
½ tsp salt
⅛ tsp white pepper
1 Tbsp cracker crumbs
2 Tbsp sherry
¼ cup whipping cream, whipped
Ground nutmeg

Thaw crabmeat and retain liquid. Heat butter in top of double boiler over rapidly boiling water and blend in flour. Add milk and half-and-half, stirring constantly. Add Worcestershire sauce, grated lemon rind, mace, crab, and liquid. Stir well and cook slowly for 20 minutes. Season with salt and white pepper; add cracker crumbs. Allow to stand 10–15 minutes. Serve in heated soup bowls, add ½ Tbsp sherry to each bowl. Top with dollop of whipped cream. Sprinkle with nutmeg. Serves 3–4.

COURTESY PACIFIC PEARL SEAFOODS.

Doxsee New England Clam Chowder

2 cans DOXSEE Minced Clams
¼ cup butter
1 large onion, chopped
2 large potatoes, peeled and diced
Juice from canned clams
2 cups rich milk or light cream
Salt and pepper to taste

Drain clams, reserving liquid. Heat butter in a saucepan. Cook onion in it until golden. Add potatoes, clam liquid. Cover and simmer slowly until potatoes are tender, about 15 minutes. Add minced clams and seasonings. Cook 3 minutes. Add milk. (Heat but do not boil.) Serve at once with crisp crackers. Makes 8 servings.

FROM THE DOXSEE KITCHENS.

Gorton's New England Clam Chowder

1 can GORTON'S Clams
1 cup pared diced potatoes
2 Tbsp butter
¼ cup chopped onion
2 cups milk
Salt and pepper to taste

Drain clams. Cook onion in butter. Add potatoes and clam juice and cook until tender. Add clams and milk. Heat and season. Do not boil. Yield: 4 servings.

COURTESY GORTON'S OF GLOUCESTER.

Campbell's Southern Style Vegetable Soup

3 smoked pork hocks (about 2 lb)
2 cans (11¼ oz each) CAMPBELL'S Condensed Green Pea Soup
1 can (10½ oz) CAMPBELL'S Condensed Old Fashioned Vegetable Soup
3 soup cans water
1 pkg (9 oz) frozen chopped collard greens
¼ cup chopped onion
¼ tsp cayenne pepper

In large heavy pan, cover hocks with water. Bring to boil; cover. Reduce heat; simmer 1 hour. Drain. Blend in soup; gradually stir in 3 soup cans water. Add remaining ingredients. Simmer 2 hours. Stir occasionally. Makes about 6 cups.

COURTESY CAMPBELL SOUP COMPANY.

Enrico's Minestrone (Italian Vegetable Soup)

1 cup dried beans
5 cups water
1 Tbsp minced onion
1 tsp parsley
½ cup chopped celery
½ clove garlic, minced
½ pepper, diced
½ red pepper, diced
¾ cup olive oil
Thyme to taste
½ tsp salt
⅛ tsp pepper
1 cup diced cooked potatoes
1 cup chopped cabbage
½ cup cooked macaroni
1 cup ENRICO'S Spaghetti Sauce
Grated Parmesan cheese, or any Italian-style cheese

Soak beans overnight, drain. Add water, cover, and simmer 2 or 3 hours or until tender. Add water as necessary. Sauté onion, parsley, celery, garlic, and peppers in oil. Add to beans with crushed thyme, salt, pepper, remaining vegetables, and macaroni. Simmer 30 minutes more. Add ENRICO'S Spaghetti Sauce and simmer for 5 minutes more. Serve in soup bowls and sprinkle cheese over top. Serves 6.

COURTESY VENTRE PACKING COMPANY, INC.

Hunt's®

Hunt's® Meal-in-Itself Minestrone

- *1 lb stewing beef, cut in bite-size pieces*
- *5 cups water*
- *1 onion, chopped*
- *1 clove garlic, minced*
- *1 (14½ oz) can HUNT'S® Whole Tomatoes (generic term: peeled whole tomatoes)*
- *2 (8 oz) cans HUNT'S® Tomato Sauce (generic term: tomato sauce)*
- *1 tsp seasoned salt*
- *1 tsp basil leaves*
- *1 tsp marjoram leaves*
- *Pepper to taste*
- *2 carrots, sliced*
- *1 zucchini, sliced*
- *¼ head cabbage, shredded*
- *1 (15½ oz) can HUNT'S® Small Red Beans (generic term: small red beans)*
- *1½ cups cooked corkscrew macaroni*
- *Parmesan cheese*

In a 4-qt (or larger) slow cooker, combine beef, water, onion, garlic, HUNT'S Whole Tomatoes, HUNT'S Tomato Sauce, and seasonings. Cook on LOW 9–10 hours. Add vegetables and beans. Cook on HIGH 1 hour. Just before serving, stir in cooked macaroni. Garnish with Parmesan cheese. Makes 8–10 servings.

For a quick-and-easy meal, add hot sourdough rolls, fruit salad, milk, and cake.

COURTESY HUNT-WESSON FOODS, INC.

Dole®

Dole® Hungarian Cream Soup

- 1 cup thinly sliced DOLE® Fresh Mushrooms
- ¼ cup thinly sliced green onion
- 2 Tbsp butter
- 2½ Tbsp flour
- 1 tsp paprika
- ¾ tsp salt
- ⅛ tsp white pepper
- ⅛ tsp garlic powder
- 1 can (10¾ oz) condensed chicken broth
- 1 cup milk
- ½ cup dairy sour cream

Sauté mushrooms and onion in butter. Stir in flour, paprika, salt, pepper, and garlic powder. Gradually blend in broth and milk. Cook, stirring, until mixture boils and thickens slightly. Stir a little of the hot soup into sour cream, blending smooth. Combine with remaining soup and serve at once. Makes 3–4 servings.

Variation: blend ½ to 1 cup mashed potatoes into soup, along with the sour cream. Makes about 3⅔ cups.

COURTESY OF CASTLE & COOKE FOODS (DOLE®).

Stokely's Hamburger Vegetable Soup

- 1 lb ground beef
- ⅔ cup chopped onion
- 1 can (46 oz) STOKELY'S Finest® Tomato Juice
- 2 cans (1 lb each) STOKELY'S Finest® Mixed Vegetables
- 2 beef bouillon cubes
- 1 tsp seasoned salt
- 1 tsp sugar

In large saucepan, brown ground beef and onion; drain excess fat. Add remaining ingredients and bring soup to a boil. Lower heat and simmer for 30 minutes. Makes 6 servings.

COURTESY STOKELY-VAN CAMP, INC.

Chiffon Creamy Cauliflower Soup

2 pkg (10 oz each) frozen cauliflower
2 to 3 Tbsp water
Salt
¼ cup chopped green onion
¼ cup CHIFFON Margarine
3 Tbsp flour
1 qt milk
2 tsp salt
Dash of pepper
Paprika
Chopped parsley

Cover and simmer cauliflower in small amount of water with salt until tender. Cut up or mash. Sauté onion in CHIFFON Margarine. Stir in flour. Cook 1 minute, stirring constantly. Blend in milk, salt, pepper, and cauliflower. Cook and stir until thickened. Garnish with paprika and chopped parsley. For a satin-smooth soup, use a blender. Makes 8 (¾ cup) servings.

For *creamy asparagus soup*, use 2 pkg (10 oz each) frozen cut asparagus in place of cauliflower. Makes 8 (¾ cup) servings.

For *creamy broccoli soup*, use 2 pkg (10 oz each) frozen cut broccoli in place of cauliflower. Makes 8 (¾ cup) servings.

COURTESY OF ANDERSON CLAYTON FOODS.

Holland House® Oxtail Soup

2 large onions, chopped
3 Tbsp butter
3 lb oxtails, cut in 1-inch lengths
1¾ cups HOLLAND HOUSE Red Cooking Wine
1¾ cups beef stock or broth
1 6-oz can tomato paste
2 medium carrots, finely chopped
1 small turnip, finely chopped
1 tsp sugar
½ bay leaf
1 tsp thyme or basil

In a large frying pan, sauté onions in 2 Tbsp of butter until transparent. Place in a 4-qt pan. Melt remaining butter in frying pan and brown oxtails. Add to onions. Pour wine into frying pan and bring to boil, scraping free all browned particles. Add wine to soup pan, along with remaining ingredients. Cover and simmer over low heat for 3 hours, or until meat falls from bones and broth is very thick. Serves 4.

RECIPE SUPPLIED BY HOLLAND HOUSE BRANDS CO.

Christian Brothers French Onion Soup

- 4 *medium-sized onions, thinly sliced*
- ¼ *cup butter*
- 3 *cups bouillon or soup stock*
- 1½ *cups CHRISTIAN BROTHERS Burgundy*
- 1 *tsp salt*
- 1 *tsp pepper*
- 1 *Tbsp CHRISTIAN BROTHERS Dry Sherry*
- 4 *slices French bread, toasted and buttered*
- 1 *cup shredded Parmesan cheese*

Sauté onions in butter slowly until clear. Add bouillon, wine, and seasonings; cover and simmer 20 minutes. Stir in sherry. Pour into 4 heat-proof casseroles. Float bread on top; sprinkle with Parmesan cheese. Broil until cheese is lightly browned. Serve additional grated Parmesan cheese, if desired. Serves 4.

FROM THE CHRISTIAN BROTHERS OF NAPA VALLEY, CALIFORNIA.

Almadén Jug of Soup

- 3 *medium onions, chopped*
- ¼ *cup butter or margarine*
- 4 *beef bouillon cubes*
- 2 *cups water*
- ¼ *tsp pepper*
- 1 *bay leaf*
- 2 *Tbsp freeze-dried soup greens*
- 4 *cups ALMADÉN Ruby Cabernet*
- *Grated Parmesan cheese*

In a large, deep saucepan, sauté onions, chopped in butter or margarine, stirring often, until onions are soft and lightly browned. Add bouillon cubes, 2 cups water, pepper, bay leaf, soup greens, and ALMADÉN Ruby Cabernet. Stir to dissolve bouillon cubes, bring to boiling, reduce heat, cover, and simmer for 45 minutes. Remove bay leaf. Transfer soup to a Thermos jug, cover tightly and serve 1–5 hours later. Pour into mugs and sprinkle with grated Parmesan cheese to taste. Makes 6 servings, 1 cup each.

COURTESY ALMADEN VINEYARDS.

Steero Italian Zucchini Soup

- 2 Tbsp olive oil
- 3 scallions, chopped
- 1 clove garlic, minced
- ½ tsp basil
- 4 tsp STEERO Instant Beef Bouillon or 4 STEERO Cubes dissolved in 4 cups boiling water
- Grated Parmesan cheese
- 4 cups zucchini, finely chopped
- 2 tsp salt
- ⅛ tsp pepper
- 2 Tbsp parsley flakes
- 1 Tbsp butter

Combine the first 4 ingredients in a 2½-to-3-qt saucepan and cook on medium heat for about 10 minutes or until slightly softened. Add all remaining ingredients except the cheese. Cover and cook over medium heat for 35 minutes, or until zucchini is tender. Serve with cheese.

COURTESY AMERICAN KITCHEN PRODUCTS INC., JERSEY CITY, NJ.

Eveready® Cream of Carrot Soup

- 2 Tbsp HOLLYWOOD Safflower Margarine
- 2 Tbsp flour
- 2 cups milk
- ½ cup chopped onion
- 1 can EVEREADY® Carrot Juice (12-oz can)
- 1 tsp sea salt
- ⅛ tsp pepper
- ⅛ tsp celery salt

Measure margarine and flour in saucepan or part of double boiler. Heat, stirring, until mixture is smooth. Slowly blend in milk; add onion, carrot juice, and seasonings. Heat, stirring. frequently, just to boiling point. Serve topped with crisp croutons or sprigs of parsley. Makes 4 servings.

COURTESY H. & J. FOODS.

Miller Beer-Pea Soup

- 1½ cups split peas
- 3 cups water
- 3 cups MILLER High Life
- 1 large onion, sliced
- 1 large carrot, peeled and sliced
- 1½ tsp salt
- Freshly ground pepper
- ½ tsp basil
- 1 beef bouillon cube, crumbled
- 1 bay leaf
- ¾ lb sausage, cut into cubes (frankfurters, knockwurst, or bauernwurst)

In a large nonmetal bowl, combine split peas, water, and MILLER High Life and soak peas overnight. Turn into a

saucepan and place over low heat. Add onion, carrot, salt, pepper, basil, bouillon cube, and bay leaf. Simmer for 2 hours. Add sausage cubes and simmer for 45 minutes longer. Remove bay leaf before serving. Serves 6.
COURTESY MILLER BREWING COMPANY.

Van Camp's Butter Bean Soup

1 can (15 oz) VAN CAMP'S Butter Beans
1 can (1 lb) STOKELY'S Finest® Stewed Tomatoes
3 Tbsp butter or margarine
1 Tbsp instant minced onion
1½ tsp sugar
¼ tsp seasoned salt
Dash pepper

Combine all ingredients in a saucepan and simmer for 30 minutes. Makes 3–4 servings.
COURTESY STOKELY-VAN CAMP, INC.

Rokeach Borscht with Potato Dumplings

1 medium-size potato
2 Tbsp ROKEACH Nyafat
1 tsp salt
⅛ tsp ROKEACH Pepper
1 egg
½ cup matzo meal
1 tsp grated onion
1 jar ROKEACH Borscht

Boil potato, skin and mash. Beat in ROKEACH Nyafat, salt, ROKEACH Pepper, egg, and matzo meal. Cover and chill 2 hours. Shape into 1-inch balls. Drop into boiling, salted water. Boil 20 minutes. Drain. Add grated onion to ROKEACH Borscht, in saucepan. Bring to a boil. Pour into serving plates. Add cooked potato dumplings. Serve hot. Makes about 10 potato dumplings.
COURTESY I. ROKEACH & SONS, INC.

Herb-Ox Onion Cheese Soup

1 *large onion, sliced thin*
½ *cup butter*
¼ *cup flour*
½ *tsp dry mustard*
2 *cups boiling water*
4 *packets HERB-OX Beef Flavored Instant Broth and Seasoning*
1 *qt milk*
2 *cups grated Cheddar cheese (½ lb)*

Cook onion in butter in soup pot 5 minutes, until translucent but not brown. Sprinkle with flour and mustard; stir. Gradually add boiling water. Cook over low heat, stirring, until mixture is smooth and thickened. Add instant broth, stir to dissolve. Cover pan; simmer 15 minutes, stirring often. Add milk, heat just to boiling point. Add cheese, stir until cheese melts. Makes 8 servings.

COURTESY THE PURE FOOD COMPANY, INC.

Treasure Cave Blue Velvet Soup

2 *pkg (4 oz each) TREASURE CAVE Blue Cheese, crumbled*
1 *cup finely chopped carrots*
1 *cup finely chopped celery*
½ *cup minced onion*
2 *Tbsp butter or margarine*
1 *Tbsp flour*
1 *cup milk*
1 *8-oz pkg cream cheese*
1 *13½-oz can chicken broth*
1 *Tbsp chopped parsley*

In a saucepan, sauté carrots, celery, and onion in butter until tender. Blend in flour. Gradually blend in milk and cream cheese until smooth. Add broth, blue cheese, and parsley. Heat and serve hot. Yield: about 5½ cups.

COURTESY TREASURE CAVE BLUE CHEESE.

DANNON® YOGURT

Dannon Hot Yogurt Soup

- *1 cup semolina*
- *1 cup medium barley*
- *4 cups DANNON Plain Yogurt*
- *12 cups meat broth*
- *3 cups finely chopped onion*
- *2 Tbsp finely chopped mint*
- *¼ lb butter*
- *Salt and pepper to taste*

Soak semolina in 1 cup water for ½ hour. Soak and wash barley, cook in meat broth for 1 hour. Add semolina and cook until thick. While this goes on, fry onions golden brown in butter. Add onions, mint, salt, and pepper to soup and cook 3 more minutes. Stir yogurt well and add it very slowly. Heat until just before it comes to a boil. Serve hot. Serves 8.

COURTESY THE DANNON COMPANY.

Budweiser Beer 'n Cheese Soup

- *¾ cup shredded carrots*
- *¼ cup chopped onion*
- *¼ cup butter or margarine*
- *¼ cup flour*
- *2½ cups milk*
- *⅔ cup BUDWEISER Beer*
- *2 cups (8 oz) shredded sharp natural Cheddar cheese*
- *⅛ tsp salt*
- *Dash pepper*

Cook carrots and onion in butter or margarine until tender. Blend in flour. Stir in milk and beer. Cook until thickened. Add cheese and seasonings, stirring until melted. Yield: 4–6 servings.

REPRINTED BY PERMISSION ANHEUSER-BUSCH, INC., ST. LOUIS, MO.

Count Down® Cheese and Potato Soup

1 medium potato
½ small onion
1 Tbsp imitation bacon bits
⅓ cup COUNT DOWN® cheese, cubed
1 cup skim milk (made from cooking liquid and ⅓ cup dry milk)
1 tsp margarine

Cube peeled potato into ½-inch cubes, chop onions, and cook potato, onion, and imitation bacon bits in small amount of water until tender. Drain liquid into measuring cup and add water to make ¾ cup. Add ⅓ cup dry skim milk powder to make 1 cup skim milk. Heat milk, cheese, margarine, onions, potatoes, and imitation bacon bits in double boiler until cheese is melted. Serve with crackers or croutons. Makes 1 serving.

COURTESY FISHER CHEESE—AN AMFAC COMPANY.

Steero Homemade Bread Soup

6 slices firm white bread, toasted, buttered, cut in ½-inch strips
1 Tbsp butter or margarine
2 Tbsp all-purpose flour
6 tsp STEERO Instant Chicken Bouillon or 6 STEERO Cubes dissolved in 6 cups boiling water
¼ tsp pepper
1 cup onion, chopped
1 lb stewed tomatoes
1 cup water
2 eggs, hard-boiled and sliced
Grated Parmesan cheese

Sauté the onion in butter in a 3-qt saucepan until tender. Stir in tomatoes and heat until simmering; combine the flour, pepper, and 2–3 Tbsp of the water, making a smooth paste. Stir the paste into the tomato mixture with the rest of the water and the 6 cups of STEERO Chicken Bouillon, stirring occasionally over medium heat for 45–50 minutes. To serve: top each portion with 4 strips of buttered toast. Garnish with egg slices and cheese. Serves 6–8.

COURTESY AMERICAN KITCHEN PRODUCTS INC., JERSEY CITY, NJ.

La Choy Cantonese Soup

- *½ lb lean pork, sliced thin*
- *2 Tbsp cooking oil*
- *2 Tbsp LA CHOY Soy Sauce*
- *¼ tsp pepper*
- *1 tsp ground ginger*
- *1½ qt chicken broth*
- *3 cups thin-sliced Chinese celery cabbage*
- *LA CHOY Chow Mein Noodles*

In saucepot, lightly brown pork in hot oil, stirring frequently. Stir in soy sauce and seasonings; cook for 5 minutes. Add broth; simmer 15 minutes. Add cabbage to soup. Cook until cabbage is tender, about 5 minutes. Sprinkle a few noodles over each serving. Makes 6 servings.

COURTESY LA CHOY FOOD PRODUCTS.

Lipton®

Lipton Egg Drop Soup

- *1 envelope LIPTON Noodle Soup Mix with Real Chicken Broth*
- *3½ cups water*
- *1 egg, beaten*

In medium saucepan, combine noodle soup mix and water; bring to a boil, then simmer 2 minutes. With fork, quickly stir egg into soup until egg separates into shreds. Makes about 4 servings.

COURTESY OF THE LIPTON KITCHENS.

Snap-E-Tom® Tortilla Soup

- *6 corn tortillas*
- *½ cup oil*
- *2 cans (10½ oz each) condensed onion soup*
- *1½ cups water*
- *1 can (10 oz) SNAP-E-TOM Tomato Cocktail (or two 6-oz cans)*
- *1 can (7 oz) ORTEGA® Green Chile Salsa*
- *½ tsp ground coriander*
- *2 cups grated Monterey Jack cheese*

Cut tortillas into ½-inch-wide strips. In a skillet, heat oil and fry strips until crisp and golden. Drain on absorbent paper.

Combine remaining ingredients, except cheese, and cook until bubbly. Divide tortilla strips between large soup bowls. Ladle over soup and sprinkle with cheese. Serve at once. Serves 6.

COURTESY SNAP-E-TOM TOMATO COCKTAIL AND ORTEGA® GREEN CHILE SALSA.

Kellogg's®

Kellogg's® Gazpacho Soup

- *2 cans (10¾ oz each) condensed tomato soup*
- *2 cups water*
- *⅛ tsp rosemary leaves*
- *⅛ tsp oregano leaves*
- *⅛ tsp basil leaves*
- *1 clove garlic, finely chopped*
- *¼ cup finely chopped onion*
- *¼ cup vinegar*
- *¼ cup regular margarine or butter*
- *1 clove garlic, split*
- *2 cups KELLOGG'S® CROUTETTES® herb seasoned croutons*
- *1 medium-size tomato, peeled, coarsely chopped*
- *1 medium-size green pepper*
- *1 medium-size cucumber, coarsely chopped*
- *1 hard-cooked egg, coarsely chopped*

Measure first 8 ingredients into large mixing bowl. Stir to combine. Chill.

While soup is chilling, melt margarine in large frypan over low heat. Add split garlic and croutons, stirring until well coated. Cook, stirring frequently, until croutons are crisped and lightly browned. Remove and discard garlic. Set croutons aside to cool.

Portion tomato, green pepper, cucumber, and egg in chilled soup bowls. Pour about ¾ cup soup over each portion. Top with croutons. Yield: 8–10 servings.

COURTESY OF KELLOGG COMPANY.

Boggs Dessert Fruit Soup

- *2 cups BOGGS Cranberry Liqueur*
- *½ lb pitted dried prunes*
- *¼ lb dried apricots*
- *1 cup seedless raisins*
- *2 Tbsp quick-cooking tapioca*
- *½ cup sugar*
- *1 stick cinnamon*
- *3 apples, diced*
- *1 orange, thinly sliced*
- *1 lemon, thinly sliced*
- *4 cups water*

Place all ingredients in 4-qt saucepan. Bring to a boil. Reduce heat. Simmer, covered, 30 minutes. Chill several hours or overnight. Serves 10–12.

COURTESY BOGGS CRANBERRY LIQUEUR.

Sandwiches

Wesson® Tostada Buffet

1 (40-oz) can refried beans
8 large flour tortillas
WESSON Oil (generic term: pure vegetable oil)
2 cups cooked, shredded chicken
1 head iceberg lettuce, shredded
2 tomatoes, chopped
3 green onions, sliced
2 cups grated Cheddar cheese
1 cup sour cream
1 cup guacamole
Whole ripe olives (optional)

In a large saucepan, heat refried beans over low heat, stirring frequently. In a 12-inch skillet, heat 1 inch of WESSON Oil to 375°F. Fry tortillas, one at a time, until puffed and crisp. Drain on paper towels; keep warm. Arrange all ingredients in individual serving bowls or platters. Place buffet-style on table. To assemble: allow guests to spread tortillas with refried beans, then layer with equal amounts of chicken, lettuce, tomatoes, onions, and cheese. Top with dollops of sour cream and guacamole. Garnish with olives, if desired. Makes 8 tostadas.

COURTESY HUNT-WESSON FOODS, INC.

Bumble Bee® Broiled Tuna Mushroom Sandwich

1 can (7 oz) BUMBLE BEE® Solid White Albacore Tuna
2 Tbsp finely chopped green onion
2 tsp lemon juice
½ tsp salt
⅛ tsp pepper
1 cup finely chopped DOLE® Fresh Mushrooms
1 cup grated Cheddar cheese
2 large eggs, separated
4 slices bread, lightly toasted
Butter

Drain and flake tuna. Mix with onion, lemon juice, salt, and pepper. Add mushrooms and cheese. Beat egg whites stiff but not dry. Beat yolks lightly and fold into whites. Fold into tuna mixture. Spread hot toast with butter. Heap with tuna mixture, spreading just to edges. Broil 8 inches from heat 5–6 minutes, until puffy and browned. Makes 4 servings.

COURTESY OF CASTLE & COOKE FOODS (BUMBLE BEE® AND DOLE®).

Arnold Turkey/Chicken Salad Sandwich Deluxe

2 cups cooked turkey or chicken (diced)
¾ cup celery (diced)
¼ cup chives (chopped fine)
½ cup shredded toasted almonds
¾ cup seedless white grapes (sliced)
8 slices ARNOLD Naturel
¾ cup mayonnaise
1 tsp salt
5 Tbsp butter (soft)
4 tsp lemon juice
1 tsp grated lemon rind

Combine turkey or chicken with celery, chives, and almonds. Fold in grapes and mayonnaise. Salt to taste. Cover and refrigerate 2 hours or longer, so that flavors will mellow. Preheat broiler. Cream butter with lemon juice and grated lemon rind. Lightly toast ARNOLD Naturel slices on one side. Spread untoasted side with butter mixture and place under broiler until butter melts. Place a generous scoop of salad mixture on each piece of toast. Serve on luncheon plate. Yield: 8 sandwiches.

FROM ARNOLD, "ONE OF THE WORLD'S MOST RESPECTED BAKERS."

Land O'Lakes Toasty Turkeywiches

2 cups cooked, cubed (½ inch) LAND O LAKES® ButterMoist® Turkey Roast
1 7-oz can (1 cup) whole kernel corn, drained
½ cup chopped celery
⅔ cup salad dressing or mayonnaise
1 tsp prepared mustard
¼ tsp salt
⅛ tsp pepper
16 slices whole wheat bread, buttered
8 slices (3½ X 3½ X ⅛ inches) LAND O LAKES® Process American Cheese

Preheat oven: 425°F. In 3-qt bowl, combine turkey roast, corn, celery, salad dressing, mustard, salt, and pepper; mix well. Place 8 slices bread, buttered side down, on ungreased baking sheet.

Top each with 1 slice cheese, ⅓ cup turkey mixture, and 1 slice bread, buttered side up. Bake near center of 425°F oven 6–8 minutes, or until golden brown on the bottom. Turn, bake 2–3 minutes more until golden on second side. Yield: 8 sandwiches.

COURTESY OF THE LAND O'LAKES KITCHENS, MINNEAPOLIS, MN.

Wakefield Hot Seafood Sandwiches

- *1 (6-oz) pkg WAKEFIELD Alaska Crabmeat & Shrimp*
- *1 cup shredded mild Cheddar cheese*
- *½ cup finely chopped celery*
- *1 Tbsp chopped parsley*
- *½ cup sliced ripe olives*
- *¼ cup mayonnaise or salad dressing*
- *1 tsp lemon juice*
- *½ tsp Dijon-style mustard*
- *½ tsp Worcestershire sauce*
- *4 English muffins*
- *¼ cup butter or margarine*

Thaw crabmeat and shrimp, and drain. Combine crabmeat and shrimp, ¾ cup shredded cheese, celery, parsley, and black olives. Combine mayonnaise, lemon juice, mustard, and Worcestershire sauce. Toss seafood mixture with dressing. Split and toast English muffins; spread with butter. Place approximately ¼ cup of seafood mixture on each English muffin half; top with remaining cheese. Broil about 4 inches from source of heat 4–5 minutes or until cheese is melted and seafood mixture is heated. Serves 4.

COURTESY PACIFIC PEARL SEAFOODS.

Kretschmer Beefed Up Beef in Pocket Bread

- *4 pocket bread rounds, halved*
- *2 Tbsp cooking oil*
- *½ lb lean ground beef*
- *1 medium onion, coarsely chopped*
- *2 large cloves garlic, minced*
- *2 cartons (8 oz each) plain yogurt, divided*
- *¾ cup KRETSCHMER Regular Wheat Germ*
- *½ cup chopped celery*
- *½ cup minced parsley*
- *1½ tsp dried mint leaves, crushed*
- *1 tsp oregano leaves, crushed*
- *¾ tsp salt*
- *Chopped tomatoes*
- *Shredded romaine lettuce*
- *Thinly sliced cucumbers*

Wrap bread in foil. Heat at 350°F for 15 minutes. Prepare filling while bread heats. Heat oil in skillet. Add beef, onion, and garlic and sauté until browned. Stir in 1½ cups yogurt, wheat germ, celery, parsley, and seasonings. Stir well. Cook over low heat,

stirring, until thoroughly heated. Spoon into pocket bread. Serve with remaining yogurt, tomatoes, lettuce, and cucumbers and add to pockets. Yield: 4 servings.
COURTESY KRETSCHMER WHEAT GERM, A PRODUCT OF INTERNATIONAL MULTIFOODS.

Underwood Savory Brunch-wich

4 Tbsp butter or margarine, divided
½ cup diced onions
1 medium green pepper, diced
⅛ tsp salt
Dash pepper
4 eggs
1 can (4¾ oz) UNDERWOOD Roast Beef Spread
2 English muffins, split, toasted

In medium saucepan, melt 1 Tbsp butter; sauté onions and peppers until crisp-tender; add salt and pepper. In large skillet, fry eggs in remaining butter. Spread roast beef spread on toasted muffin halves. Top with fried egg; spoon peppers and onions over egg. Makes 4 servings.
REPRINTED WITH PERMISSION OF WM. UNDERWOOD CO., WESTWOOD, MA.

Stokely's Reuben Sandwiches

12 slices rye bread
6 Tbsp Thousand Island dressing
6 slices Swiss cheese
1 can (16 oz) STOKELY'S Finest® Bavarian Style Sauerkraut, drained
1 lb thinly sliced corned beef
2 eggs, slightly beaten
½ cup milk
Dash salt
Dash sugar
Butter or margarine

Spread 6 slices rye bread with Thousand Island dressing; top with Swiss cheese, STOKELY'S Sauerkraut, corned beef, and second bread slice. Mix together eggs, milk, salt, and sugar. Melt butter in skillet. Dip each side of sandwich into egg mixture and brown each side in skillet until golden. Makes 6 sandwiches.
COURTESY STOKELY-VAN CAMP, INC.

THOMAS'®

Thomas' Pepperoni Pizza

2 Tbsp marinara sauce
2 toasted THOMAS' English Muffins
Mozzarella cheese, shredded
Pepperoni, sliced

Spoon marinara sauce on each of 4 toasted THOMAS' English Muffin halves. Top with cheese and sliced pepperoni. Broil until cheese melts.

COURTESY S. B. THOMAS, INC.

Lipton Sloppy Joey

1 lb ground beef
2 envelopes LIPTON Tomato Cup-a-Soup
1 envelope LIPTON Onion Cup-a-Soup
1¼ cups water
⅓ cup sweet pickle relish (optional)
Toasted hamburger rolls

In medium skillet, brown ground beef; stir in LIPTON Tomato and LIPTON Onion Cup-a-Soup, water, and relish. Simmer, stirring occasionally, 5 minutes or until sauce is slightly thickened. Serve on hamburger rolls. Makes about 4 servings.

COURTESY OF THE LIPTON KITCHENS.

Salads

Tender chicken, crunchy nuts, marinated beans and grains, chunks of seafood, potatoes and pasta, fresh fruit—these are just a few of the ingredients that make up the great salad recipes on the following pages. So, if you think a salad is just a bowl of greens splashed with oil and vinegar—think again!

What makes a salad a salad? The ancient Romans, who popularized the custom of serving salads, knew only one type: raw greens mixed with herbs and dipped in a "dressing" of salt. In fact, our word "salad" comes from the Latin "sal" for salt.

Over the years, the definition of salads has expanded. Greens are now decked with more elaborate dressings including the classic French, Italian, and other national specialties.

Of course, salad dressings do not have to be based on a blend of oil and vinegar. Lemon juice may be used instead of vinegar, or, for a low-calorie dressing, lemon juice may be used by itself. Other fine dressings originate with sour cream, mayonnaise, milk, cheese, yogurt—the choice of toppings is almost as varied as the salads themselves.

Yet even with all the variety available, salads still generally include some type of greens served chilled with a dressing. Tossed salads depend upon the quality of the greens used, raw vegetables add crunch and flavor to seafood and meat salads, and even jellied salads usually are served on a bed of crisp lettuce.

To make sure your salads are always crisp and perfect, chill, wash, and thoroughly dry all the greens well in advance. Tear rather than cut lettuce and other fragile greens into bite-sized pieces, and place them into a bowl large enough to allow you plenty of room to mix all the ingredients. Add only enough dressing so that the ingredients are seasoned, not overwhelmed.

If you give the greens all the respect they deserve, it is hard to go wrong when you make a salad. So the next time you decide that a salad is just what you need to brighten your meal, try some salad ideas in this chapter that go beyond the basic bowl of greens.

Kellogg's® Croutettes® Tossed Salad Deluxe

- 1/4 cup regular margarine or butter
- 1/8 tsp garlic powder
- 1 Tbsp sesame seed
- 2 cups KELLOGG'S® CROUTETTES® herb seasoned croutons
- 1 qt romaine or iceberg lettuce, torn into bite-sized pieces
- 1 qt spinach leaves, torn into bite-sized pieces
- 1/2 cup small sweet onion rings
- 1 tsp salt
- 1/4 tsp pepper
- 1/2 tsp dry mustard
- 3 Tbsp vinegar
- 1 Tbsp honey
- 1/2 cup vegetable oil
- 3 medium-size tomatoes, cut into wedges

Melt margarine in large frypan over low heat. Stir in garlic powder and sesame seed. Add croutons, stirring until well coated. Cook, stirring frequently, until croutons are crisp and golden. Remove from heat. Set aside. In large salad bowl, toss salad greens with onion rings. Chill. For dressing, combine salt, pepper, dry mustard, vinegar, and honey in small mixing bowl. Add oil slowly while beating with rotary beater or electric mixer. Chill. Just before serving, combine salad greens, tomato wedges, dressing, and crisp croutons. Toss lightly. Yield: 8–10 servings.

COURTESY OF KELLOGG COMPANY.

Minute Maid®

Lemon-zesty Spinach Salad

- 1 lb fresh spinach
- 1 16-oz can Chinese vegetables without celery, drained and rinsed
- 2/3 cup salad oil
- 1/4 cup sugar
- 1/4 cup catsup
- 1/4 cup MINUTE MAID® 100% Pure Lemon Juice
- 1/4 cup Worcestershire sauce
- 2 Tbsp coarsely chopped onion, or 1 Tbsp instant minced onion
- 6 slices crisp bacon, crumbled
- 6 large fresh mushrooms, sliced

Wash spinach thoroughly, drain and tear into bite-size pieces. Combine spinach and Chinese vegetables in a large bowl, cover tightly and chill. Combine next 6 ingredients in an electric blender and blend well; store in refrigerator. At serving time, pour dressing over vegetables, add sliced mushrooms, and sprinkle bacon on top; toss lightly. Yield: 6–8 servings.

MINUTE MAID IS A REGISTERED TRADEMARK OF THE COCA-COLA COMPANY COURTESY THE COCA-COLA COMPANY FOODS DIVISION.

Friendship Spinach Salad

1 lb fresh spinach
2 hard-boiled eggs (diced)
2 red apples (unpeeled and diced)
1 red onion (sliced fine)
¼ lb blue cheese (crumbled)
1 cup mayonnaise
½ pint FRIENDSHIP Sour Cream

Wash spinach and tear into bite-sized pieces. Place spinach, eggs, apples, and onion in large bowl. In a separate bowl, mix together cheese, mayonnaise, and FRIENDSHIP Sour Cream. Toss salad with dressing and serve immediately.

RECIPE COURTESY OF FRIENDSHIP FOODS' HOME ECONOMIST, HELEN SCHWARTZ.

Diamond Walnuts Picture-Pretty Waldorf

2 medium-size Golden Delicious apples
2 medium-size Red Delicious apples
Lemon Water (see below)
⅔ cup coarsely chopped DIAMOND Walnuts
½ cup thinly sliced celery
Crisp lettuce leaves
Mayonnaise

Core apples. Cut one of each color into 16 wedges; dip in Lemon Water. Dice remaining apples; dip in Lemon Water; drain well; mix with walnuts and celery. Spoon onto 4 lettuce-lined salad plates. Arrange 8 apple wedges of alternating colors around each serving. Top each with a dollop of mayonnaise. Decorate with a walnut piece. If preferred, toss salad mixture with ½ cup mayonnaise. Decorate as directed. Makes 4 servings.

Lemon Water

Combine 1 Tbsp lemon juice with ½ cup cold water.

COURTESY DIAMOND WALNUT GROWERS, INC., STOCKTON, CALIFORNIA.

MICHELOB®

Michelob Beer Cabbage Slaw

- *1 medium-size head of cabbage*
- *1 green pepper, shredded*
- *2 Tbsp celery seed*
- *1 tsp minced onion*
- *1 tsp salt*
- *¼ tsp pepper*
- *1 cup mayonnaise*
- *½ cup MICHELOB Beer*

Shred cabbage. Add green pepper, celery seed, onion, and seasonings. Thin mayonnaise with beer. Add to cabbage. Toss thoroughly. Chill. Yield: about 6 servings.

Friendship Cucumber Salad

- *4 large cucumbers*
- *2 cloves garlic, pressed*
- *3 8-oz containers FRIENDSHIP Plain Yogurt*
- *Salt*
- *Freshly ground pepper*

Peel the cucumbers and cube. Add the garlic and seasonings to taste to the yogurt. Marinate cucumbers in yogurt mixture overnight. Drain excess water from salad. Serve chilled, garnished with fresh dill or mint. Yield: 6–8 servings.

RECIPE COURTESY OF FRIENDSHIP FOODS' HOME ECONOMIST, HELEN SCHWARTZ.

La Choy Chinese Vegetable Salad

LA CHOY®

- *½ cup salad oil*
- *2 Tbsp vinegar*
- *½ tsp dry mustard*
- *¼ tsp paprika*
- *1 Tbsp sugar*
- *1 tsp salt*
- *Freshly ground pepper*
- *1 clove garlic, crushed*
- *3 cups finely sliced Chinese celery cabbage*
- *½ cup thinly sliced carrots*
- *½ cup sliced green onions*
- *1 cup rinsed, drained LA CHOY Bean Sprouts*
- *½ cup sliced LA CHOY Water Chestnuts*

Combine oil, vinegar, seasonings, and garlic; mix well. Chill for at least 1 hour. In a salad bowl, combine remaining ingredients.

Pour salad dressing over vegetables. Toss lightly until vegetables are coated with salad dressing. Serve immediately. Makes 6 servings.

COURTESY LA CHOY FOOD PRODUCTS.

Ortega® Guacamole Salad

2 Tbsp red wine vinegar
1 Tbsp chili powder
2 tsp salt
3 medium avocados, seeded and peeled
¼ cup minced onion
1 can (4 oz) ORTEGA Diced Green Chiles
1 small firm tomato, diced
¾ cup cooked and crumbled bacon (approx. ¾ lb)
4 cups shredded iceberg lettuce
Corn chips
Ripe olives (optional)

Combine vinegar, chili powder, and salt. In a large bowl, mash avocado with chili dressing. Fold onion, chiles, tomato, and bacon into mixture. Line individual plates with shredded lettuce. Mound avocado mixture onto centers and arrange corn chips around edges. Garnish with slices of ripe olives or reserved diced tomato, if desired. Serves 6.

COURTESY OF HEUBLEIN, INC.

Pompeian Greek Salad

1 head lettuce
2 medium tomatoes
1 onion, sliced
1 chopped green pepper
1 cucumber, sliced
½ cup POMPEIAN Olive Oil
¼ cup vinegar
Fillets of anchovies or herring

Section lettuce. Add quartered tomatoes, onion, pepper, and cucumber. Salt, pepper to taste; mix well. Add POMPEIAN Olive Oil and vinegar; toss lightly. Garnish with anchovies or herring bits. Serves 6.

COURTESY OF POMPEIAN OLIVE OIL.

Planters Crunchy Chicken Salad

4 cups cubed cooked chicken
1 cup chopped celery
1 cup halved seedless green grapes
1 cup PLANTERS® Slivered Almonds, toasted
1 tsp salt
¼ tsp pepper
¾ cup mayonnaise
¼ cup sour cream
Lettuce

Combine cubed cooked chicken, chopped celery, halved green grapes, and toasted PLANTERS Slivered Almonds in a large mixing bowl. Sprinkle salt and pepper over mixture. Add mayonnaise and sour cream and mix thoroughly. Chill well. Serve on lettuce. Makes 4–5 servings.

COURTESY OF STANDARD BRANDS INCORPORATED.

Stokely's Chicken Cocktail Salad

½ cup mayonnaise or salad dressing
1 Tbsp cream or milk
1 tsp lemon juice
¼ tsp nutmeg
⅛ tsp curry powder
2 whole cooked chicken breasts, diced
1 can (1 lb 14 oz) STOKELY'S Finest® Fruit Cocktail, drained and chilled
¼ cup slivered toasted almonds

Combine first 5 ingredients. Fold in chicken and chill 30 minutes. Add STOKELY'S Fruit Cocktail and almonds. Serve on lettuce leaves. Makes 5 servings.

COURTESY STOKELY-VAN CAMP, INC.

La Rosa Tuna, Mushroom, and Macaroni Salad

½ lb fresh mushrooms, thinly sliced
2 tsp lemon juice
¼ tsp thyme
¼ cup thinly sliced scallion greens
3 Tbsp olive oil
½ tsp salt
8 oz LA ROSA Elbow Macaroni (½ pkg)
1 7-oz can tuna, in chunks
8 to 10 black olives, sliced

In a serving bowl, toss the mushrooms with lemon juice until the slices are lightly moistened. Then add scallions, oil, salt, and thyme and toss again. Cook LA ROSA Macaroni as directed on package; drain. Add macaroni, tuna, and olives and set aside to chill until serving.

COURTESY V. LA ROSA & SONS, INC.

SeaPak Shrimp Salad Louis

1 lb SEAPAK Frozen, Peeled and Deveined Shrimp

Prepare by package directions and arrange on lettuce. Serve with Louis Dressing.

Louis Dressing

1 cup mayonnaise
¼ cup French dressing
1 tsp horseradish
1 tsp Worcestershire sauce
1½ tsp salt
½ tsp Tabasco

Combine all ingredients and mix thoroughly. Serves 4–5.

COURTESY RICH-SEAPAK CORPORATION.

Swift's Turkey Salad Supreme

2 cups diced roasted Butter Basted SWIFT'S Premium Turkey Roast, White Meat
1 cup dairy sour cream
1 cup yogurt or mayonnaise
½ cup sliced ripe or green olives
¼ cup chopped parsley
¼ cup finely chopped onion
1 medium unpared cucumber, chopped
1 large tomato, seeded and chopped
1 tsp salt
Lettuce cups

Mix together all ingredients except lettuce. Chill and serve in lettuce cups. Yield: 6 servings (6 cups).

COURTESY SWIFT & COMPANY.

Lindsay Salad Nicoise

2 hard-cooked eggs, sliced
1 can tuna, chunk style
1 can green beans, drained
1 can LINDSAY Ripe Olives, drained
Crisp romaine lettuce
Anchovies (optional)

Toss all the above ingredients with an oil and lemon dressing. A hearty "meal in a salad bowl."

COURTESY LINDSAY INTERNATIONAL, INC., LINDSAY, CALIFORNIA 93247.

MUSSELMAN'S®

Musselman's Mexican White Fish

- 2 lb halibut or cod steaks, ¾ inch thick
- ½ cup lemon juice
- ⅔ cup flour
- 2 Tbsp plus 1 tsp paprika, divided usage
- 2½ tsp salt, divided usage
- 1½ tsp ground cumin, divided usage
- 1½ tsp oregano leaves, crushed, divided usage
- 1 tsp ground nutmeg, divided usage
- ¼ tsp garlic powder, divided usage
- Dash ground red pepper
- ⅓ cup salad oil
- 2 cups MUSSELMAN'S Distilled White Vinegar
- ½ cup chopped onion
- 3 bay leaves

Cut fish into 8 to 12 portions. Place fish in a shallow pan in a single layer. Pour lemon juice over all; let stand for 15 minutes. In a shallow pan, combine: flour; 1 tsp paprika; ½ tsp each salt, cumin, and oregano; ¼ tsp nutmeg; ⅛ tsp garlic powder; and red pepper. Coat fish with the seasoned flour mixture. In a large skillet, heat oil until hot. Add fish; sauté until opaque on the inside and lightly browned on the outside, about 45 seconds on each side. Place close together in pan in a single layer. In a small saucepan, combine vinegar, onion, bay leaves, and remaining 2 Tbsp paprika, 2 tsp salt, 1 tsp each cumin and oregano, ¾ tsp nutmeg, and ⅛ tsp garlic powder. Bring to a boil; simmer, covered, 5 minutes. Pour over fish. Cover and refrigerate overnight. Serve on a bed of iceberg lettuce leaves garnished with lemon wedges, stuffed olives, and radish roses, if desired. Serve as an appetizer or luncheon salad. Makes 8–12 servings.

PET, AN IC INDUSTRIES COMPANY, HOME ECONOMICS DEPT., P.O. BOX 392, ST. LOUIS, MO 63166.

King Oscar Delicious Sardine Salad

- 2 cans KING OSCAR Sardines, drained
- 2 large Delicious apples, peeled, cored, chopped
- 2 large oranges, peeled and cut into bite-size pieces
- 1 large sweet Spanish onion, peeled and chopped
- ½ cup walnuts, chopped
- ½ cup sour cream
- ¼ cup lemon juice
- 1 tsp chopped chives
- Lettuce
- Parsley

In large salad bowl, toss together sardines, apple, orange, onion, and walnuts. Make dressing by mixing together sour

cream, lemon juice, and chives. Pour dressing over salad and toss gently. Serve on bed of lettuce and garnish with parsley. Serves 6.
COURTESY KING OSCAR SARDINES.

Stokely's Tangy Bean Salad

- *½ cup white vinegar*
- *½ cup sugar*
- *½ cup salad oil*
- *½ cup chopped onion*
- *½ cup chopped green pepper*
- *1 can (1 lb) STOKELY'S Finest® Green Beans, drained*
- *1 can (1 lb) STOKELY'S Finest® Cut Wax Beans, drained*
- *1 can (1 lb) STOKELY'S Finest® Shellie® Beans, drained*

Combine first 5 ingredients and mix well. Drain STOKELY'S Beans and add to dressing. Refrigerate overnight. Makes 9–10 servings.
COURTESY STOKELY-VAN CAMP, INC.

IGA Garbanzo Salad

- *2 cans IGA Garbanzos, drained*
- *4 Tbsp olive oil*
- *4 Tbsp wine vinegar*
- *2 Tbsp chopped parsley*
- *2 small jars chopped pimientos*
- *3 chopped green onions*
- *½ tsp salt*
- *¼ tsp pepper*

In a bowl, combine oil, vinegar, onions, salt, and pepper. Add IGA Garbanzos, pimientos, and parsley. Let stand for 3 hours. Serves 6.
COURTESY OF IGA, INC.

San Giorgio Macaroni Salad

- *½ lb (2 cups dry) SAN GIORGIO Elbow Macaroni*
- *½ Tbsp salt*
- *3 qt boiling water*
- *½ cup chopped celery*
- *¼ cup diced green pepper*
- *2 Tbsp thinly sliced radishes*
- *¾ cup salad dressing*
- *2 Tbsp prepared mustard*
- *¼ tsp onion salt*

Cook SAN GIORGIO Elbows in salt and boiling water for about 10 minutes. Rinse in cold water and drain. Combine with the remaining ingredients and toss lightly. Refrigerate for several hours. Serve.

COURTESY SAN GIORGIO-SKINNER, INC.

Kretschmer Veggie Salad

- *1 can (7–8¾ oz) whole kernel corn, drained*
- *⅓ cup KRETSCHMER Regular Wheat Germ*
- *⅓ cup finely sliced green onion*
- *⅓ cup minced parsley*
- *⅓ cup chopped carrots*
- *⅓ cup chopped celery*
- *3 Tbsp cooking oil*
- *2 Tbsp lemon juice*
- *½ tsp basil leaves, crushed*
- *¼ tsp oregano leaves, crushed*
- *¼ tsp salt*
- *Salad greens*
- *Sliced cucumber*

Combine all ingredients except salad greens and cucumber. Mix well. Line salad bowl with greens. Spoon corn mixture into center of greens. Garnish with cucumber. Yield: 4 servings.

COURTESY KRETSCHMER WHEAT GERM, A PRODUCT OF INTERNATIONAL MULTIFOODS.

Hellmann's Old-Fashioned Potato Salad

- *1 cup HELLMANN'S or BEST FOODS Real Mayonnaise*
- *1 cup minced onion*
- *3 Tbsp white vinegar*
- *2 tsp salt*
- *¼ tsp pepper*
- *2 hard-cooked eggs, chopped*
- *3 lb potatoes, cooked, peeled, cubed (about 6 cups)*
- *2 cups sliced celery*

In large bowl, stir together HELLMANN'S Real Mayonnaise, onion, vinegar, salt, pepper, and eggs. Add potatoes and celery; toss to coat well. Cover; refrigerate at least 4 hours. If desired, sprinkle with paprika. Makes about 8 cups.

COURTESY HELLMANN'S REAL MAYONNAISE.

Quaker® Barley Salad Vinaigrette

- *1 cup QUAKER® Scotch Brand Quick Pearled Barley*
- *1 tsp salt*
- *3 cups boiling water*
- *2 cups mushroom slices*
- *1 cup thin carrot slices*
- *¼ cup green onion slices*
- *½ cup vegetable oil*
- *⅓ cup lemon juice*
- *1½ tsp garlic salt*
- *1 tsp prepared mustard*
- *½ tsp tarragon leaves, crushed*
- *⅛ tsp pepper*

Cook barley in salted boiling water according to package directions. Drain; cool. Combine barley, mushrooms, carrot, and onion. Add combined remaining ingredients; mix well. Chill about 3–4 hours; serve on lettuce leaves. Makes 6–8 servings.

RECIPE REPRODUCED WITH THE PERMISSION OF THE QUAKER OATS COMPANY.

Uncle Ben's®

Uncle Ben's® It's-Better-Than-Potato Salad

1 cup UNCLE BEN'S® CONVERTED® Brand Rice
2 cups mayonnaise or salad dressing
2 cups sliced celery
1 medium onion, finely chopped
4 tsp prepared mustard
½ tsp salt
4 hard-cooked eggs, chopped
8 radishes, sliced
1 cucumber, pared and diced

Cook rice according to package directions. Chill. Add mayonnaise or salad dressing, celery, onion, mustard, and salt; mix well. Chill. Stir in eggs, radishes, and cucumber before serving. Makes 6–8 servings.

COURTESY UNCLE BEN'S FOODS.

Kraft Fiesta Mac Salad

1 7¼-oz pkg KRAFT Macaroni and Cheese Dinner
1 cup chopped tomato
½ cup chopped cucumber
½ cup shredded carrot
½ cup MIRACLE WHIP Salad Dressing
¼ tsp salt

Prepare Dinner as directed on package. Add remaining ingredients; mix lightly. Chill. Add additional salad dressing before serving, if desired. Yield: 4–6 servings.

COURTESY OF KRAFT, INC.

Del Monte Confetti Fruit Salad

1 can (15¼ oz) DEL MONTE Pineapple Chunks
1½ cups diced cooked ham
1 cup Cheddar cheese, cubed
2 oranges, peeled and sectioned
Lettuce
⅓ cup mayonnaise
⅓ cup dairy sour cream

Drain pineapple, reserving ¼ cup syrup. Toss pineapple, ham, cheese, and oranges. Place in lettuce-lined bowl. Chill. Mix together mayonnaise, sour cream, and reserved pineapple syrup. Serve as dressing with salad. Yield: 4 servings.

COURTESY DEL MONTE KITCHENS, DEL MONTE CORPORATION, P.O. BOX 3575, SAN FRANCISCO, CA 94119.

Knox Blox

4 envelopes KNOX Unflavored Gelatine
3 pkg (3 oz each) flavored gelatine
4 cups boiling water

In large bowl, mix KNOX Unflavored Gelatine with flavored gelatine; add boiling water and stir until gelatine is completely dissolved. Pour into 13 X 9-inch baking pan and chill until firm. To serve, cut into 1-inch squares. Makes about 9 dozen blox.

Variation

For double-decker blox, reduce water to 3 cups; after gelatine is dissolved, stir in 1 cup (½ pint) whipping, or heavy, cream.
COURTESY OF KNOX GELATINE, INC.

DANNON® YOGURT

Dannon Knox Nature Blox

4 envelopes Knox Unflavored Gelatine
2 cups (8 oz each) DANNON Dutch Apple Yogurt
½ cup apple juice
1 cup boiling water
¼ cup honey
½ cup chopped walnuts or raisins

In large bowl, sprinkle unflavored gelatine over apple juice; add boiling water and stir until gelatin is completely dissolved. With wire whisk or rotary beater, blend in yogurt and honey. Pour into 8- or 9-inch-square pan and sprinkle with walnuts; chill until firm. Cut squares to serve. Makes 5–6 dozen squares.

Variation

Pineapple-orange yogurt and orange juice.
COURTESY THE DANNON COMPANY.

Lucky Leaf Apple Salad Mold

6 oz lemon-flavored gelatin
1 cup hot LUCKY LEAF Apple Juice
1 cup ginger ale
½ cup chopped nuts
½ cup chopped celery
1 Tbsp ground ginger or 2 Tbsp chopped crystallized ginger
1 25-oz jar LUCKY LEAF Apple Sauce

Dissolve gelatin in hot apple juice. Cool, add ginger ale. When it cools and begins to thicken, add other ingredients. Pour into mold. Refrigerate at least 2 hours, 4 hours is better. Unmold onto bed of lettuce leaves.

COMPLIMENTS OF KNOUSE FOODS—MAKERS OF LUCKY LEAF QUALITY FRUIT PRODUCTS.

PET®

Pet Cranberry Salad

1 can (8 oz) crushed pineapple
1 pkg (3 oz) strawberry-flavored gelatin
⅓ cup mayonnaise
¼ tsp salt
2 Tbsp vinegar
1 small can (⅔ cup) PET Evaporated Milk
1 can (16 oz) whole cranberry sauce

Drain juice from pineapple into a measuring cup. Add enough water to make ¾ cup liquid. Heat to boiling. Dissolve gelatin in liquid. Cool slightly. Combine mayonnaise, salt, and vinegar. Gradually add cooled gelatin mixture. Stir until smooth. Mix in evaporated milk, pineapple, and cranberries. Pour into oiled 4-cup gelatin mold. Chill until firm. Turn out onto lettuce. Serve. Makes 6 servings.

PET, AN IC INDUSTRIES COMPANY, HOME ECONOMICS DEPT., P.O. BOX 392, ST. LOUIS, MO 63166.

Campbell's Tomato Aspic

- *2 envelopes unflavored gelatine*
- *3 cups CAMPBELL'S Tomato Juice*
- *2 Tbsp vinegar*
- *½ tsp celery salt*
- *½ tsp Worcestershire sauce*
- *¼ tsp onion powder*
- *Generous dash pepper*

In saucepan, sprinkle gelatine over 1 cup cold juice to soften. Place over low heat, stirring until gelatine is dissolved. Remove from heat; add remaining juice, vinegar, and seasonings. Pour into 4-cup mold. Chill 4 hours or until firm. Unmold on salad greens. Makes about 3 cups.

COURTESY CAMPBELL SOUP COMPANY.

Dannon Cold Salmon & Cucumber Soufflé

- *2 envelopes unflavored gelatin*
- *1½ cups chicken broth*
- *½ cup mayonnaise*
- *2 cups DANNON Plain Yogurt*
- *2 Tbsp lemon juice*
- *2 Tbsp minced onion*
- *2 Tbsp chopped dill*
- *1 1-lb can salmon, drained, with skin and bones removed*
- *2 cucumbers peeled, seeds removed, and chopped*
- *Salt to taste*

Stir gelatin and chicken broth over low heat until gelatin is dissolved. Beat in mayonnaise and lemon juice. Chill until the mixture is thick and syrupy. Fold in yogurt, dill, onion, cucumbers, and salmon. Pour into mold. Chill until set. Unmold, garnish with hard-boiled eggs, parsley, and tomatoes and put on a bed of cooked rice or lettuce.

COURTESY THE DANNON COMPANY.

Under-The-Sea Salad

- *1 can (16 oz) pear halves*
- *1 pkg (3 oz) JELL-O® Brand Lime Flavor Gelatin*
- *¼ tsp salt (optional)*
- *1 cup boiling water*
- *1 Tbsp lemon juice*
- *2 pkg (3 oz each) cream cheese*
- *⅛ tsp cinnamon (optional)*

Drain pears, reserving ¾ cup of the syrup. Dice pears and set aside. Dissolve gelatin and salt in boiling water. Add reserved syrup and lemon juice. Pour 1¼ cups into an 8 X 4-inch loaf pan or 4-cup mold. Chill until set but not firm, about 1 hour. Meanwhile, soften cheese until creamy. Very slowly blend in remaining gelatin, beating until smooth. Add cinnamon and pears and spoon into pan. Chill until firm, about 4 hours. Unmold. Garnish with crisp salad greens, mayonnaise, and additional pears, if desired. Makes about 3½ cups or 6 servings.

Note: recipe may be doubled, using a 9 X 5-inch loaf pan. Garnish may be pear-half fan or slices and maraschino cherries.

Mazola Basic French Dressing

- *1 cup MAZOLA Corn Oil*
- *⅓ to ½ cup vinegar (lemon juice may be substituted for all or part of the vinegar, if desired)*
- *1 to 3 Tbsp sugar*
- *1½ tsp salt*
- *½ tsp paprika*
- *½ tsp dry mustard*
- *1 clove garlic*

Measure into jar, corn oil, vinegar, sugar, salt, paprika, mustard, and garlic. Cover tightly and shake well. Chill several hours, then remove garlic. Shake thoroughly before serving. Makes 1⅓–1½ cups.

Zesty Dressing

Follow recipe for Basic French Dressing, adding 2 Tbsp catchup, 1 Tbsp lemon juice, and 1 tsp Worcestershire sauce.

Mystery Dressing

Combine ingredients for Zesty Dressing in small bowl. Add 1 unbeaten egg white. Beat with rotary beater until thoroughly blended. Cover; refrigerate. (Dressing thickens slightly on standing.) Stir well before serving. Makes about 1½ cups.

Spicy Dressing

Heat ⅓ to ½ cup vinegar. Add 1 Tbsp pickling spices (tied in cheesecloth , if desired). Let stand until vinegar is cool. Remove spices. Follow recipe for Basic French Dressing, using this vinegar.

Lemon Herb Dressing

Follow recipe for Basic French Dressing, using lemon juice for ¾ of the vinegar, reducing range of sugar to 1–2 Tbsp and substituting ½ tsp salad herbs for dry mustard.

Creamy Dressing

Follow recipe for Basic French Dressing, increasing sugar to ¼ cup, omitting dry mustard and garlic, and adding ½ cup dairy sour cream and ¼ cup catchup. Makes 2 cups.

Diet French Dressing

Follow recipe for Basic French Dressing, decreasing vinegar to ¼ cup, adding 2 Tbsp water, and decreasing sugar and salt to 1 tsp each.

COURTESY MAZOLA CORN OIL.

Campbell's Piquant Salad Dressings

1 can (10¾ oz) CAMPBELL'S Condensed Cream of Celery Soup
3 eggs
¼ cup vinegar
1 tsp dry mustard
1 tsp sugar
¼ tsp salt
Dash cayenne pepper
1½ cups salad oil

In blender, combine all ingredients except oil. Cover; blend on high speed a few seconds. With blender still on high speed, remove cover. *Very slowly* pour oil in a steady stream into soup mixture. Chill. Makes about 4 cups basic salad dressing.

For *blue cheese sour cream dressing*, gradually stir 1 cup basic salad dressing into 2 Tbsp sour cream. Add ¼ cup crumbled blue cheese; chill. Serve on salad greens, baked potatoes, hamburgers, or vegetable salads. Makes about 1 cup.

For *green goddess dressing*, combine 1 cup basic salad dressing, 1 Tbsp chopped anchovy fillets, 1 Tbsp finely chopped parsley, and ¼ tsp crushed tarragon leaves. Chill. Serve on salad greens. Makes about 1 cup.

COURTESY CAMPBELL SOUP COMPANY.

Sunkist® Lemon Sesame Dressing

⅔ cup salad oil
Juice of 1 Sunkist® Lemon
2 Tbsp vinegar
2 Tbsp toasted sesame seed
1 Tbsp sugar
½ tsp onion salt
½ tsp salt

In jar with lid, combine all ingredients; shake well. Makes about 1 cup. Serve over any crisp green, tuna, chicken or fruit salad.

COURTESY SUNKIST GROWERS, INC.

Hunt's® Thousand Island Dressing

1 8-oz can HUNT'S Tomato Sauce
½ cup mayonnaise
¼ cup sweet pickle relish
2 hard-cooked eggs, chopped
1 Tbsp minced onion
½ tsp dry mustard
½ tsp salt
¼ tsp leaf basil
¼ tsp pepper

In a small bowl, combine all ingredients. Store in refrigerator in airtight container. Makes 1 pint.

COURTESY HUNT-WESSON FOODS, INC.

Colombo Blue Cheese Dressing

1 cup plain COLOMBO Whole-Milk Yogurt
3 Tbsp crumbled blue cheese
¼ tsp garlic powder
1 Tbsp minced onion
Dash pepper

Combine all ingredients and chill in a covered container.

PERMISSION TO REPRODUCE GRANTED BY AMERICA'S ORIGINAL YOGURT COMPANY, COLOMBO, INC.

Kikkoman Creamy Salad Dressing

1 cup dairy sour cream
½ cup mayonnaise
4 tsp KIKKOMAN Soy Sauce
1 tsp parsley flakes
¼ tsp onion powder
Dash paprika

Combine all ingredients until well blended. Let stand 10 minutes before serving. Makes 1½ cups.

COURTESY KIKKOMAN INTERNATIONAL INC.

Puritan Zesty Salad Dressing

¾ cup PURITAN Oil
¼ cup cider vinegar
1 tsp garlic salt
1 tsp sugar
⅛ tsp pepper
1 tsp paprika
1 tsp prepared mustard, regular or Dijon style

Combine all ingredients in container with tight fitting cover. Shake vigorously to blend. Store covered in refrigerator. Shake well before serving with green salads.

COURTESY OF THE PROCTER & GAMBLE COMPANY.

Breads

Bread making is a satisfying art that is too important to be left to the professionals. Commercially prepared breads are a great convenience, but store-bought bread can not give you the sense of satisfaction that comes from turning your own crusty brown loaves out of the oven.

Yet many otherwise adventurous cooks shy away from making their own bread. Believing that bread making is too complicated, too likely to fail, or just too time-consuming, these cooks miss out on the fun—and great flavor—of fresh, homemade loaves.

If you have avoided bread making in the past, remember that breads did not become the staple of our diets by being too complicated to cook. Now, thanks to convenience foods and new shortcut methods, it is easier than ever to make delicious breads. The flours you buy in the store are presifted; the yeasts are dated so that you know when to use them; mixes take all the worry out of quick breads. Best of all, the manufacturers' carefully tested recipes give such precise directions that it is hard to go wrong.

If you have always thought that bread making has to be an all-day affair, remember that there are many different types of bread. It is still possible to devote a whole afternoon to making an old-fashioned rye bread, but it is also possible to whip up a quick nut bread in less than an hour. You may choose to knead and shape elaborate loaves of yeast bread, or you may pick a coffeecake recipe that simply calls for you to pour batter into a pan.

The art of bread making allows you to be as creative as you want—but like other arts bread making does require you to use your own judgment and taste. Some of the following recipes, for example, offer only a range of flour amounts instead of specifying a single measurement. This vagueness is deliberate, because individual flours vary in the amount of liquid they will absorb. Try beginning with the smaller amount of flour suggested, and then add more only as you feel it is necessary.

Fleischmann's White Bread

- 2 *cups milk*
- ¾ *cup sugar*
- 8 *tsp salt*
- ¾ *cup (1½ sticks) FLEISCHMANN'S® Margarine*
- 6 *cups warm water (105°–115°F)*
- 4 *pkg FLEISCHMANN'S® Active Dry Yeast*
- 24 *cups unsifted flour (about)*

Scald milk; stir in sugar, salt, and FLEISCHMANN'S Margarine. Cool to lukewarm. Measure warm water into large warm bowl. Sprinkle in FLEISCHMANN'S Yeast; stir until dissolved. Add lukewarm milk mixture and 12 cups flour; beat until smooth. Add enough additional flour to make a stiff dough. Turn out onto lightly floured board; knead until smooth and elastic, about 10–12 minutes. Place in greased bowl, turning to grease top. Cover; let rise in warm place, free from draft, until doubled in bulk, about 1 hour. Punch dough down. Cover; let rest 15 minutes. Divide dough into 6 equal pieces. Roll each piece to a 14 X 9-inch rectangle. Shape into loaves. Place in 6 greased 9 X 5 X 3-inch loaf pans. Cover; let as many as will fit in the oven rise in warm place, free from draft, until doubled in bulk, about 1 hour. Cover remaining loaves and put in cooler place, free from draft, until doubled in bulk, about 1½ hours. Bake at 400°F about 30 minutes, or until done. Remove from pans and cool on wire racks.

COURTESY OF STANDARD BRANDS INCORPORATED.

Quaker® Oatmeal Bread

- 2 *pkg active dry yeast*
- ½ *cup warm water*
- 1¼ *cups milk*
- 1 *cup cold water*
- ¼ *cup butter or margarine*
- ¼ *cup sugar*
- 2½ *tsp salt*
- 6 *to 6¼ cups all-purpose flour*
- 2 *cups QUAKER® Oats (quick or old fashioned, uncooked)*

Dissolve yeast in warm water. Combine milk and cold water; heat. Pour hot liquid over butter, sugar, and salt. Stir until butter melts. Cool to lukewarm. Stir in 2 cups flour to make soft dough.

Turn out onto lightly floured surface; knead about 8–10 minutes or until smooth and elastic. Shape to form ball; place in greased bowl, turning to coat surface of dough. Cover; let rise in warm place about 1 hour or until double in size. Punch dough down. Cover; let rest 10 minutes. Shape to form 2 loaves. Place in 2 greased 9 X 5-inch loaf pans. Brush lightly with melted butter. Cover; let rise about 45 minutes or until nearly double in size. Bake in preheated moderate oven (375°F) 45–50 minutes. Makes 2 loaves.

Note: For 4 loaves, recipe may be doubled. For ease in handling, divide dough in half before kneading; proceed as directed.

RECIPE REPRODUCED WITH THE PERMISSION OF THE QUAKER OATS COMPANY.

Elam's 100% Whole Wheat Flour Bread

2 cups milk, scalded
2 Tbsp soft shortening or butter
¼ cup molasses or fructose
*1 pkg (¼ oz) active dry yeast**
¼ cup warm water (105°–115°F)
About 5½ cups ELAM'S Stone Ground 100% Whole Wheat Flour

Combine first 3 ingredients in bowl; mix well and cool to lukewarm. Dissolve yeast in warm water; stir into milk mixture. Gradually stir in flour as needed to make a stiff dough; beat well after each addition. Cover bowl with damp towel. Let rise in warm draftless area until double in size; punch down. Knead dough until smooth and elastic on a board lightly sprinkled with whole wheat flour. Divide dough in half; shape into 2 loaves. Place loaves in greased loaf pans (8½ X 4½ X 2⅝ inches). Brush tops lightly with additional cooking oil or melted butter. Cover; let rise until almost double in size. Bake in moderate oven (375°F) until done, 40–45 minutes. Remove from pans; cool on wire racks. Yield: 2 loaves.

*1 cake (0.6 oz) compressed yeast can be substituted for dry yeast and dissolved in lukewarm water (about 95°F).
COURTESY ELAM'S STONE GROUND 100% WHOLE WHEAT FLOUR.

Miller Country Beer Bread

1 pkg active dry yeast
½ cup warm water
1½ cups hot MILLER High Life
2 tsp salt
¼ cup sugar
¼ cup honey
2 Tbsp corn oil
4½ cups soy or wheat flour

Preheat oven to 325°F. Dissolve yeast in warm water and set aside. In a greased mixing bowl combine hot MILLER High Life, salt, sugar, honey, and corn oil. Add yeast mixture and stir in flour, a little at a time, until a stiff dough is formed. Turn dough to grease thoroughly on all sides. Remove to a floured board and knead with floured hands for 5 minutes, or until smooth and elastic.

Reduce oven to 250°F and return the dough to the bowl, covering with a cloth. Place in the closed oven for 20 minutes. Remove and knead again on a floured board for 10 minutes, or until dough is resilient. Fold in half 4 or 5 times, pounding down on it with your fists in a beating motion, then refolding anew. Flour dough so it won't stick to board. Again return to bowl, cover, and return to oven (250°F), closing oven door. Let stand for 50 minutes or until doubled in bulk.

Increase oven temperature to 350°F. Shape dough into 2 loaves and place in 2 greased 9 X 5-inch loaf pans. Bake for 50 minutes, or until crusts are brown and a tester inserted in the center comes out clean. Cool on racks before slicing. Makes 2 loaves.

COURTESY MILLER BREWING COMPANY.

Ralston Purina Batter Bran Bread

2¾ cups all-purpose flour (divided)
2 tsp salt
2 pkg active dry yeast
1¼ cups milk
½ cup water
3 Tbsp butter or margarine
2 Tbsp honey
2 cups BRAN CHEX® cereal

In large mixer bowl, combine 1¼ cups flour, salt, and undissolved yeast. Combine milk, water, butter, and honey in saucepan. Heat over low heat until very warm (120°–130°F). (Butter does not need to melt.) Stir in Chex. Add to dry ingredients. Beat 2 minutes on medium speed of electric mixer. Add ¾ cup flour. Beat 2 minutes on high speed. Scrape bowl occasionally. Mix in remaining flour. Cover. Let rise in warm place, free from draft, until doubled in bulk, 35–45 minutes. Stir batter down. Beat vigorously about ½ minute or until batter is reduced to almost its original size. Turn into greased, deep 1½-qt casserole. Bake in preheated 375°F oven about 35–40 minutes or until done. (Top will sound hollow when lightly tapped.) Remove from casserole. Cool. For a special treat, serve with honey butter. Makes 1 loaf.

CREATED AND TESTED AT CHECKERBOARD KITCHENS. REPRINTED COURTESY OF RALSTON PURINA COMPANY.

Pat Uhlmann's Old-Fashioned Wheatena Bread

1¾ cups milk
1 cake (1 oz) compressed yeast or 2 pkg active dry yeast
½ cup water
6 to 6½ cups sifted flour
1 cup WHEATENA
2 Tbsp sugar
1 Tbsp honey
1 Tbsp salt
2 Tbsp soft shortening

Scald milk; cool to lukewarm. Soften compressed yeast in *lukewarm* (80°–85°F) water (use *warm*, 105°–115°F for active dry yeast). Add scalded milk, half the flour, WHEATENA, sugar, honey, salt, and shortening to yeast mixture. Beat until smooth; add remaining flour. Turn out onto floured board; knead until smooth and elastic. Place in greased bowl; cover; let rise in warm (80°–85°F) draft-free place 1 hour (or until doubled). Punch down; cover; let rise again for 30 minutes. Divide into 2 equal pieces and roll each into ball. Let rest 10 minutes. Shape into loaves. Place each loaf in well-greased 9 X 5 X 3-inch loaf pan. Return to warm place; let rise until sides reach top of pan and center is well-rounded (about 50–55 minutes). Bake in preheated 425°F oven about 30–35 minutes, or until tests done. Remove from pans; cool on rack. Brush tops with melted butter. Makes 2 loaves.

COURTESY STANDARD MILLING COMPANY.

Red Star® No-Time-To-Bake™ 90-Minute Buttercrust Bread

5½ to 6 cups all-purpose flour
2 pkg RED STAR® Instant Blend Dry Yeast
2 Tbsp sugar
1 Tbsp salt
1 cup milk
1¼ cups water
3 Tbsp butter or margarine
1 Tbsp butter or margarine, melted

Oven 400°F. In large mixer bowl, combine 2½ cups flour, yeast, sugar, and salt; mix well. In saucepan, heat milk, water, and 3 Tbsp butter until warm (120°–130°F; butter does not need to melt); add to flour mixture. Beat at low speed until moistened; beat 3 minutes at medium speed. By hand, gradually stir in enough remaining flour to make a firm dough. Knead on floured surface 5–10 minutes until smooth and elastic. Place in greased bowl, turning to grease top. Cover; let rise in warm oven (Turn oven to lowest setting for 1 minute, turn off.) for 20 minutes. Punch down dough; divide into 2 parts. On lightly floured surface, roll or pat each half to a 7 X 14-inch rectangle. Starting with the shorter side, roll up tightly, pressing dough into roll with each turn. Pinch edges and ends to seal. Place in 2 greased 8 X 4-inch bread pans. Cover; let rise in warm oven until doubled—about 30 minutes. With a very sharp knife, make a slash across the top of each loaf and pour melted butter into each slash. Bake at 400°F for 25–30 minutes until golden brown. Remove from pans; cool. Makes 2 loaves.

NO-TIME-TO-BAKE™ TRADEMARKED BY UNIVERSAL FOODS CORPORATION. AN EXCLUSIVE BAKING PROCESS BY THE MAKERS OF RED STAR® YEAST, THE ALL-NATURAL YEAST THAT LETS YOU BAKE FROM SCRATCH WITH YEAST IN ABOUT HALF THE USUAL TIME.

Blue Ribbon Jewish Light Rye Bread

Sour

1 pkg active dry yeast
1 cup water, warm
2 cups rye flour

Dissolve yeast in water. Mix in flour. Cover and let stand for 24 hours.

Sponge

1 pkg active dry yeast
1 cup water, warm
3 cups rye flour

Dissolve yeast in water and mix in flour. Add to sour mixture and mix to a fine consistency. Cover and let rise for 2 hours.

Dough

1 Tbsp salt
1 cup water, warm
1 Tbsp BLUE RIBBON Malt
Ground caraway seeds (optional)
2 cups unbleached flour (or all-purpose), blended with
1 cup rye flour

Mix all ingredients and add to sponge; completely incorporate but do not overmix. Round up dough and let it recover for a few minutes. Make it up into long or round loaves and place on corn mealed pans or earthenware. Proof for 12 minutes. Bake in a moist 375°F oven for 55 minutes.

COURTESY PREMIER MALT PRODUCTS—MILWAUKEE, WI.

Brer Rabbit Scandinavian Rye Bread

2 pkg active dry yeast
2 cups warm water (105°–115°F)
½ cup BRER RABBIT Light Molasses
3 tsp salt
2 Tbsp coarsely grated orange peel
1 tsp anise or fennel seed (optional)
3 cups whole rye flour
¼ cup vegetable shortening, softened
3 to 3½ cups all-purpose flour

In large mixing bowl, dissolve yeast in warm water. Stir in molasses, salt, orange peel, anise seed, rye flour, and shortening. Beat until smooth. Gradually stir in enough of the all-purpose flour to make a stiff dough. Turn dough out onto a floured surface; knead until smooth and no longer sticky, about 5 minutes. Place in bowl; cover with towel; let rise in warm place until doubled, about 1½ hours. Punch dough down; divide in half. Shape each into an oval loaf. Place loaves on large greased cookie sheet, 5 inches apart. Cover; let rise 1 hour or until doubled. Bake in a preheated moderate oven (375°F) 30–35 minutes or until loaves sound hollow when tapped. Cool on wire racks. Makes 2 loaves.

COURTESY PREPARED FOOD AND BEVERAGE PRODUCTS GROUP OF DEL MONTE CORPORATION.

Gold Medal® Cinnamon Coffee Rolls

1 pkg active dry yeast
¼ cup warm water (105°–115°F)
*4 cups GOLD MEDAL® All-Purpose Flour**
¼ cup sugar
1 tsp salt
1 cup margarine or butter, softened
3 egg yolks, beaten
1 cup lukewarm milk (scalded then cooled)
2 Tbsp margarine or butter, melted
½ cup sugar
1½ tsp ground cinnamon
Creamy Glaze (below)

Dissolve yeast in warm water. Mix flour, ¼ cup sugar, and the salt in large mixing bowl. Cut in 1 cup margarine until mixture resembles fine crumbs. Mix in yeast, egg yolks, and milk until dough is smooth. Cover and refrigerate at least 8 hours. (Dough can be refrigerated at 45°F or below for up to 3 days. Keep covered.)

Grease 24 muffin cups, 2½ X 1¼ inches. Divide dough into halves. Roll 1 half into rectangle, 12 X 10 inches, on well-floured surface; brush with 1 Tbsp melted margarine. Mix ½ cup sugar and the cinnamon; sprinkle half of the mixture on rectangle. Roll up, beginning at 12-inch side. Pinch edge of dough into roll to seal well. Stretch roll to make even; cut into 1-inch slices. Place in muffin cups. Repeat with remaining dough. Cover rolls and let rise until double, 1–1½ hours.

Heat oven to 375°F. Bake until golden, 15–20 minutes. Spread with Creamy Glaze while warm. Yield: 2 dozen rolls.

Creamy Glaze

Mix 1½ cups powdered sugar, 2 Tbsp margarine or butter, softened, 1½ tsp vanilla, and 1–2 Tbsp hot water until smooth and of spreading consistency.

*If using self-rising flour, omit salt.
COURTESY BETTY CROCKER FOOD & NUTRITION CENTER, GENERAL MILLS, INC. REGISTERED® TRADEMARK OF GENERAL MILLS, INC.

Red Star® No-Time-To-Bake™ Deep-Fried Cinnamon Puffs

2½ cups all-purpose flour
1 pkg RED STAR® Instant Blend Dry Yeast
½ tsp salt
½ tsp cinnamon
¼ cup sugar
½ cup milk
¼ cup water
¼ cup butter or margarine
2 eggs
Oil for frying

In mixer bowl, combine flour, yeast, salt, cinnamon, and sugar; mix well. In saucepan, heat milk, water, and butter until warm (120°–130°F; butter does not need to melt); add to flour mixture. Add eggs. Beat at low speed until moistened; beat 3 minutes at medium speed. Cover; let rise in warm oven (turn oven to lowest setting for 1 minute, turn off) for 20 minutes. Heat oil to 400°F. Drop batter by tablespoonfuls into oil and fry about 2 minutes, until golden brown. Drain on absorbent paper towels and roll warm puffs in cinnamon-sugar mixture. Makes about 42 puffs.

NO-TIME-TO-BAKE™ TRADEMARKED BY UNIVERSAL FOODS CORPORATION. AN EXCLUSIVE BAKING PROCESS BY THE MAKERS OF RED STAR® YEAST, THE ALL-NATURAL YEAST THAT LETS YOU BAKE FROM SCRATCH WITH YEAST IN ABOUT HALF THE USUAL TIME.

Sun-Maid® Back-To-Nature Raisin Bread

1 cup SUN-MAID® Golden Seedless Raisins (gold box)
1¾ cups water
⅓ cup shortening
2 pkg active dry yeast
⅓ cup brown sugar (packed)
2 tsp salt
½ tsp ginger
½ tsp cinnamon
2 cups sifted all-purpose flour
2 cups whole wheat flour
⅓ cup wheat germ

Combine raisins, 1¼ cups water, and shortening. Heat to boiling, stirring until shortening melts. Remove from heat and cool to lukewarm. Soften yeast in remaining ½ cup warm water. Add sugar, salt, spices, and 1 cup all-purpose flour, and mix well. Add raisin mixture. Gradually mix in remaining all-purpose and whole wheat flours and wheat germ. Turn out onto *well floured* board, and knead 3 minutes. Return to mixing bowl, and brush top of dough with oil. Cover and let rise until doubled, about 1¾ hours. Punch down and shape into loaf. Place in greased pan (9 X 5 X 3 inches) and brush top with oil. Let rise until doubled, about 45 minutes. Bake below oven center, in moderately hot oven (375°F) about 40 minutes, until nicely browned. Turn out onto wire rack to cool. Makes 1 large loaf.

COURTESY SUN-MAID GROWERS OF CALIFORNIA, KINGSBURG, CALIFORNIA.

Souptime Onion Cheese Loaf

2 cups unsifted flour
2 tsp baking powder
2 tsp dry mustard
1/8 tsp salt
1 cup (4 oz) shredded Swiss cheese
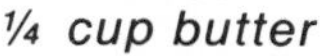
1/4 cup butter
1 cup milk
2 envelopes SOUPTIME Instant French Onion Soup
2 eggs

Preheat oven to 375°F. In small bowl, combine flour, baking powder, mustard, and salt. Stir in Swiss cheese; set aside. In small saucepan, melt butter. Add milk; heat until foamy. Remove from heat; stir in SOUPTIME Instant French Onion Soup. Cool at room temperature 5 minutes. In large bowl, beat eggs slightly. Stir in onion-milk mixture. Blend in flour-cheese mixture. Spread into greased 9 X 5 X 3-inch loaf pan. Bake at 375°F 50–55 minutes. Makes 1 loaf.

COURTESY THE NESTLÉ COMPANY, INC.

Clabber Girl Southern Corn Bread

1/4 cup vegetable shortening
2 cups white cornmeal
2 Tbsp all-purpose flour
2 tsp CLABBER GIRL Baking Powder
1 tsp baking soda
1 tsp salt
2 cups buttermilk
1 egg

Melt shortening in a 9-inch iron skillet or a 9-inch square baking pan in the oven, brushing sides of pan with melted shortening.

Sift together dry ingredients. Combine egg and buttermilk and stir into the dry ingredients along with melted shortening. Pour batter into a hot pan. Bake in a 450°F (hot) oven 20–25 minutes, or until browned. Cut in squares or wedges, serve hot with plenty of butter.

Campbell's

Campbell's Ham Spoonbread

1 cup finely chopped ham
¼ cup finely chopped onion
2 Tbsp butter or margarine
1 can (10¾ oz) CAMPBELL'S Condensed Cream of Mushroom Soup
½ soup can milk
Dash cayenne pepper
½ cup corn meal
3 eggs, separated
Syrup or butter

In saucepan, brown ham and cook onion in butter until tender. Stir in soup, milk, and cayenne. Add corn meal. Bring to boil; reduce heat. Cook until thickened, stirring. Remove from heat. Beat egg yolks until thick and lemon-colored; stir into corn meal mixture. Using clean egg beater, beat egg whites until stiff but not dry. Gradually fold into corn meal mixture. Pour into buttered 1½-qt casserole. Bake at 350°F for 1 hour. Serve with syrup. Makes 4 servings.

Aunt Jemima® Hush Puppies

1½ cups QUAKER® or AUNT JEMIMA® Enriched White Corn Meal
½ cup all-purpose flour
2 tsp baking powder
1 tsp salt
¾ cup milk
1 egg, beaten
1 small onion, finely chopped

Combine corn meal, flour, baking powder, and salt. Add milk, egg, and onion; mix well. Drop by rounded teaspoonfuls into deep hot oil (375°F), frying only a few at a time until golden brown. Drain on absorbent paper. Makes about 2 dozen.

Arm & Hammer® Irish Soda Bread

- *4 cups sifted all-purpose flour*
- *1 Tbsp sugar*
- *1½ tsp ARM & HAMMER Baking Soda*
- *1 tsp salt*
- *1 tsp baking powder*
- *¼ cup butter or margarine*
- *1 cup seedless raisins*
- *1½ cups buttermilk*

Sift together flour, sugar, baking soda, salt, and baking powder into large bowl. Cut in butter until crumbly. Stir in raisins. Add buttermilk and stir to make a soft dough. Turn onto lightly floured board and knead to form a smooth ball.

Pat by hand on greased baking sheet to 1¼-inch thickness. With sharp knife score into 4 sections. Bake in 350°F oven 1 hour or until bread is browned and a toothpick inserted in the center comes out clean. Serve warm with butter. Makes 1 loaf.

RECIPE COURTESY OF ARM & HAMMER DIVISION, CHURCH & DWIGHT CO., INC.

Carnation Toasted Almond Bread

Carnation

- *2½ cups flour*
- *1 cup sugar*
- *3½ tsp baking powder*
- *1 tsp salt*
- *¼ tsp almond extract*
- *1 Tbsp grated orange rind*
- *3 Tbsp salad oil*
- *¾ cup undiluted CARNATION® Evaporated Milk*
- *½ cup water*
- *1 egg*
- *¾ cup toasted chopped almonds*
- *¾ cup sifted confectioners' sugar*
- *2½ tsp water*
- *Toasted sliced almonds*

Combine flour, sugar, baking powder, salt, almond extract, orange rind, oil, CARNATION® Evaporated Milk, water, and egg in large mixer bowl. Beat at high speed for 30 seconds. Fold in chopped almonds. Pour batter into buttered 9 X 5 X 3-inch loaf pan. Bake in moderate oven (350°F) 50–60 minutes or until toothpick inserted in center comes out clean. Remove from pan; cool on wire rack. Combine confectioners' sugar and water in a small bowl. Drizzle icing over bread. Sprinkle toasted almonds on top, if desired. Makes 1 loaf.

LABEL ART AND RECIPE PROVIDED COURTESY CARNATION COMPANY.

Colombo Yogurt Honey Bread

- 2 cups plain COLOMBO Whole-Milk Yogurt
- 2½ cups whole wheat flour
- 2½ tsp baking powder
- ½ tsp salt
- ½ cup honey
- 1 cup brown sugar
- 3 eggs
- Juice of 1 lemon

Combine yogurt, lemon juice, eggs, and honey just enough to mix. Add flour, salt, baking powder, and sugar. Do not overmix. Pour into a "brownie" pan greased with butter. Bake in a preheated 350°F oven for 1 hour. Cool and slice thinly. Serve with your favorite jellies, jams, or preserves.

PERMISSION TO REPRODUCE GRANTED BY AMERICA'S ORIGINAL YOGURT COMPANY, COLOMBO, INC.

Bordo Date-Nut Bread

- 1 tsp baking soda
- 1 cup boiling water
- 1 cup BORDO Pitted Dates, cut up
- ¾ cup raisins
- 2 Tbsp soft butter
- 1 cup sugar
- 1 tsp vanilla
- 1 egg
- 1⅓ cups sifted flour
- ¾ cup chopped pecans

Pour soda and boiling water over dates and raisins. Set aside. Cream butter and sugar. Add vanilla, then egg. Beat well. Add flour and mix. Pour in fruit mixture (including water) and pecans. Mix. Bake in a buttered 9 X 5-inch loaf pan at 350°F 45–55 minutes.

COURTESY THE BORDO PRODUCTS COMPANY.

Diamond Walnuts Old-Fashioned Diamond Nut Bread

- 1½ cups DIAMOND Walnuts
- 3 cups sifted all-purpose flour
- 1 cup granulated sugar
- 4 tsp baking powder
- 1½ tsp salt
- 1 egg, lightly beaten
- ¼ cup shortening, melted
- 1½ cups milk
- 1 tsp vanilla

Coarsely chop walnuts. Resift flour with sugar, baking powder, and salt. Add egg, shortening, milk, and vanilla to dry mixture. Stir just until all of flour is moistened. Stir in walnuts. Turn

into greased 9 X 5 X 3-inch loaf pan, or divide batter between 2 greased #2½ cans. Bake at 350°F about 1 hour 20 minutes for rectangular loaf or 1 hour 10 minutes for round loaves.
COURTESY DIAMOND WALNUT GROWERS, INC., STOCKTON, CALIFORNIA.

Dole® Speedy Whole Banana Bread

1 cup sifted all-purpose flour
1 tsp baking powder
1 tsp baking soda
¼ tsp salt
1 cup whole wheat flour
½ cup butter
¾ cup brown sugar, packed
1 large egg
3 medium ripe DOLE® Bananas
¼ cup plain yogurt

Resift flour with baking powder, soda, and salt. Add whole wheat flour. Cream butter and sugar together well. Beat in egg. Mash DOLE® Bananas to make 1¼ cups. Add to yogurt, and beat again. (Mixture will appear curdled.) Add flour mixture and mix just until well blended. Turn into greased 9 X 5 X 2¾-inch loaf pan. Bake below oven center at 350°F about 55 minutes, until loaf tests done. Let stand in pan 10 minutes, then turn out onto wire rack to cool. Makes 1 loaf.
COURTESY OF CASTLE & COOKE FOODS (DOLE®).

Libby's Pumpkin Nut Bread

2 cups sifted flour
2 tsp baking powder
½ tsp soda
1 tsp salt
1 tsp cinnamon
½ tsp nutmeg
1 cup LIBBY'S Solid Pack Pumpkin
1 cup sugar
½ cup milk
2 eggs
¼ cup softened butter
1 cup chopped pecans

Preheat oven to 350°F. Sift together first 6 ingredients. Combine pumpkin, sugar, milk, and eggs in mixing bowl. Add dry ingredients and butter; mix until well blended. Stir in nuts. Spread in well-greased 9 X 5 X 3-inch loaf pan. Bake at 350°F 45–55 minutes or until toothpick inserted in center comes out clean. Yields 1 loaf.
COURTESY, LIBBY'S.

Ocean Spray's Cranberry Fruit-Nut Bread Recipe

2 cups all-purpose flour
1 cup sugar
1½ tsp baking powder
1 tsp salt
½ tsp baking soda
2 Tbsp shortening
1 Tbsp grated orange peel
¾ cup orange juice
1 egg, well-beaten
1½ cups OCEAN SPRAY® Fresh or Frozen Cranberries, coarsely chopped
½ cup nuts, chopped

Preheat oven to 350°F. In a bowl, mix together flour, sugar, baking powder, salt, and baking soda. Stir in orange juice, orange peel, shortening, and egg to dry ingredients. Mix until well blended. Stir in cranberries and chopped nuts. Turn into a 9 X 5-inch loaf pan, greased on bottom only. Bake 55–60 minutes, until toothpick inserted in center comes out clean. Cool on rack 15 minutes; remove from pan, cool thoroughly before slicing.

COURTESY OCEAN SPRAY CRANBERRIES, INC.

Stokely's Apricot Coffee Cake

¼ cup shortening
¼ cup sugar
1 egg
1¼ cups flour
1¾ tsp baking powder
½ tsp salt
⅓ cup milk
1 can (1 lb) STOKELY'S Finest® Apricot Halves, drained
½ cup sugar

2 Tbsp butter or margarine, softened
1 tsp cinnamon

Cream shortening and sugar; beat in egg. Sift together next 3 ingredients and add alternately with milk. Spread dough into a greased 8 X 8 X 2-inch pan. Arrange STOKELY'S Apricot Halves, cut side down, atop dough. Combine remaining ingredients and sprinkle over apricots. Bake at 375°F for 30 minutes. Makes 9 servings.

COURTESY STOKELY-VAN CAMP, INC.

Aunt Jemima® Blueberry Pecan Coffee Cake

1 10½-oz pkg AUNT JEMIMA® Easy Mix Coffee Cake
1 egg, unbeaten
½ cup milk
¼ cup fresh or frozen blueberries, drained
1 Tbsp chopped pecans

Put egg and milk into large bag of mix. Squeeze upper part of bag to force air out. Close top of bag by holding tightly between thumb and index finger. With bag resting on table, mix by working bag vigorously with fingers. Mix about 40 seconds or until egg is completely blended.

Squeeze bag to empty batter into special aluminum foil pan contained in package. (Do not grease pan.) Sprinkle blueberries, pecans and topping over coffee cake batter. Bake in preheated moderate oven (375°F) about 25 minutes. Makes 8 servings.

RECIPE REPRODUCED WITH THE PERMISSION OF THE QUAKER OATS COMPANY.

Dole® Banana Streusel Coffee Cake

1 cup sifted all-purpose flour
½ cup sugar
1 tsp baking powder
½ tsp salt
¼ tsp baking soda
⅛ tsp nutmeg
2 medium ripe DOLE® Bananas
1 large egg, beaten
¼ cup melted butter
1 Tbsp milk
½ tsp vanilla
Streusel Crumbs (below)

Resift flour with sugar, baking powder, salt, soda, and nutmeg. Mash bananas to make ¾ cup. Combine with egg, butter, milk, and vanilla. Add to dry mixture, and mix well. Spread half the batter in a greased 8-inch layer cake pan. Sprinkle with half the Streusel Crumbs. Spoon remaining batter over, spreading to cover streusel, and sprinkle with remaining crumbs. Bake in a 375°F oven about 25 minutes, just until cake tests done. Serve warm, cut into wedges. Makes 6–8 servings.

Streusel Crumbs

½ cup brown sugar, packed
3 Tbsp flour
¼ tsp cinnamon
3 Tbsp butter

Combine sugar, flour, and cinnamon. Cut in butter until crumbly.

COURTESY OF CASTLE & COOKE FOODS (DOLE®).

Campbell's Peachy Brunch Cake

1 pkg (2 layer) yellow cake mix
1 can (11 oz) CAMPBELL'S Condensed Cheddar Cheese Soup
½ cup water
2 eggs
½ tsp almond extract
2 cans (16 oz each) sliced peaches, well-drained and chopped
½ cup chopped almonds
3 Tbsp butter or margarine, softened
½ cup all-purpose flour
¼ cup packed brown sugar
1 tsp ground cinnamon

Preheat oven to 350°F. Generously grease and flour a 3-qt shallow baking pan (13 X 9 X 2 inches). In large bowl of electric mixer, combine cake mix, soup, water, eggs, and almond extract. Beat, following package directions. Stir in peaches and almonds. Spread batter evenly in pan. Meanwhile, to make topping, cut butter into flour, sugar, and cinnamon until crumbly. Sprinkle over batter. Bake 50 minutes or until done. Serve warm.

COURTESY CAMPBELL SOUP COMPANY.

Kretschmer Layered Streusel Coffee Cake

2 cups biscuit mix
¾ cup KRETSCHMER Regular or Brown Sugar & Honey Wheat Germ
¼ cup granulated sugar
¾ cup milk
1 egg
2 Tbsp butter or margarine, melted
¼ cup unsifted all-purpose flour
¼ cup firmly packed brown sugar
¼ cup finely chopped nuts
1 tsp cinnamon
2 Tbsp butter or margarine, melted

Combine biscuit mix, wheat germ, and granulated sugar in bowl. Stir well to blend. Add milk, egg, and 2 Tbsp butter. Beat until well mixed (about ½ minute). Combine flour, brown sugar, nuts, and cinnamon for streusel. Add 2 Tbsp butter. Toss together with fork. Spread half the batter (1¼ cups) in lightly greased 9-inch square pan. Sprinkle with half the streusel mixture (½ cup). Top with remaining batter and streusel.

Bake at 375°F for 25–30 minutes until wooden pick inserted in center comes out clean. Serve warm with butter if desired. Yield: 9–12 servings.

COURTESY KRETSCHMER WHEAT GERM, A PRODUCT OF INTERNATIONAL MULTIFOODS.

Clabber Girl Light, Tasty Biscuits

- *2 cups all-purpose flour*
- *2½ tsp CLABBER GIRL Baking Powder*
- *½ tsp salt*
- *⅓ cup shortening*
- *¾ cup milk*

Sift together dry ingredients. Cut in shortening with fork until mixture resembles coarse corn meal. Add milk and blend lightly with fork only until flour is moistened and dough pulls away from sides of bowl. Turn out on lightly floured board. Knead lightly (30 seconds) and roll ¾ inch thick. Place on lightly greased pan and brush tops of biscuits with butter or margarine. Bake at 475°F (very hot oven) for 12–15 minutes.

Aunt Jemima® Quick Drop Biscuits

- *2 cups AUNT JEMIMA® Original Pancake & Waffle Mix*
- *⅔ cup milk*
- *⅓ cup vegetable oil*

Combine all ingredients; mix just until dry ingredients are moistened. Spoon dough by rounded tablespoonfuls onto lightly greased cookie sheet. Bake in preheated hot oven (425°F) about 12 minutes. Makes 8–10 biscuits.

Elam's Old-Fashioned Buckwheat Cakes

- *3½ cups milk, scalded*
- *1 pkg (¼ oz) active dry yeast*
- *1 tsp fructose or honey*
- *3 cups ELAM'S Pure Buckwheat Flour*
- *1 Tbsp molasses*
- *¼ tsp baking soda*
- *1 Tbsp cooking oil or melted and cooled butter*
- *½ cup warm water (105°–115°F)*

Cool milk to lukewarm. Soften yeast in warm water. Stir yeast, fructose or honey into milk. Add flour and stir until batter is lump free. Cover; let stand in warm area 30 minutes. Stir batter to remove bubbles; cover and refrigerate overnight. In the morning, transfer 1 cup of batter to covered container. Store in refrigerator and use in place of yeast when making the next batch of buckwheat pancakes.* Let remaining batter warm at room temperature 30 minutes. Add remaining ingredients; stir until well mixed. For each cake, pour ¼ cup batter onto hot lightly greased griddle. Bake until top is covered with bubbles and edges look cooked. Turn and brown second side. Yield: About eighteen 4½-inch pancakes or 6 servings, 3 pancakes each.

*To make cakes using starter, follow above recipe except do not scald milk, and omit yeast. Combine all dry ingredients in bowl; mix well. Mix liquids and starter and add to dry ingredients. Stir just until batter is smooth. Yield: About 22 cakes, 4 inches in diameter.
COURTESY ELAM'S PURE BUCKWHEAT FLOUR.

Arm & Hammer® Griddle Cakes

2 cups all sifted all-purpose flour
1 Tbsp sugar
1 tsp ARM & HAMMER Baking Soda
1 tsp salt
2 eggs
2 cups buttermilk
2 Tbsp vegetable shortening, melted

Sift together flour, sugar, baking soda, and salt. In large bowl, beat eggs until light and fluffy; stir in buttermilk and melted shortening. Add dry ingredients to liquid, beating until smooth.

Pour a scant ¼ cup batter for each griddle cake onto hot griddle. (For thin griddle cakes, spread batter with spoon.) Turn griddle cakes as soon as they are puffed and full of bubbles but before bubbles break. Turn and bake other side until golden brown. Serve immediately with butter and hot maple syrup. Makes about 2 dozen 4-inch cakes.
RECIPE COURTESY OF ARM & HAMMER DIVISION, CHURCH & DWIGHT CO., INC.

PDQ Egg Nog Crepe

2 eggs
¾ cup PDQ Egg Nog
2 cups milk
1⅓ cups flour

Beat eggs and milk together. Add PDQ and flour, beat with electric mixer or whisk until smooth. Refrigerate at least 1 hour. (Variation: substitute 2 cups milk with 1¾ cups milk and ¼ cup rum.)

Heat crepe pan, brush lightly with melted butter. Pour ¼ cup batter into pan, tilting pan so batter covers bottom completely. As crepes' edges brown, flip, cook until golden. Serve with favorite filling. Makes 20–24 crepes.

Rokeach Matzo Meal Pancakes

3 egg yolks
3 egg whites
½ cup cold water
½ tsp salt
1 Tbsp sugar
½ cup matzo meal
ROKEACH Nyafat (for frying)

Beat yolk until light—add sugar and salt. Beat egg whites until stiff. Fold in matzo meal with the whites and blend yolks. Drop mix by tablespoonful into ROKEACH Nyafat that has been heated to about 370°F in frying pan. Brown on both sides. Drain on absorbent paper. Serve with ROKEACH Honey or ROKEACH Preserves.

COURTESY I. ROKEACH & SONS, INC.

Clabber Girl Spicy Apple Waffles

1¼ cups sifted all-purpose flour
2 tsp CLABBER GIRL Baking Powder
½ tsp salt
1 tsp ground nutmeg
3 Tbsp sugar
2 Tbsp shortening
2 eggs, separated
1 cup milk
1½ cups pared, coarsely grated apple

Sift together flour, baking powder, salt, nutmeg, and sugar into a mixing bowl. Cut in shortening until mixture is fine. Beat together egg yolks and milk and add all at once to dry ingredients. Blend ingredients and beat just until smooth. Stir in apples. Beat egg whites until stiff but not dry. Fold into batter. Bake in waffle maker, following manufacturer's directions. Yield: 4 servings.

Oroweat Wheat Berry French Toast with Maple Pecan Syrup

2 eggs, beaten
½ cup milk
½ tsp salt
¼ tsp nutmeg
8 slices OROWEAT Honey Wheat Berry Bread
1 cup pancake syrup
2 Tbsp chopped pecans

For French toast, beat together eggs, milk, salt, and nutmeg in flat, shallow dish. Dip each bread slice into egg mixture, coating both sides. Fry on preheated, greased skillet until brown, turning once. Meanwhile, for syrup, combine syrup and pecans. Serve over hot French toast with butter or margarine.

FROM OROWEAT, "ONE OF THE WORLD'S MOST RESPECTED BAKERS"

Wilderness Texas French Toast with Blueberries

1 loaf unsliced white bread
1 pkg (3¼ oz) regular vanilla pudding
3 eggs
1¼ cups milk
⅛ tsp cardamom (optional)
1 can (21 oz) WILDERNESS Blueberry Fruit Filling

Slice bread at least an inch thick. Make a batter by beating eggs until thick and lemon-colored; add milk, pudding, cardamom, beating until well blended. Dip bread in batter, turning to coat each side. Fry on hot buttered griddle or skillet on each side until golden brown. Serve with butter and blueberry fruit filling. Also delicious with strawberry fruit filling.

COURTESY OF WILDERNESS FOODS.

Arm & Hammer® Breakfast Muffins

1¾ cups sifted all-purpose flour
2 Tbsp sugar
1 tsp baking powder
½ tsp ARM & HAMMER Baking Soda
½ tsp salt
1 cup buttermilk
1 egg, slightly beaten
3 Tbsp butter or margarine, melted

Sift together flour, sugar, baking powder, baking soda, and salt into large bowl. Combine buttermilk, egg, and butter; add to flour mixture and stir just until all ingredients are moistened. Fill greased 2½-inch muffin cups about ⅔ full. Bake in 400°F oven 20–25 minutes. Serve warm with butter or preserves. Makes about 1 dozen muffins.

RECIPE COURTESY OF ARM & HAMMER DIVISION, CHURCH & DWIGHT CO., INC.

Kellogg's®—Our Best Bran Muffins

1¼ cups regular all-purpose flour
3 tsp baking powder
½ tsp salt
½ cup sugar
1½ cups KELLOGG'S® ALL-BRAN® cereal
1¼ cups milk
1 egg
⅓ cup soft shortening or vegetable oil

Stir together flour, baking powder, salt, and sugar. Set aside. Measure cereal and milk into mixing bowl. Stir to combine. Let stand 1–2 minutes or until cereal is softened. Add egg and shortening. Beat well. Add dry ingredients to cereal mixture, stirring *only until combined.* Portion batter evenly into 12 greased 2½-inch muffin-pan cups. Bake in oven at 400°F about 25 minutes or until muffins are golden brown. Serve warm. Yield: 12 muffins.

COURTESY OF KELLOGG COMPANY.

Lea & Perrins Corn Oysters

1 can (1 lb 1 oz) whole kernel corn, drained
2 eggs, separated
1 Tbsp minced onion
1 Tbsp LEA & PERRINS Worcestershire Sauce
⅓ cup sifted all-purpose flour
½ tsp baking powder
½ tsp salt
Fat for frying

In a medium bowl combine corn, egg yolks, onion, and LEA & PERRINS; mix well. Sift flour, baking powder, and salt; stir into corn mixture. Beat egg whites until stiff but not dry. Gently fold into corn mixture. Drop by the teaspoonful into deep fat preheated to 350°F. Fry until golden, about 3 minutes, turning once. Drain on absorbent paper. Serve immediately as a main dish accompaniment or appetizer. Yield: About 3 dozen.

COURTESY LEA & PERRINS WORCESTERSHIRE SAUCE, A PRODUCT OF LEA & PERRINS, INC.

Pillsbury Speedy Doughnuts

1 8-oz can PILLSBURY Refrigerated Buttermilk or Country Style Biscuits
Sugar or cinnamon sugar

Separate dough into 10 biscuits. Cut hole in center of each biscuit. Fry biscuits and holes in hot shortening or oil (375°F) until golden brown, about 1½ minutes on each side. Drain. Sprinkle with sugar or cinnamon sugar. Serve warm. Yield: 10 doughnuts.

COURTESY OF THE PILLSBURY COMPANY.

Main Dishes

"What's for dinner?"

When members of your family ask that question, you know they are not interested in what the vegetable will be, what type of salad will be served, or what is planned for dessert. What they really want to know is: "What's the main dish?"

The main dish plays such an important role that it can make or break your whole dinner. Too often, however, cooks find themselves making the same main dishes over and over. These are the dishes that first come to mind because they are easy to fix, the ingredients are usually on hand, and the results are consistently satisfying.

The following wide selection of savory main dishes probably includes some recipes that are already family favorites, recipes that you first tried years ago and have been cooking ever since. Yet the dozens of dishes in every category also undoubtedly include potential favorites you have not yet tried.

Even if you think you do not have time to cook anything out of the ordinary, you will find that many manufacturers have specially developed recipes with the busy cook in mind. Often these recipes will give valuable hints on how to use packaged sauce mixes, prepared soups, canned and frozen foods, and other conveniences to the best advantage.

For your convenience, the main dishes here are divided into four basic categories:

Meats: There are recipe suggestions for those occasions when you want to splurge, but there are also budget-saving recipes that will help you stretch your meat dollars.

Poultry: The delicious chicken dishes in this section come from every part of the world, and you will most definitely want to try the tempting turkey and duck recipes.

Seafood: Whether frozen, fresh, or canned, fish and shellfish offer attractive, low-calorie alternatives to meat and potatoes.

Eggs and Cheese: Quiches, omelets, fondues—plenty of low-meat or meatless dinners are included that are appealing and easy to prepare.

Meats

Holland House® Steak Diablo

- 3 lb round steak, either 1 or 2 steaks, pounded thin
- Salt and pepper to taste
- ½ tsp paprika
- ½ cup fresh mushrooms, sliced
- 1 large onion, sliced thin
- 2 garlic cloves, crushed
- ¼ cup grated Parmesan cheese
- ¼ cup pimento
- 1 cup fine bread crumbs
- ½ cup melted butter or margarine
- 1 Tbsp boiling water
- 1 egg
- 10 large stuffed green olives
- ¼ cup butter or margarine
- 2 Tbsp flour
- 1½ cups HOLLAND HOUSE Red Cooking Wine
- 2 tomatoes, quartered
- Parsley sprigs

Rub steaks with salt, pepper, and paprika. If 2 steaks are being used, overlap to make 1 large piece of meat. Spread with layers of mushroom, onion, garlic, cheese, and pimento; cover with bread crumbs. With an electric mixer or whisk, combine melted butter or margarine with water and egg. Dribble egg mixture over bread crumbs. Arrange olives in a row along one edge of the steak and roll meat from that edge. Tie firmly with string. Melt ¼ cup butter or margarine in a Dutch oven. Dust steak with flour and brown on all sides in melted butter or margarine. Add wine, cover, and roast in 350°F oven for 2 hours, or until meat is tender. When done, place on serving platter and garnish with quartered tomatoes and parsley sprigs. Serves 6.

RECIPE SUPPLIED BY HOLLAND HOUSE BRANDS CO.

Domino® Steak Teriyaki

⅓ cup soy sauce
⅓ cup saki or sherry wine
3 Tbsp DOMINO® Brownulated® Brown Sugar
1 tsp ground ginger
Salt to taste
1 (2–3 lb) steak 2 inches thick

Combine soy sauce, wine, sugar, ginger, and salt; stir well. Pour over steak and marinate 4 hours or more; turn occasionally. Broil steak, turning once until done as desired, about 5 minutes each side for medium rare. Baste occasionally with marinade. Serve immediately. Makes 3–4 servings.

COURTESY AMSTAR CORPORATION, AMERICAN SUGAR DIVISION.

Heinz Spicy Pot Roast

4 tsp salt
2 tsp ground mace
1 tsp minced garlic
½ tsp pepper
4 lb rolled rump roast
½ cup HEINZ Apple Cider Vinegar
1 Tbsp salad oil
¾ cup HEINZ Tomato Ketchup
¼ cup water
1 cup chopped green pepper
1 cup chopped onions

Combine first 4 ingredients, rub thoroughly into meat on all sides. Place meat in bowl; pour vinegar over meat. Cover; marinate in refrigerator overnight, turning meat occasionally. Drain meat well; discard marinade. Brown meat on all sides in oil in Dutch oven. Combine ketchup and remaining ingredients; spoon over meat. Cover; bake in 350°F oven, 2½–3 hours or until meat is tender, basting occasionally. Skim excess fat from sauce; thicken sauce, if desired. Makes 8–10 servings.

COURTESY OF HEINZ U.S.A., DIVISION OF H.J. HEINZ COMPANY.

Mogen David Concord Beef Roast

- 2 *cups MOGEN DAVID Concord Wine*
- 1 *cup Tribuno Dry White Vermouth*
- ¼ *cup oil*
- 1 *medium onion, chopped*
- 2 *carrots, chopped*
- 1 *tsp dry mustard*
- 1 *tsp thyme*
- 1 *bay leaf*
- ½ *tsp salt*
- ¼ *tsp pepper*
- 1 *stalk celery, chopped*
- 2 *garlic cloves, crushed*
- 1 *rolled rump roast (3½–4 lb)*

Combine all ingredients in large plastic bag. Squeeze out all air and tie bag tightly. Place in large bowl, if desired, in case of leakage. Refrigerate at least 6 hours or up to 2 days. Remove roast from marinade and place in roasting pan. Strain marinade and pour 1 cup over roast, reserving remainder for gravy if desired. Discard chopped vegetables. Insert meat thermometer into roast. Cook, uncovered, at 325°F to desired degree of doneness, about 1½ hours for medium rare. Serves 6.

COURTESY MOGEN DAVID WINE CORPORATION.

A.1.® Beef Roulade

- 5 *Tbsp butter*
- ½ *cup finely chopped onion*
- 1 *cup packaged stuffing mix*
- 2 *Tbsp water*
- 6 *cube steaks*
- ¼ *cup A.1. Sauce Steak*
- 1 *medium clove garlic, minced*
- ¼ *cup red cooking wine*
- 1 *cup (13¾ oz) beef broth*

In skillet, soften ¼ cup onion in 3 Tbsp butter. Mix in stuffing mix and water. Brush each steak lightly with A.1. Spoon stuffing over A.1. Roll steaks, securing with toothpicks. In skillet, brown meat in remaining butter. Set aside. Soften remaining onion and garlic in drippings. Deglaze pan with wine. Add broth and remaining A.1. Place meat in pan. Simmer, covered, 45 minutes. Turn occasionally. Remove meat. Keep warm. Boil sauce to reduce by ½. Serves 6.

COURTESY OF HEUBLEIN, INC.

French's Savory Steak Strips

1 lb round steak, cut about 1 inch thick
1 envelope (¾ oz) FRENCH'S Au Jus Gravy Mix
1 cup tomato juice
½ cup water
1 Tbsp FRENCH'S Worcestershire Sauce
1 Tbsp vinegar

Cut steak into very thin slices; weave back and forth on 6 skewers. Stir together contents of gravy mix envelope, tomato juice, water, Worcestershire sauce, and vinegar; spoon or brush about half of mixture over steak. Broil steak 5-10 minutes, turning once until done. Heat remaining gravy mixture; serve as sauce over steak strips. Yield: 6 servings.

COURTESY THE R.T. FRENCH COMPANY.

Kikkoman Sukiyaki

2 lb boneless beef sirloin, sliced as thin as possible
4 stalks celery, cut diagonally into ½-inch-thick slices
2 medium onions, thinly sliced
1 bunch green onions and tops, cut in 2-inch lengths
1 cup fresh mushrooms, sliced
1 can (8½ oz) bamboo shoots, sliced
1 can (8½ oz) shirataki
1 can (11 oz) tofu, cut in 1-inch cubes
¾ cup beef broth
½ cup KIKKOMAN Soy Sauce
¼ cup sherry
3 Tbsp sugar
2 pieces beef suet (or 1 Tbsp salad oil)

Arrange beef and vegetables attractively on large platter. Turn electric skillet setting to 300°F. Blend together beef broth, soy sauce, sherry, and sugar. Melt suet in skillet, stirring until pan is well coated; remove. (Or, heat salad oil in skillet.) Add about

⅓ of the meat and cover with ½ of the sauce. Add ⅔ of each vegetable, keeping meat and vegetables separate. Turn ingredients over gently while cooking 5–6 minutes. Add another ⅓ of the meat and cook 1–2 minutes longer. Serve immediately in individual bowls or plates. Replenish skillet with remaining ingredients as needed. Makes 4–6 servings.

COURTESY KIKKOMAN INTERNATIONAL INC.

Planters® Beef with Broccoli

- *2 pkg (10 oz each) frozen broccoli spears, partially thawed, or 1 bunch fresh broccoli (if using fresh broccoli, break flowerets with stems from large stems; peel skin from large and small stems)*
- *½ lb flank steak, thinly sliced across grain*
- *2 tsp cornstarch*
- *1 tsp sugar*
- *¼ tsp ground ginger*
- *1 Tbsp soy sauce*
- *Water*
- *1 clove garlic, crushed*
- *5 Tbsp PLANTERS® Peanut Oil*
- *1 can (8 oz) sliced bamboo shoots, drained*
- *½ cup sliced fresh mushrooms*
- *1 tsp salt*

Cut broccoli flowerets and stems into 1½-inch lengths, about ½-inch thick; set aside. Cut steak slices into 2-inch lengths. In a small bowl, combine 1 tsp cornstarch, ¼ tsp sugar, ginger, soy sauce, 1½ tsp water, and garlic; blend well. Mix beef with marinade; set aside. (Meat will absorb marinade.) Preheat wok or large skillet; add 2 Tbsp PLANTERS® Peanut Oil and heat 30 seconds. Add beef and brown until just slightly pink. Return beef to bowl. Heat remaining 3 Tbsp peanut oil in wok or skillet. Stir in broccoli, bamboo shoots, and mushrooms; stir-fry until broccoli is tender, 2–5 minutes. Add salt, remaining sugar, 3 Tbsp water, and remaining cornstarch; mix well. Bring to a boil, stirring constantly until slightly thickened. Return meat and heat 1 minute. Serve immediately. Makes 4 servings.

COURTESY OF STANDARD BRANDS INCORPORATED.

Uncle Ben's®

Uncle Ben's® Pepper Steak with Brown & Wild Rice

1 *lb beef round steak, about 1 inch thick*
2 *Tbsp butter or margarine*
1 *Tbsp flour*
1 *tsp salt*
1 *can (about 10 oz) tomatoes*
1 *medium onion, chopped*
1 *beef bouillon cube, crushed*
1 *pkg (5 oz) UNCLE BEN'S® Brown & Wild Rice*
1 *medium green pepper, cut in thin strips*

Cut meat into very thin strips. Brown well in butter or margarine in 10-inch skillet. Stir in flour and salt. Drain and cut up tomatoes, reserving liquid. Add water to liquid to make 1 cup. Add liquid, onion, and bouillon cube to meat; stir. Cover and cook over low heat, stirring occasionally, until meat is tender, about 1 hour. Meanwhile, prepare rice according to package directions. Add green pepper and tomatoes to cooked meat; cover and heat about 5 minutes. Serve over rice. Makes 4 servings.

COURTESY UNCLE BEN'S FOODS.

Campbell's Saucy Liver Strips

1 *lb sliced beef liver, cut in strips*
1 *large clove garlic, minced*
½ *tsp oregano leaves, crushed*
2 *Tbsp butter or margarine*
1 *can (10¾ oz) CAMPBELL'S Condensed Tomato Soup*
¼ *cup water*
Cooked rice

In skillet, brown liver with garlic and oregano in butter. Add remaining ingredients except rice. Cover; cook over low heat 20 minutes or until done. Stir occasionally. Serve over cooked rice. Makes about 2½ cups.

COURTESY CAMPBELL SOUP COMPANY.

Savory Beef Stew with VEG-ALL

- *1 can VEG-ALL Mixed Vegetables*
- *1½ lb beef stew meat, cut into ¾-inch cubes*
- *2 Tbsp fat*
- *2 cups boiling water*
- *1 tsp salt*
- *¼ tsp pepper*
- *1 tsp Worcestershire sauce*
- *2 Tbsp butter or margarine*
- *2 Tbsp flour*

Drain VEG-ALL thoroughly, saving liquid. Brown meat thoroughly on all sides in the 2 Tbsp fat. Add the liquid from VEG-ALL and the boiling water. Add salt, pepper, and Worcestershire sauce. Place over low heat and simmer for 1½ hours. Combine butter and flour. Add to the stew in a lump and cook until slightly thickened. Add VEG-ALL and continue cooking 10–15 minutes.

COURTESY OF THE LARSEN COMPANY, 520 N. BROADWAY, GREEN BAY, WI 54305.

Heinz Saucy Meatballs

- *1 lb lean ground beef*
- *⅔ cup grated Parmesan cheese*
- *½ cup seasoned dry bread crumbs*
- *½ cup milk*
- *1 egg, slightly beaten*
- *2 Tbsp shortening*
- *1 Tbsp flour*
- *1 can (28 oz) tomatoes, cut into bite-size pieces*
- *⅓ cup HEINZ 57 Sauce*
- *1 Tbsp sugar*
- *½ tsp salt*
- *Hot buttered noodles*

Combine first 5 ingredients. Shape into 20 meatballs, using a rounded tablespoon for each. Brown well in shortening. Drain excess fat. Sprinkle flour over meatballs; stir gently to coat meatballs. Combine tomatoes, HEINZ 57 Sauce, sugar, and salt; pour over meatballs. Simmer, uncovered, 25 minutes or until sauce is desired consistency, stirring occasionally. Serve meatballs and sauce over noodles. Makes 5 servings (about 3 cups sauce).

COURTESY OF HEINZ U.S.A., DIVISION OF H.J. HEINZ COMPANY.

Quaker Oats® Prize-Winning Meat Loaf

1½ lb ground beef
1 cup tomato juice
¾ cup QUAKER OATS® (quick or old fashioned, uncooked)
1 egg, beaten
¼ cup chopped onion
1½ tsp salt
¼ tsp pepper

Combine all ingredients; mix well. Press firmly into ungreased 8½ X 4½ X 2½-inch loaf pan. Bake in preheated moderate oven (350°F) about 1 hour. Let stand 5 minutes before slicing. Makes 8 servings.

Ac'cent® "World's Greatest Meat Loaf"

1 egg
1 tsp AC'CENT Flavor Enhancer
1 tsp salt
¼ tsp pepper
½ tsp dried leaf basil
½ tsp dried leaf thyme
¼ cup ketchup
2 tsp prepared mustard
1½ cups soft bread crumbs
2 beef bouillon cubes
1 cup boiling water
½ cup finely chopped celery
½ cup finely chopped onion
1 cup shredded Cheddar or Swiss cheese
2 lb ground beef chuck

Beat egg lightly in medium bowl, add AC'CENT Flavor Enhancer, salt, pepper, basil, thyme, ketchup, mustard, and bread crumbs. Dissolve bouillon cubes in boiling water, add to bowl, and mix well until all ingredients are very well blended. Mix in celery, onion, and cheese. Break up ground beef and add to bowl, mix lightly but thoroughly with fork. In a shallow baking pan, shape mixture into a 12 X 5-inch oval loaf pan or press meat mixture lightly into a 9 X 5 X 3-inch loaf pan. Bake uncovered in 375°F oven 1 hour to 1 hour 10 minutes. Yield: 8 servings.

Campbell's Best Ever Meat Loaf

1 can (10¾ oz) CAMPBELL'S Condensed Cream of Mushroom or Golden Mushroom Soup
2 lb ground beef
½ cup fine dry bread crumbs
1 egg, slightly beaten
⅓ cup finely chopped onion
1 tsp salt
⅓ cup water

Mix thoroughly ½ cup soup, beef, bread crumbs, egg, onion, and salt. Shape *firmly* into loaf (8 X 4 inches); place in shallow baking pan. Bake at 375°F for 1 hour 15 minutes. In saucepan, blend remaining soup, water, and 2–3 Tbsp drippings. Heat; stir occasionally. Serve with loaf. Makes 6–8 servings.

Frosted Meat Loaf: Prepare loaf as above; bake for 1 hour. Frost loaf with 4 cups mashed potatoes; sprinkle with shredded Cheddar cheese. Bake 15 minutes more.

Swedish Meat Loaf: Add ½ tsp nutmeg to loaf. Blend remaining soup with ⅓ cup sour cream; omit drippings and water. Serve over loaf; sprinkle with additional nutmeg. Garnish with thinly sliced cucumber.

Meat Loaf Wellington: Crescent rolls (refrigerated)—prepare loaf as above. Bake at 375°F for 1 hour. Spoon off fat. Separate 1 pkg (8 oz) refrigerated crescent dinner rolls; place crosswise over top and down sides of meat loaf, overlapping slightly. Bake 15 minutes more.

Patty Shells: Thaw 1 pkg (10 oz) frozen patty shells. Prepare loaf as above. Bake at 375°F for 30 minutes. Spoon off fat. Increase oven temperature to 400°F. On floured board, roll 5 patty shells into rectangle (12 X 8 inches); prick several times with fork. Cover top and sides of loaf with pastry. Decorate top with remaining patty shell, rolled and cut into fancy shapes. Bake 45 minutes more or until golden brown. Serve with sauce.

COURTESY CAMPBELL SOUP COMPANY.

Hamburger Helper

Hamburger Helper® Layered Cheeseburger Casserole

1 pkg HAMBURGER HELPER® Mix for Cheeseburger Macaroni
1 lb ground beef
1 medium stalk celery, chopped (about ½ cup)
1 small onion, chopped (about ¼ cup)
1 tsp seasoned salt
¼ tsp pepper
2½ cups milk
4 eggs
1 tsp dry mustard

Heat oven to 350°F. Cook Macaroni in 6 cups boiling salted water 8 minutes; drain. Cook and stir ground beef, celery, and onion until beef is brown; drain. Stir in seasoned salt and pepper. Grease baking pan, 9 X 9 X 2 inches, or baking dish, 12 X 7½ X 2 inches. Spread macaroni in pan; top with beef mixture. Beat Sauce Mix and remaining ingredients. (Sauce mix will be slightly lumpy.) Pour over beef mixture. Bake uncovered until knife inserted in center comes out clean, 40–50 minutes. Let stand 5 minutes before serving. Yield: 6–8 servings.

COURTESY BETTY CROCKER FOOD & NUTRITION CENTER, GENERAL MILLS, INC. REGISTERED® TRADEMARK OF GENERAL MILLS, INC.

Chiffon Slim Jim Stroganoff

4 cups sliced fresh mushrooms
1 cup sliced onion
¼ cup CHIFFON Margarine
2½ lb top round beef, ¼ inch thick cut in 1-inch strips
¼ cup flour
2 cups hot water
2 Tbsp dried parsley flakes
2 tsp salt
2 tsp Worcestershire sauce
2 cloves garlic, minced
1 tsp paprika

½ tsp pepper
2 beef bouillon cubes
2 cups buttermilk
6 to 8 cups cooked noodles

Place mushrooms, onion, and CHIFFON in large skillet. Sauté until onion is tender; remove and set aside. Add beef strips and sauté. Stir in flour, water, and seasonings. Cover and simmer about 20 minutes, until meat is fork tender. Stir occasionally. Add mushroom mixture and buttermilk. Heat through but do not boil. Serve over noodles. Makes 8 servings.

COURTESY OF ANDERSON CLAYTON FOODS.

Mueller's® Hamburger Stroganoff

- *½ lb lean ground beef*
- *1 Tbsp butter or margarine*
- *1 can (4 oz) mushroom stems and pieces, drained, reserving liquid*
- *2 Tbsp chopped onion*
- *2 Tbsp flour*
- *1½ cups beef broth*
- *½ tsp salt*
- *Dash pepper*
- *1 Tbsp ketchup*
- *½ cup sour cream*
- *8 oz (7½ cups) MUELLER'S Hearty Egg Noodles*
- *Minced parsley*

In skillet, lightly brown beef in butter, stirring to separate particles. Add mushrooms and onion; cook a few minutes. Remove from heat; blend in flour. Add beef broth, reserved mushroom liquid, salt, pepper, and ketchup; cook over low heat 10 minutes, stirring occasionally. Blend in sour cream; heat 1 minute longer. Meanwhile, cook noodles as directed; drain. Serve stroganoff over noodles; sprinkle with parsley. Makes 4 generous servings.

COURTESY OF C. F. MUELLER COMPANY.

Campbell's Noodleburger Scallop

- *2 lb ground beef*
- *½ cup chopped celery*
- *2 medium cloves garlic, minced*
- *1 tsp salt*
- *⅛ tsp pepper*
- *1 can (11 oz) CAMPBELL'S Condensed Cheddar Cheese Soup*
- *1 can (10¾ oz) CAMPBELL'S Condensed Cream of Mushroom Soup*
- *⅔ cup milk*
- *½ cup sour cream*
- *4 cups cooked noodles*
- *4 tomato slices, halved*
- *Shredded process cheese*

In skillet, brown beef and cook celery with garlic until tender. Pour off fat. Add salt and pepper. In large bowl, blend soups, milk, and sour cream. In two 1½-qt casseroles, layer noodles,

meat, and soup mixture. Bake at 400°F for 25 minutes. Top with tomato and cheese. Bake until cheese melts. Makes 8 servings.
COURTESY CAMPBELL SOUP COMPANY.

Stokely's Swedish Cabbage Casserole

(Similar to cabbage rolls, but easier to make)

1 lb ground beef
½ cup chopped onion
1 can (1 lb) STOKELY'S Finest® Stewed Tomatoes
½ cup instant rice
1 can (8 oz) STOKELY'S Finest® Tomato Sauce
½ cup (2 oz) cubed pasteurized process cheese spread
1 Tbsp Worcestershire sauce
½ tsp salt
¼ tsp garlic salt
3 cups shredded cabbage

In skillet, brown ground beef and onion; drain excess fat. Add stewed tomatoes and rice, stirring to break tomatoes and blend ingredients. Bring to a boil; cover and turn off heat. Let stand 10 minutes. Stir in next 5 ingredients and heat until cheese is melted. Arrange cabbage in bottom of an 11½ X 7½ X 2-inch pan. Spread hamburger mixture over cabbage. Cover and bake at 350°F for 30 minutes. Makes 6 servings.
COURTESY STOKELY-VAN CAMP, INC.

Gebhardt's Chili Lover's Chili

1½ lb lean ground beef
2 cups chopped onion
1 medium green pepper, chopped
2 large garlic cloves, chopped
1 can (28 oz) whole peeled tomatoes, broken up
1 can (8 oz) tomato sauce
2 cups water
2 Tbsp GEBHARDT'S Chili Powder
1 Tbsp salt

1 bay leaf
¼ tsp GEBHARDT'S Hot Sauce
2 cans (15 oz each) GEBHARDT'S Mexican Style Chili Beans

Cook beef, onion, green pepper, and garlic in large saucepan or Dutch oven until meat loses its red color. Stir in all remaining ingredients except beans. Cook over low heat, covered,

1½ hours. Add beans and cook ½ hour longer. Serve with cheese cutouts. Yield: 6 servings.
FROM THE KITCHENS OF GEBHARDT MEXICAN FOODS.

Mr. McIlhenny's Chili

- 3 *lb lean stewing beef, well trimmed, cut in 1-inch cubes*
- ¼ *cup salad oil*
- 1 *cup chopped onion*
- 3 *cloves garlic, minced*
- 4 *to 6 Tbsp chili powder*
- 2 *tsp salt*
- 2 *tsp ground cumin*
- 2 *tsp TABASCO Pepper Sauce*
- 1 *can (4 oz) green chilies, seeded and chopped*
- 1 *qt water*
- ¼ *cup chopped onion*

In large saucepan, brown beef in oil. Add remaining ingredients and mix well. Bring to a boil, reduce heat, and simmer uncovered 1½ to 2 hours, until meat is tender. Garnish with chopped onion and serve with a bottle of TABASCO Pepper Sauce on the side. Yield: 4–6 servings.
RECIPE COURTESY MCILHENNY COMPANY, AVERY ISLAND, LOUISIANA, 70513.

Uncle Ben's® Taco Rice Skillet

- 1 *lb ground beef*
- 1 *medium onion, chopped*
- 1 *can (16 oz) tomatoes*
- 1 *cup UNCLE BEN'S® CONVERTED® Brand Rice*
- 1 *pkg (1¼ oz) taco seasoning mix*
- 1 *cup shredded Cheddar cheese*
- 2 *cups shredded lettuce*

Brown beef with onion in 10-inch skillet; drain off fat. Drain and cut up tomatoes, reserving juice. Add water to juice to make 2½ cups liquid. Add tomatoes, liquid, rice, and taco seasoning to beef in skillet; stir. Bring to boil. Reduce heat, cover, and let simmer until liquid is absorbed, about 25 minutes. Stir occasionally. Top with shredded cheese and lettuce before serving. Makes 4–6 servings.
COURTESY UNCLE BEN'S FOODS.

Lawry's Tijuana Torte

- 1 *lb ground beef*
- 1 *medium onion, chopped*
- 1 *can (1 lb) stewed tomatoes*
- 1 *can (8 oz) tomato sauce*
- 1 *can (4 oz) chopped green chiles (optional)*
- 1 *pkg (1¼ oz) LAWRY'S Taco Seasoning Mix*
- 12 *corn tortillas*
- 1 *lb Cheddar cheese, grated*

Brown ground beef and onion in skillet. Drain excess fat. Add stewed tomatoes, tomato sauce, green chiles, and taco seasoning mix. Combine thoroughly and simmer 10–15 minutes. Place about ¼ cup meat mixture in the bottom of a 13 X 9-inch baking dish. Place 2 tortillas side by side on the meat mixture. Top each tortilla with some meat mixture and grated cheese. Repeat until each stack contains 6 tortillas layered with meat and cheese. Bake in 350°F oven 20–25 minutes or until cheese is bubbly. Cut each torte (stack) into quarters with a sharp knife before serving. Makes 4–6 servings.

COURTESY LAWRY'S FOODS, INC.

Hormel Mexicale Casserole

- ¼ *cup chopped green pepper*
- 2 *Tbsp butter or margarine*
- 1 *can (15 oz) HORMEL Chili—No Beans (or With Beans)*
- ½ *cup chopped celery*
- 1 *can (15 oz) HORMEL Tamales*
- ½ *cup shredded Cheddar cheese*
- 1 *pkg (8½ oz) corn muffin mix*

Sauté green peppers and celery in butter until tender. Remove papers from tamales and slice into bite-size pieces. Combine cut-up tamales, chili, green pepper, and celery. Spoon ½ tamale/chili mixture into an 8-inch round or square baking pan. Sprinkle with cheese and top with remaining mixture. Prepare corn muffin mix according to package directions; drop batter by spoonfuls atop the mixture. Bake in a preheated 375°F oven for 25 minutes. Makes 4 servings.

COURTESY GEO. A. HORMEL & CO.

Almadén Burgundy Burgers

1 cup soft bread crumbs
¾ cup ALMADÉN Mountain Red Burgundy
2 lb lean ground beef
1 can (4 oz) mushroom stems and pieces, drained
2 tsp onion salt
1 tsp dry mustard
1 tsp Worcestershire sauce
¼ tsp pepper
¼ tsp garlic powder
Onion or sesame seed rolls

In a bowl lightly mix 1 cup bread crumbs, ¾ cup ALMADÉN Mountain Red Burgundy, 2 lb ground beef, 1 can (4 oz) mushroom stems and pieces, 2 tsp onion salt, 1 tsp each dry mustard and Worcestershire sauce, and ¼ tsp each pepper and garlic powder. Shape into 8–10 patties. Cover with waxed paper and refrigerate until ready to cook (for best flavor, prepare ground beef mixture at least 2 hours ahead). Barbecue over low coals to desired doneness, turning once. Serve on onion or sesame seed rolls. Makes 8–10 burgers.

COURTESY ALMADEN VINEYARDS.

A.1.® Savory Cheese & Bacon Burgers

1½ lb ground beef
½ cup minced onion
¼ lb sharp Cheddar cheese, grated
¼ cup A.1. Steak Sauce
¾ tsp basil
1 tsp salt
¼ tsp pepper
6 slices bacon
6 slices tomato
6 hamburger rolls

In large bowl, mix lightly beef, onion, cheese, A.1. Steak Sauce, basil, salt, and pepper. Form into 6 patties. Wrap a slice of bacon around each patty and secure with a toothpick. Grill burgers until bacon is cooked. Remove toothpicks. Top each with a slice of tomato and place in rolls. Serves 6.

COURTESY OF HEUBLEIN, INC.

Pepperidge Farm Individual Beef Wellingtons

1 Tbsp butter
1 onion, minced
¼ lb mushrooms, chopped
1 can (4¾ oz) liver spread or paté
2 Tbsp minced parsley
½ tsp fine herbs
4 filet mignons, about 1½ inches thick
1 pkg (17¼ oz) PEPPERIDGE FARM Frozen "Bake It Fresh" Puff Pastry
1 egg, well beaten

In a skillet, heat butter and sauté onion until golden. Add mushrooms and sauté for 5 minutes. Remove from heat and cool. Stir in liver spread, parsley, and herbs; chill. Sprinkle filet mignons with salt and pepper and broil just until brown on both sides and very rare; cool. Thaw puff pastry 20 minutes and unfold. With a sharp knife, cut both sheets in half. On a lightly floured board, roll out each sheet to an 8-inch square. Spread pastry with liver mixture. Place 1 filet on each sheet of pastry. Wrap pastry around filet, enclosing it completely. Brush top with egg. Bake in a preheated 400°F oven seam sides down for 20–25 minutes or until puffed and brown. Serve as is or topped with your favorite red wine sauce. Makes 4 servings.
COURTESY PEPPERIDGE FARM, INC.

Dole® Budget Wellington

1 cup finely chopped DOLE® Fresh Mushrooms
⅓ cup chopped green onion
3 Tbsp butter
1½ tsp salt
¼ cup soft bread crumbs
¼ cup water
1 tsp prepared mustard
¼ tsp sweet basil, crumbled
¼ tsp pepper
1 lb ground chuck
Oil
1 pkg (8 oz) refrigerated crescent rolls
Dairy sour cream (optional)

Sauté mushrooms and onion in 2 Tbsp butter until mixture is dry. Remove from heat; mix in ¼ tsp salt and set aside. Combine remaining salt, bread crumbs, water, mustard, basil, and pepper. Add beef and mix thoroughly. Shape into 4 patties about 3½ inches in diameter. Brush skillet lightly with 1 tsp oil. Brown over moderately high heat, cooking 1 minute on each side for medium rare, or 2 minutes each side for well done. Remove patties from skillet. Separate crescent roll dough into 4 rectangles. Pinch each together at perforations. Roll each on lightly floured board to form 6-inch square. Place a patty in center, topping each with about 1½ Tbsp of mushroom mixture. Bring edges of dough to center, overlapping to seal. Place on ungreased baking sheet. Melt remaining butter and brush over tops. Bake in 375°F oven 20–25 minutes, until nicely browned. Serve with dairy sour cream, if desired. Makes 4 servings.

COURTESY OF CASTLE & COOKE FOODS (DOLE®).

Underwood Beef & Biscuit Casserole

2 cans (16 oz each) mixed vegetables, drained
2 cans (4¾ oz each) UNDERWOOD Roast Beef Spread
1 can (10¾ oz) condensed golden mushroom soup
1 cup buttermilk biscuit mix
¼ cup cold water

Preheat oven to 350°F. In a large bowl, mix together vegetables, roast beef spread, and soup. Spoon mixture into a 2-qt baking dish. Bake 15 minutes. Meanwhile, in a small bowl, mix biscuit mix and water with a fork to make a soft dough. Increase oven temperature to 425°F. Remove casserole from oven and top with spoonfuls of dough. Return to oven and continue baking for 10 minutes. Makes 4 servings.

REPRINTED WITH PERMISSION OF WM. UNDERWOOD CO., WESTWOOD, MA.

Mrs. Smith's® Beef Pie Supreme

1 9- or 9⅝-inch MRS. SMITH'S® Pie Crust Shells
1½ lb beef round
2 cups carrots, sliced
2 cups potatoes, sliced
1 cup mushrooms, sliced (optional)
½ cup celery, finely chopped
¼ cup onion, finely chopped
1 can tomato paste
⅓ cup liquid brown sugar
¼ cup vinegar or red wine
1 Tbsp lemon juice
1 Tbsp prepared mustard
1 clove garlic, minced
1 Tbsp parsley, chopped

Thaw pie shell at room temperature. Cut beef into ¾-inch cubes. Spray large skillet with vegetable cooking spray. Add beef and brown over medium heat. Add carrots, potatoes, mushrooms, celery, onion. Cook for 10 minutes. Mix together tomato paste, liquid brown sugar, vinegar, lemon juice, mustard, garlic, and parsley. Stir into meat and vegetable mixture. Pour all ingredients into pie shell. Bake in a preheated 375°F oven for 40–45 minutes or until filling is bubbly and crust is richly browned. Serves 6.

COURTESY MRS. SMITH'S FROZEN FOODS CO.

Berio Veal Cutlet Parmesan

1 lb veal cutlets
½ lb mozzarella cheese
1 cup dry bread crumbs
2 beaten eggs
1 can tomato sauce
1 tsp salt
Dash of pepper

Dip cutlets in beaten eggs combined with seasoning, then in mixture of Parmesan cheese and bread crumbs. Fry in FILIPPO BERIO Olive Oil until brown (about 8 minutes). Then place cutlets in baking dish, spread tomato sauce and slices of mozzarella cheese over them. Bake in moderate oven 10–15 minutes. Serves 4.

COURTESY BERIO IMPORTING CORP.

Dorman's Swiss Veal Dormandia

1 slice white bread, crust removed
¼ cup white wine
1 lb ground veal
1½ tsp salt
¼ cup chopped onion
1 egg
1 pkg (6 oz) DORMAN'S Swiss
5 or 6 midget sweet gherkins

2 Tbsp vegetable oil
1 cup water
1 Tbsp flour
¼ cup cold milk

Soak bread in wine until completely absorbed. Combine veal, soaked bread, 1 tsp salt, 1 Tbsp chopped onion, and egg; mix well. Spread mixture onto large sheet of waxed paper, into a rectangle ½ inch thick. Cover with cheese slices. Place gherkins along narrow edge of meat. Starting at this end, roll meat layer up, jelly-roll fashion. If necessary, use waxed paper to help roll meat. Gently slice roll into 5 equal pieces. Coat rolls with flour. In a medium-size skillet, heat oil. Sauté remaining 3 Tbsp chopped onion until tender. Add water and ½ tsp salt;

bring to a boil. Add veal rolls; bring to a boil. Lower heat; cover and steam for 15 minutes. Remove rolls; keep warm. Dissolve flour in cold milk. Add to skillet, stirring constantly. Bring to a boil. Grate remaining cheese in electric blender. Add to sauce; continue stirring until cheese melts. Serve sauce with warm veal rolls. Makes 5 servings.
COURTESY DORMAN CHEESE CO.

Promise Veal Piccata

1½ lb veal, cut in thin slices for scaloppine
1 tsp salt
¼ cup PROMISE Margarine
⅓ cup water, white wine, or vermouth
6 thin lemon slices
1 tsp dried leaf tarragon
3 cups hot cooked rice
2 Tbsp chopped parsley

Sprinkle veal with salt. Melt margarine in a large skillet. Add veal slices, half at a time, and brown lightly on both sides. Add desired liquid, lemon slices, and tarragon to all of veal. Cover and simmer 2 or 3 minutes. To serve, spoon veal and sauce over hot cooked rice; sprinkle with parsley. Yield: 6 servings.
COURTESY LEVER BROTHERS COMPANY.

TAYLOR®

Taylor Veal Ala Suisse

1 lb veal—sliced from leg (as for scaloppine)
3 Tbsp butter
2 Tbsp minced onion
1 tsp minced garlic (less if put through press)
¾ cup TAYLOR American Chablis
1 cup heavy cream
Flour
Salt
Pepper

Pound veal slices until ¼ inch thick. Slice veal *across* grain into narrow strips about ½ inch wide. Slice strips into 2-inch lengths. Discard sinews and fat as you cut; set veal aside. Heat butter in a heavy skillet or fry pan until hot but not smoking. Add onion and garlic; cook slowly until onion is soft and golden. Add veal and cook until veal is tender and *lightly* browned. Remove veal and onion with a perforated spoon; keep warm. Pour chablis into pan. Bring to a boil; simmer 2–3 minutes. Scrape pan to stir in glaze. Dust meat with flour and return to pan. Simmer slowly, stirring until liquid thickens. Stir in cream and continue to cook until hot; do not boil. Season to taste. Serve over noodles or rice. Garnish with fresh parsley or as desired. Yield: 4–6 servings.

COURTESY THE TAYLOR WINE COMPANY, INC., HAMMONDSPORT, NY 14840.

Widmer Spring Lamb Chops with Wine Marinade

- *12 rib lamb chops*
- *2 cups WIDMER Lake Niagara Red Wine*
- *1 clove garlic, mashed*
- *⅓ cup oil*
- *2 tsp salt*
- *½ tsp pepper*
- *1 tsp crumbled rosemary*
- *1 onion, grated*

Place chops side by side into a shallow glass or earthenware dish. Combine remaining ingredients in a bowl and beat until well blended. Pour mixture over chops. Let stand at room temperature for 1 hour. Drain chops and place under broiler. Broil 5–6 minutes on each side or until brown and crusty on the outside and pink and juicy inside. Place chops on a platter and surround with hot, cooked, baby whole onions, tiny peas, and fresh carrot slices. Serves 6.

COMPLIMENTS OF WIDMER'S WINE CELLARS, INC., NAPLES, NEW YORK. RECIPES DEVELOPED AND COMPILED BY SUE BARRA AND PAT CALAHAN, HOME ECONOMISTS.

Gold's Lamb Patties with Savory Sauce

- *1 lb chopped lamb*
- *1 tsp salt*
- *¼ tsp pepper*
- *2 Tbsp fat*
- *¼ cup finely diced onion*
- *¼ cup tomato purée*
- *1 Tbsp steak sauce*
- *½ tsp salt*
- *½ tsp prepared GOLD'S Horseradish*

Combine lamb, 1 tsp salt, and pepper and shape into 4 patties. Melt fat in saucepan. Add onion and cook over moderate heat until tender. Stir in purée, steak sauce, ½ tsp salt, and prepared GOLD'S Horseradish and heat thoroughly. Brush patties with a bit of fat and place on a rack in preheated broiler. Broil 4 inches from moderate heat until lightly browned, about 10 minutes. Turn, brush with more fat, and continue broiling until done, about 10 minutes longer. Top with sauce and serve. Serves 4.

COURTESY GOLD PURE FOOD PRODUCTS, BROOKLYN, NY.

Imperial Moussaka

- 1½ lb ground lamb or beef
- 3 lb eggplant
- ¾ cup IMPERIAL Margarine
- 2 onions, chopped
- 1 clove garlic, minced
- 1 tsp salt
- ½ tsp thyme
- ½ tsp crushed rosemary
- ¼ tsp black pepper
- 1 (10½ oz) can beef gravy
- 3 Tbsp tomato paste
- 4 Tbsp flour
- ¼ tsp salt
- ⅛ tsp nutmeg
- 2 cups milk
- 2 egg yolks, slightly beaten

Brown meat in large skillet, breaking up meat with a fork. Remove with slotted spoon; drain on absorbent paper. Discard fat. Peel and chop eggplant. Melt 4 Tbsp margarine in same skillet. Brown eggplant lightly, adding 2 Tbsp more margarine if needed. Place in 13 X 9 X 2-inch baking pan. Melt 2 Tbsp margarine in same skillet. Sauté onions, garlic, salt, thyme, rosemary, and pepper until onions are transparent. Add meat, gravy, and tomato paste; mix lightly. Spoon over eggplant. Press mixture firmly into baking pan with back of spoon. Melt remaining 4 Tbsp margarine in saucepan. Stir in flour, salt, and nutmeg until well blended. Add milk. Cook quickly, stirring constantly, until thickened. Add a small amount of hot sauce to eggs; mix well. Quickly stir egg mixture into sauce until well blended. Spread sauce evenly over meat mixture in baking pan. Bake in a moderately hot oven (375°F) 25–30 minutes or until bubbly and sauce is lightly browned. Makes 10–12 servings.

COURTESY LEVER BROTHERS COMPANY.

Progresso Lamb Shanks Mediterranean*

- 2 Tbsp PROGRESSO Olive Oil
- 3 lb lamb shanks, cut in serving pieces
- 1 jar (21 oz) PROGRESSO Italian Style Cooking Sauce
- 2 cups water
- 1 cup dry white wine
- 6 carrots, sliced ½ inch thick
- 4 celery ribs with leaves, coarsely chopped
- 2 Tbsp chopped fresh parsley
- 1 tsp dried mint leaves
- 1 tsp salt
- ½ tsp ground black pepper
- 1 bay leaf, crumbled
- 1 chicken bouillon cube

Preheat oven to 350°F. In a large heavy saucepot or Dutch oven, heat oil until hot. Add lamb; brown on all sides. Drain fat.

Add remaining ingredients. Stir well to scrape bottom of pot. Cover and bake in preheated oven until meat easily comes off the bones, about 1½ hours, turning occasionally. If necessary, skim fat from sauce before serving. Serves 6.

*May be prepared in advance of serving.
COURTESY PROGRESSO QUALITY FOODS.

Mrs. Butterworth's Oven Baked Pork Shoulder

- *1 (2½–3 lb) smoked boneless pork shoulder roll*
- *6 sweet potatoes*
- *Dijon-type mustard*
- *1 large onion, sliced*
- *½ cup MRS. BUTTERWORTH'S Syrup*

Place meat in large pot; cover with water. Bring to a boil; simmer 20 minutes per pound or until tender. Drain. Place sweet potatoes in a large pot; cover with water. Bring to a boil; simmer until tender when pierced with a fork. Drain and peel. Make 5 or 6 slashes ¾ way through meat; spread cut sides with mustard. Insert onion slice in each slash. Arrange sweet potatoes around meat. Bake in a 375°F oven 20 minutes. Pour MRS. BUTTERWORTH'S Syrup over meat and potatoes. Bake 10–15 minutes longer until meat is glazed. Makes 6–8 servings.
COURTESY LEVER BROTHERS COMPANY.

Karo Sweet and Sour Pork

- *2 Tbsp corn oil*
- *1 lb boneless pork, cut in 1-inch cubes*
- *1 can (20 oz) pineapple chunks in own juice*
- *½ cup KARO Light or Dark Corn Syrup*
- *¼ cup cider vinegar*
- *2 Tbsp catchup*
- *2 Tbsp soy sauce*
- *1 clove garlic, crushed*
- *1 small pepper, cut in 1-inch squares*
- *2 Tbsp corn starch*
- *2 Tbsp water*
- *Hot cooked rice or Chinese noodles*

In large skillet, heat corn oil over medium-high heat; add pork and brown on all sides. Add pineapple, corn syrup, vinegar, catsup, soy sauce, and garlic. Bring to boil. Reduce heat; simmer uncovered, stirring occasionally, 10 minutes or until pork is tender. Add green pepper. Mix corn starch and water;

stir into pork mixture. Stirring constantly, bring to boil over medium heat and boil 1 minute. Serve over rice or noodles. Makes 4 servings.
COURTESY KARO CORN SYRUP.

Heinz Sweet Sour Pork Chops

- *6 rib pork chops, ½ inch thick*
- *1 Tbsp shortening*
- *Salt and pepper*
- *½ cup HEINZ Tomato Ketchup*
- *½ cup pineapple juice*
- *1 Tbsp brown sugar*
- *1 Tbsp lemon juice*
- *2 Tbsp minced onion*
- *1 tsp HEINZ Worcestershire Sauce*
- *½ tsp salt*
- *⅛ tsp ground cloves*

Brown chops in shortening; drain excess fat. Sprinkle lightly with salt and pepper. Combine ketchup and remaining ingredients; pour over chops. Cover; simmer 45 minutes, basting occasionally or until meat is tender. Skim excess fat from sauce. Makes 6 servings (about 1 cup sauce).
COURTESY OF HEINZ U.S.A., DIVISION OF H.J. HEINZ COMPANY.

Schlitz Caribbean Pork Back Ribs

- *6 lb pork back ribs*
- *1 Tbsp cornstarch*
- *1½ tsp salt*
- *½ tsp ginger*
- *1 can (8 oz) SCHLITZ Malt Liquor*
- *3 Tbsp orange juice concentrate*
- *2 Tbsp dark molasses*
- *1 tsp lemon juice*
- *1 tsp imitation rum extract*

Combine cornstarch, salt, and ginger in a saucepan. Stir in SCHLITZ Malt Liquor, orange juice concentrate, molasses, and lemon juice and cook slowly, stirring constantly until mixture thickens. Lower heat and cook slowly 2–3 minutes, stirring occasionally. Stir in rum extract. Place ribs on grill, rib ends down, as far as possible from heat. Broil 1 hour over low to moderate heat, turning occasionally. Brush sauce on both sides of ribs and continue broiling, turning and brushing occasionally, for 20–30 minutes longer or until ribs are done. Yield: 6 servings.
COURTESY JOS. SCHLITZ BREWING CO.

Sun-Maid® Sweet 'N Spicy Pork Chops

- 4 pork chops, 1 inch thick
- 2 onions, sliced
- 1 cup orange juice
- 1 Tbsp lemon juice
- 2 Tbsp brown sugar
- 1 tsp ginger
- ½ tsp poultry seasoning
- ½ tsp marjoram
- ½ cup SUN-MAID® Golden Seedless Raisins (gold box)
- Salt
- Pepper

Render a small amount of fat from pork chops in a heavy skillet; brown pork chops. Remove from pan, add onions and cook until soft. Return chops to pan with remaining ingredients; salt and pepper to taste. Cover, cook until pork is tender and thoroughly cooked, about 30 minutes. Makes 4 servings.

COURTESY SUN-MAID GROWERS OF CALIFORNIA, KINGSBURG, CALIFORNIA.

PROGRESSO®

Progresso Pork Chops Pizzaiola

- 6 loin pork chops
- 2 Tbsp PROGRESSO Olive Oil
- 1 jar (16 oz) PROGRESSO Meat Flavored Spaghetti Sauce
- ¾ cup water
- ½ tsp oregano
- Salt and pepper to taste
- 1 clove garlic
- 1 small green pepper, diced

Sauté the chops in oil in a large skillet until golden. Pour off fat and add meat-flavored spaghetti sauce, water, oregano, and garlic; salt and pepper to taste. Cover and simmer 40 minutes. Add the green pepper and cook 10 minutes more. Serves 6.

COURTESY PROGRESSO QUALITY FOODS.

Orange Crush® Ham

- 1 slice (1 lb) ready-to-eat ham
- 1 Tbsp butter or margarine
- 1 bottle (10 oz) Orange CRUSH®
- ⅓ cup seedless raisins
- ⅓ cup water
- ¼ cup light brown sugar, firmly packed
- 4 tsp cornstarch
- 1 Tbsp orange rind, grated
- 1 Tbsp vinegar

Brown ham lightly on both sides in butter or margarine. Remove ham from frypan and keep hot. Add remaining ingredients to frypan; cook over low heat until slightly thickened, stirring constantly. Return ham to frypan; cover and heat 5–10 minutes. Yields: 4 servings.

THIS RECIPE HAS BEEN PROVIDED AND IS PUBLISHED WITH PERMISSION OF CRUSH INTERNATIONAL INC., EVANSTON, ILLINOIS, MANUFACTURER OF THE FAMOUS CRUSH® SOFT DRINK PRODUCTS. CRUSH IS A REGISTERED TRADEMARK OF CRUSH INTERNATIONAL INC., EVANSTON, IL 60202.

French's Ham and Colcannon Bake

- 1 ham slice, about 1½ lb FRENCH'S Whole Cloves
- 3 Tbsp butter
- 4 cups coarsely chopped cabbage
- 1½ cups water
- 1 tsp salt
- ½ cup milk
- 1 envelope (5 servings) FRENCH'S Idaho Mashed Potato Granules

Pierce ham slice with 4 or 5 cloves; place on bake-and-serve pan. Melt 2 Tbsp butter in medium-size saucepan. Add cabbage, cover, and cook 5 minutes, stirring occasionally. Add water, salt, and milk; bring to a boil. Remove from heat. Gradually add contents of potato envelope, stirring briskly with fork. Spoon around edge of ham slice; dot with remaining 1 Tbsp butter. Bake at 400°F for 20 minutes, until hot. Yield: 5–6 servings.

COURTESY THE R. T. FRENCH COMPANY.

B&M Bean and Ham Roll-Ups

1 28-oz can B&M Brick Oven Baked Beans
12 slices baked or boiled ham
2 Tbsp butter or margarine
¼ cup brown sugar
1½ Tbsp prepared mustard

Preheat oven to 350°F. Spoon beans into a strip at narrow end of ham slices. Roll up ham slices, beginning at narrow end so that beans are enclosed in the roll. In a small saucepan, melt butter or margarine. Add sugar and mustard. Cook over low heat and stir until well blended. Arrange ham rolls in a shallow baking dish. Baste tops of rolls with mustard glaze. Bake for about 25 minutes, basting occasionally. Makes 6 servings.
REPRINTED WITH PERMISSION OF WM. UNDERWOOD CO., WESTWOOD, MA.

Pillsbury Cheese 'N Wiener Crescents

8 wieners
8 strips of sharp natural Cheddar cheese
1 8-oz can PILLSBURY Refrigerated Quick Crescent Dinner Rolls

Heat oven to 375°F. Slit wieners to within ½ inch of ends; insert cheese strips. Separate crescent dough into 8 triangles. Place wiener on shortest side of triangle; roll up. Place on ungreased cookie sheet, cheese side up. Bake at 375°F for 12–15 minutes or until golden brown. To reheat, wrap in foil; heat at 350°F for 10–15 minutes. Yield: 8 sandwiches.
COURTESY OF THE PILLSBURY COMPANY.

Rathskeller Stuffed German Wieners

1 lb RATHSKELLER German Brand Wieners, split lengthwise
2 servings prepared instant mashed potatoes
¼ cup salad dressing
1 tsp prepared mustard
2 hard-cooked eggs, chopped

2 Tbsp chopped onion
2 Tbsp sweet pickle relish

Prepare mashed potatoes according to package directions for 2 servings. Mix in salad dressing and mustard until thoroughly blended. Fold eggs, onion, and pickle relish into potato mixture. Season to taste. Fill split RATHSKELLER German Brand Wieners with potato mixture. Bake at 375°F 15–20 minutes. Makes 4 servings.
COURTESY THE RATH PACKING COMPANY.

Hunt's®

Hunt's® Easy Zucchini Sausage Bake

- ½ lb Italian sausage
- ½ cup chopped onion
- 3 zucchini, cut in ½-inch slices
- 1 (6 oz) can HUNT'S Tomato Paste*
- 1 cup water
- 3 cups hot cooked rice
- 1 tsp sweet basil
- 1 tsp seasoned salt
- ½ cup shredded mozzarella cheese
- ¼ cup grated Parmesan cheese

In 10-inch skillet, cook sausage and onion until sausage loses redness. Remove and drain on paper towel. Sauté zucchini in remaining fat in skillet until transparent. Cover; cook 5 minutes or until almost done; reserve. Combine HUNT'S Tomato Paste with water. Combine *half* with rice-and-sausage mixture in 2-qt baking dish. Add basil and salt; mix well. Arrange slices of zucchini over top. Sprinkle with mozzarella and Parmesan; spoon *remaining* paste mixture over all. Bake, *covered*, at 350°F 20 minutes. Makes 4–6 servings.

*Generic term: tomato paste.
COURTESY HUNT-WESSON FOODS, INC.

Armour Kulbassy-Potato Combo

- 6 cups chopped cooked potatoes
- 2 hard-cooked eggs, sliced
- 2 Tbsp sliced green onions
- 1 lb ARMOUR Star Kulbassy, thinly sliced
- 6 slices ARMOUR Star Bacon, chopped
- 3 Tbsp sugar
- 1 Tbsp cornstarch
- 1 Tbsp salt
- ¾ cup water
- ⅓ cup vinegar

Combine potatoes, eggs, and green onions; set aside. Brown sausage; add to potato mixture. Cook bacon until crisp. Combine sugar, cornstarch, salt, water, and vinegar; slowly add to bacon, stirring constantly until thickened. Pour over potato mixture; toss slightly. Yield: 6 servings.

COURTESY ARMOUR AND COMPANY.

Lawry's Sausage and Eggplant Creole

1½ lb mild Italian sausage
1 large onion, chopped
1 green pepper, chopped
1 cup sliced celery
3 zucchini, halved lengthwise and cut in ½-inch slices
1 large eggplant, cut in 1-inch cubes
1 can (1 lb 12 oz) tomatoes
1 tsp LAWRY'S Garlic Salt
1 tsp LAWRY'S Seasoned Salt
1 tsp sugar
1 tsp LAWRY'S Pinch of Herbs
½ lb fresh mushrooms, sliced and sautéed in butter
½ lb grated Monterey Jack cheese
¼ cup chopped parsley

Brown sausage until crumbly; drain fat. Add onion, green pepper, celery, zucchini, eggplant, tomatoes, garlic salt, seasoned salt, sugar, and pinch of herbs. Cover and bring to a boil. Reduce heat and simmer 1½ to 2 hours, stirring occasionally. Top with layer of sautéed mushrooms, cheese, and parsley. Cover and cook about 5 minutes or until cheese is melted. Serve over buttered noodles or rice. Makes 6–8 servings.

COURTESY LAWRY'S FOODS, INC.

La Choy Chinese Fire Pot

1 lb beef sirloin, sliced thin
1 lb boned chicken, sliced thin
8 oz uncooked, cleaned, medium shrimp
1 lb fresh mushrooms, sliced
1 lb fresh spinach, washed, drained
1 lb celery cabbage, cut into 1-inch pieces
2 cans (8 oz each) LA CHOY Water Chestnuts, drained, sliced
2 pkg (6 oz each) frozen LA CHOY Chinese Pea Pods, thawed
2 oz fine egg noodles, cooked
2 cans (10 oz each) concentrated chicken broth
2½ cups water
LA CHOY Soy Sauce, Chinese Hot Mustard, and Sweet & Sour Sauce
Chopped parsley or green onions

Arrange meats and vegetables on a large platter or on individual platters. Heat chicken broth and water to simmer in deep electric frypan. With slotted spoons, forks, or Chinese wire ladles, each diner drops food into the simmering broth to poach. Then dip cooked food into one of the sauces. When all food is cooked, stir noodles into the broth. Serve in soup bowls and garnish with parsley or green onions. Makes 6–8 servings.

COURTESY LA CHOY FOOD PRODUCTS.

Minute Maid®

Curried Kabobs with Lemon Marinade

- *2 lb lamb, pork, or beef, cut into 2-inch cubes*
- *½ cup MINUTE MAID® 100% Pure Lemon Juice*
- *¼ cup salad oil*
- *2 Tbsp grated onion*
- *1 clove garlic, crushed*
- *1 tsp ground ginger*
- *1 tsp salt*
- *1½ tsp curry powder*
- *½ tsp cayenne pepper*
- *16 fresh mushroom caps*
- *2 large green peppers, seeded and cut into 1-inch squares*
- *2 Tbsp butter*
- *16 cherry tomatoes*
- *4 onions, quartered*
- *32 pineapple chunks (16-oz can)*

Place the meat cubes in a glass dish; cover with a marinade made of MINUTE MAID® 100% Pure Lemon Juice, oil, and seasonings. Marinate for at least 4 hours. When ready to cook the kabobs, sauté the mushrooms and peppers in butter over medium heat and remove the meat from the marinade. Using skewers 12 inches or longer, assemble 8 kabobs, alternating meat, vegetables, and pineapple on the skewers. Grill over medium heat or 2–3 inches from heat in a broiler 10–15 minutes, turning and brushing with marinade several times. Serve over cooked brown rice. Yield: 8 servings.

MINUTE MAID IS A REGISTERED TRADEMARK OF THE COCA-COLA COMPANY. COURTESY THE COCA-COLA COMPANY FOODS DIVISION.

Poultry

Crisco Oil Crispy Fried Chicken

2½ to 3½ lb frying chicken cut into pieces
*½ cup flour**
½ tsp poultry seasoning
CRISCO OIL for frying
1 tsp garlic salt
½ tsp black pepper
½ tsp paprika

Combine dry ingredients. Coat each piece of chicken. Brown on all sides in hot (365°–375°F) CRISCO OIL. Reduce heat and cook uncovered about 30–45 minutes, until chicken is tender. Makes 4–6 servings.

*For crispier-tasting chicken, use half flour and half bread crumbs.
COURTESY OF THE PROCTER & GAMBLE COMPANY.

Wish-Bone Easy Broiled Chicken Italiano

2 to 2½ lb chicken, cut into serving pieces
Salt and pepper
½ cup WISH-BONE Italian Dressing

On broiler pan, place chicken; salt and pepper to taste and brush with Italian dressing. Grill or broil 45 minutes or until tender, basting with remaining dressing and turning frequently. Makes about 4 servings.
COURTESY OF THE LIPTON KITCHENS.

Aunt Jemima® Savory Oven Fried Chicken

- ¾ *cup AUNT JEMIMA® Original Pancake & Waffle Mix*
- ⅓ *cup grated Parmesan cheese*
- ½ *tsp salt*
- ¼ *tsp garlic powder*
- 1 *2½–3-lb broiler-fryer, cut up*
- 1 *egg, beaten*
- ¼ *cup milk*
- ⅓ *cup butter or margarine, melted*

Combine mix, cheese, salt, and garlic powder. Dip chicken pieces in combined egg and milk; coat with pancake mix mixture. Place in large shallow baking pan; let stand 10 minutes. Drizzle butter over chicken. Bake in preheated hot oven (400°F) 45–50 minutes or until tender and golden brown. Makes 4 servings.

RECIPE REPRODUCED WITH THE PERMISSION OF THE QUAKER OATS COMPANY.

Carolina Wild Chicken Amandine

- 3 *whole chicken breasts, split*
- *Salt and pepper*
- ¼ *cup butter*
- ½ *medium onion, sliced*
- 2 *Tbsp diced pimiento (optional)*
- 2½ *cups water*
- ½ *cup American cheese, grated*
- 1 *6-oz pkg CAROLINA Long Grain & Wild Rice*
- ¼ *cup sliced almonds*

Season chicken to taste with salt and pepper. In a heavy skillet, brown chicken in melted butter. Add onion and sauté lightly. Drain chicken and onion well. Pour off excess drippings. Stir pimiento, water, cheese, and contents of 1 pkg of CAROLINA Long Grain & Wild Rice (both envelopes) into a skillet. Bring to a boil and pour into a shallow baking dish (approx. 13 X 8 X 1½ inches). Place the chicken breasts on top and bake at 350°F for about 30 minutes. Sprinkle the almonds over the chicken and rice; continue to bake an additional 15 minutes. Makes 6 servings.

COURTESY RIVIANA FOODS INC.

Widmer Vineyard Chicken Casserole

- 1 *chicken, 3–4 lb*
- 1½ *cups WIDMER Lake Niagara Wine*
- 1½ *cups water*
- 1½ *tsp salt*
- ¼ *tsp French's Black Pepper*
- 1½ *cups small shell macaroni*
- 2 *Tbsp butter*
- 2 *Tbsp flour*
- 1 *cup light cream or half-and-half*
- ¼ *cup chopped pimiento*
- ¼ *cup chopped green pepper*
- 1 *can (about 4 oz) sliced mushrooms, drained*
- 1 *cup soft bread crumbs*
- 1 *cup grated mild Cheddar cheese*
- 3 *Tbsp French's Prepared Mustard*

Cook chicken with wine, water, salt, and pepper. When tender, remove from broth; discard skin and bones and cut chicken into large chunks. Reserve 1 cup of the broth. Add water to remaining broth to make about 6 cups liquid; bring to a boil, add macaroni, and cook until tender. Drain, discarding liquid. Place chicken and macaroni in shallow 2-qt baking dish. Meanwhile, make a sauce by melting butter, blending in flour, cream, and the cup of reserved broth. Cook, stirring constantly, until thickened. Add pimiento, green pepper, and mushrooms; pour over chicken and macaroni. Combine bread crumbs, cheese, and mustard; spoon over chicken mixture. Bake in 350°F oven 20–30 minutes or until bubbling hot. Serves 6–8.

COMPLIMENTS OF WIDMER'S WINE CELLARS, INC., NAPLES, NEW YORK.

Enrico's®

Enrico's Chicken Cacciatori

- 1 *frying chicken cut into pieces*
- ¼ *cup olive oil*
- 1 *medium onion, chopped*
- 1 *green pepper, chopped*
- ½ *red pepper, minced*
- ½ *clove garlic, minced*
- 2 *Tbsp sour wine (or vinegar)*
- 1 *tsp salt*
- ⅛ *tsp black pepper*
- 1 *cup ENRICO'S Spaghetti Sauce*

Brown the pieces of chicken thoroughly in hot olive oil. Add onion, peppers, and garlic and brown lightly. Add the remaining ingredients except ENRICO'S Spaghetti Sauce and simmer ½ hour or until chicken is very tender. If necessary, add a very little amount of water to simmer. During the last 5 minutes of cooking, add 1 cup of ENRICO'S Spaghetti Sauce and simmer. Cubes of veal or beef may be substituted in place of the chicken.

COURTESY VENTRE PACKING COMPANY, INC.

Kraft Chicken Marseilles

1 2½- to 3-lb broiler-fryer, cut up
CATALINA Brand French Dressing
1 16-oz can tomatoes
8 onion slices, ¼ inch thick
1 tsp salt
½ tsp celery seed
¼ tsp pepper
¼ cup wine or water
2 Tbsp flour

Brown chicken in ⅓ cup dressing over low heat. Add ¼ cup dressing, tomatoes, onion, and seasonings. Cover; simmer 45 minutes. Remove chicken and vegetables to serving platter. Gradually add wine (or water) to flour, stirring until well blended. Gradually add flour mixture to hot liquid in pan; cook, stirring constantly until mixture boils and thickens. Simmer 3 minutes, stirring constantly. Serve with chicken and vegetables. Yield: 4 servings.

COURTESY KRAFT, INC.

Hunt-Wesson Foods Chicken Oriental

2 lb chicken breasts, boned and cut into strips
2 cloves garlic, minced
*2 Tbsp WESSON® Buttery Flavor® Oil**
1 onion, cut into large chunks
2 large green peppers, cut in squares
*1 (15 oz) can HUNT'S® Tomato Sauce with Tomato Bits***
2 Tbsp cornstarch
⅛ tsp pepper
¼ cup soy sauce
1 Tbsp sherry
3 cups cooked rice

In 10-inch skillet, brown chicken and garlic in WESSON Oil. Add onion and peppers; cook 5 minutes, stirring constantly. Combine remaining ingredients, except rice; stir into chicken-vegetable mixture. Cook 5 minutes longer, stirring constantly. Serve over rice. Makes 4 servings.

*Generic term: buttery flavor oil.
**Generic term: tomato sauce with tomato bits.
COURTESY HUNT-WESSON FOODS, INC.

Ragu´ Chicken Parmesan

- *¾ cup seasoned bread crumbs*
- *¼ cup grated Parmesan cheese (reserve 2 Tbsp)*
- *1 tsp basil*
- *½ tsp garlic powder*
- *Salt and pepper to taste*
- *6 chicken cutlets, pounded thin (about 1½ lb)*
- *2 eggs, beaten*
- *Vegetable oil*
- *1 jar (15½ oz) RAGU´ Classic Combinations Spaghetti Sauce with Mushrooms and Onions*
- *1 cup shredded mozzarella cheese*

Preheat oven to 375°F. In large bowl, combine bread crumbs, 2 Tbsp Parmesan cheese, basil, garlic powder, salt, and pepper; set aside. In small bowl, dip cutlets in egg and coat with bread mixture. In large skillet, brown cutlets thoroughly on both sides in hot oil. Drain on paper towels. In an 11 X 7-inch baking dish, evenly spread ½ cup sauce. Overlap on sauce; top with remaining sauce and Parmesan cheese. Sprinkle with mozzarella cheese. Bake 20 minutes or until heated through. Serves about 6.

COURTESY RAGU´ FOODS, INC.

Progresso Arroz Con Pollo

(Literally, rice with chicken)

- *2 Tbsp vegetable oil*
- *2½ lb chicken, cut in parts*
- *1 cup regular cooking rice, uncooked*
- *1 tsp salt*
- *1 tsp chili powder*
- *2 chicken bouillon cubes*
- *1½ cups hot water*
- *1 jar (21 oz) PROGRESSO Italian Style Cooking Sauce*

In a large skillet heat oil until hot. Add chicken; brown on all sides; remove chicken and set aside. To skillet add rice, salt, and chili powder. Stir to coat rice with pan drippings. Dissolve bouillon cubes in water. Add bouillon and PROGRESSO Italian Style Cooking Sauce to skillet; stir well. Add chicken. Simmer, covered, until chicken is tender, about 40 minutes, stirring occasionally. If desired, garnish with black olives and serve with green peas. Serves 4.

COURTESY PROGRESSO QUALITY FOODS.

Imperial Chicken Rice Casserole

1 chicken, cut into 8 pieces
Water
1 Tbsp salt
½ cup IMPERIAL Margarine, melted
½ tsp salt
¼ tsp black pepper
1 tsp marjoram
1 cup rice
¼ cup chopped salted peanuts

¼ cup raisins
4 cups hot chicken broth

Place chicken in bowl; cover with water; sprinkle 1 Tbsp salt in water. Let stand. Mix melted margarine, salt, pepper, and marjoram. Pour half the margarine mixture in bottom of 13 X 9 X 2-inch pan. Sprinkle rice, nuts, and raisins over margarine mixture. Stir in 3 cups hot chicken broth. Cover with aluminum foil. Bake 20 minutes in a moderate oven (350°F). Drain chicken well; pat dry. Arrange chicken on rice; brush with half the margarine mixture. Bake 30 minutes longer; brush again with margarine mixture. Pour remaining broth over rice. Increase oven temperature to 425°F; bake 30 minutes or until chicken is browned and rice is tender. Serve immediately. Makes 6 servings.

COURTESY LEVER BROTHERS COMPANY.

Kikkoman Orange Island Chicken

½ cup orange juice
⅓ cup KIKKOMAN Soy Sauce
1 tsp ground ginger
1 tsp orange rind
½ tsp onion powder
2½ to 3 lb broiler-fryer chicken, cut up
½ cup flour
2 Tbsp salad oil

Mix first 5 ingredients; pour in plastic bag with chicken. Refrigerate 8 hours or overnight. Coat with flour; brown in hot oil. Place in baking pan; cover and bake at 350°F 30 minutes. Remove cover; bake 15 minutes longer. Makes 4–6 servings.

COURTESY KIKKOMAN INTERNATIONAL INC.

Uncle Ben's®

Uncle Ben's® Country Captain Chicken

- *1 cup UNCLE BEN'S® CONVERTED® Brand Rice*
- *1/3 cup raisins*
- *2 Tbsp butter or margarine*
- *2 tsp curry powder*
- *2½ to 3 lb chicken, cut up*
- *1 medium onion, chopped*
- *2 cups water*
- *1 can (8 oz) tomato sauce*
- *2 tsp salt*
- *1 tsp Worcestershire sauce*
- *Chopped peanuts (optional)*

Heat oven to 350°F. Combine rice and raisins in shallow, 2-qt (12 X 8 X 2-inch) baking dish. Melt butter or margarine in large skillet. Stir in curry powder. Add chicken; brown well on all sides. Arrange on rice mixture. Add onion to drippings in skillet and cook until tender. Stir in water, tomato sauce, salt, and Worcestershire sauce. Bring to boil. Pour over chicken; stir. Cover and bake in 350°F oven 40–45 minutes or until chicken is tender and rice mixture is desired consistency. Garnish with chopped peanuts, if desired. Makes 4–6 servings.

COURTESY UNCLE BEN'S FOODS.

Canada Dry Poached Chicken with Lemons and Oranges

- *4 ripe lemons*
- *3½ lb broiling chicken, cut into pieces*
- *1/8 to 1/4 tsp salt*
- *2 Tbsp melted butter or margarine*
- *1 cup chicken bouillon*
- *2 oranges, freshly squeezed*
- *1/4 tsp black pepper*
- *1 (7 oz) CANADA DRY Club Soda*

Rub chicken pieces with ½ lemon and salt. Place in lidded sauté pan; add butter and cook over medium heat for 5 minutes until pieces are golden. Turn heat to simmer; add chicken bouillon and poach for about 30 minutes. Remove chicken to warming dish. Add orange juice and pepper to sauté pan and cook for about 5 minutes. Add CANADA DRY Club Soda (at room temperature). Heat 15 seconds and serve in large soup dishes. Garnish with parsley and lemon slices. Makes 4 servings.

COURTESY OF CANADA DRY CORPORATION.

Mueller's® Stewed Chicken with Dumplings

- *2 lb chicken parts*
- *6 cups water*
- *4 carrots, cut in 1-inch pieces*
- *1 small onion, sliced*
- *⅓ cup sliced celery*
- *1 Tbsp chopped parsley*
- *1 Tbsp salt*
- *Generous dash pepper*
- *6 oz (3 cups) MUELLER'S Dumplings*
- *¼ cup flour*
- *¼ cup cold water*

Place chicken, 6 cups water, vegetables, salt, and pepper in large pot. Cover; simmer until chicken is tender—about 1–1½ hours. Remove chicken. Bring broth to a boil; add dumplings and cook about 11 minutes. Mix flour and ¼ cup cold water to form a smooth paste; slowly add to broth. Cook a few minutes, stirring, until broth thickens a little. Add chicken (meat may be removed from bones, if desired); heat 1 minute. Makes 8 cups, about 4–6 servings.

COURTESY OF C.F. MUELLER COMPANY.

Colombo Chicken Bombay

- *1 3-lb chicken, quartered*
- *1 32-oz container plain COLOMBO Whole-Milk Yogurt*
- *1 Tbsp curry powder*
- *Pinch ginger*
- *4 Tbsp apricot preserves*
- *1 clove garlic, crushed*
- *1 medium-sized onion, chopped*
- *1 cup converted long-grain rice (not instant)*
- *Salt and pepper to taste*
- *¼ cup golden raisins*

- *1 6-lb capacity brown-in-the-oven bag*
- *1 scallion, finely chopped*

Place the chicken parts in the bag, skin side down. In a mixing bowl blend together ingredients 2–10. Pour into the bag containing the chicken and close with a bag tie. Work the bag with your hands until the chicken is covered with the yogurt and rice mixture. Place in a baking pan, with the chicken skin side up. Pierce the bag to let steam escape. Bake in a preheated 350°F oven for 1 hour. Pour the cooked chicken and rice onto a platter and garnish with chopped scallions. Serves 4 generously.

PERMISSION TO REPRODUCE GRANTED BY AMERICA'S ORIGINAL YOGURT COMPANY, COLOMBO, INC.

La Choy Chicken Breasts Mandarin

- 4 large chicken breasts
- 2 cups cooked rice
- ½ cup golden raisins
- ¾ tsp salt
- Toothpicks and string
- 2 Tbsp butter, melted
- 1 can (1 lb 4 oz) pineapple tidbits
- 1 can (11 oz) Mandarin oranges
- 1½ tsp lemon juice
- 2½ Tbsp sugar
- 2 Tbsp cornstarch
- 2 Tbsp LA CHOY Soy Sauce
- 2 Tbsp butter
- 1 can (8 oz) LA CHOY Water Chestnuts, drained, sliced
- Hot cooked rice

Cut chicken breasts in half; remove bones and cut through thickest part of each breast to form a pocket. Mix rice, raisins, and salt. Stuff mixture into each piece of chicken. Fasten with toothpicks and string. Place chicken in buttered 13 X 9 X 2-inch baking pan. Brush with 2 Tbsp melted butter. Bake at 350°F for 30 minutes. Reduce heat to 325°F. Drain pineapple and oranges, saving syrups. Combine syrups in heavy saucepan with lemon juice, sugar, cornstarch, and soy sauce; blend well. Cook over medium heat, stirring constantly, until thick and transparent. Remove from heat; add remaining butter, fruit, and water chestnuts; mix well. Spoon over chicken pieces. Cover with foil. Continue baking at 325°F for 30 minutes more. Remove toothpicks and strings. Spoon sauce over chicken before serving. Serve with hot rice. Makes 8 servings.

COURTESY LA CHOY FOOD PRODUCTS.

Kikkoman Snappy-Lemon Chicken

- ¼ cup KIKKOMAN Soy Sauce
- 2 Tbsp white wine
- 2 Tbsp lemon juice
- ½ tsp liquid hot pepper sauce
- 2 green onions, finely chopped
- 1 clove garlic, crushed
- 2½ to 3 lb broiler-fryer chicken, cut up

Combine first 6 ingredients; pour into plastic bag with chicken. Refrigerate 6–8 hours or overnight. Reserving marinade, place chicken in shallow pan, skin side down. Broil 8–10 inches from heat 15 minutes. Turn, baste with sauce; broil for 15 minutes longer. Makes 4–6 servings.

COURTESY KIKKOMAN INTERNATIONAL INC.

Shasta Chicken Italiano

1 (12 oz) can Diet SHASTA Lemon-Lime
2 cups tomato juice
2 Tbsp vinegar
1 Tbsp chopped green pepper
1 tsp Worcestershire sauce
2 tsp artificial liquid sweetener
1 tsp salt
1 tsp dry mustard
1 clove garlic
1 tsp mixed Italian herbs
4 large single chicken breasts (skins removed)

Combine all ingredients except chicken in blender; whirl smooth and transfer to saucepan. Bring to a boil, lower heat, and simmer ½ hour. Arrange chicken in baking pan or casserole. Pour sauce over chicken and bake in moderate oven until tender, about 1 hour. Baste chicken every 20 minutes to keep moist. Makes 4 servings.
COURTESY SHASTA BEVERAGES.

Gebhardt's Fritada de Pollo
(Chicken Fricassee)

3 lb chicken
½ cup flour
½ cup shortening
1 onion, sliced
1 green pepper, chopped
2 cloves garlic
4 Tbsp catsup
1½ cups water
1 tsp GEBHARDT'S Chili Powder
2 tsp salt
4 Tbsp raisins (optional)
8 ripe olives, chopped (optional)

Cut chicken into serving pieces, dip in flour, brown in hot shortening. Remove to larger pan. Fry onion, green pepper, and garlic until brown in remaining hot shortening; add catsup, water, GEBHARDT'S Chili Powder; boil 5 minutes. Pour over chicken. Salt, adding water as needed; cover, allow to simmer until chicken is tender, about 1½ hours. Fifteen minutes before serving, add raisins and ripe olives. Yield: 4–6 servings.
FROM THE KITCHENS OF GEBHARDT MEXICAN FOODS.

Kretschmer Wheat Germ Picnic Chicken

Chicken

2 lb chicken wings
½ cup KRETSCHMER Regular Wheat Germ
¼ cup grated Parmesan cheese
¼ tsp pepper
⅛ tsp salt
2 Tbsp soy sauce
2 Tbsp catsup or chili sauce
2 Tbsp cider vinegar

Remove and discard wing tips from chicken. Divide each wing at joint into 2 pieces. Combine wheat germ, cheese, pepper, and salt on wax paper. Stir well to blend. Combine soy sauce, catsup, and vinegar in shallow container. Mix well. Dip each piece of chicken into soy sauce mixture, then into wheat germ mixture, turning to coat well. Place chicken in shallow baking pan lined with foil. Bake at 375°F 40–45 minutes until tender. Cover last 10 minutes to prevent overbrowning. Serve hot or cold with Dipping Sauce (below) if desired. Yield: 4–5 servings.

Dipping Sauce

½ cup chili sauce
1 Tbsp cider vinegar
1 Tbsp firmly packed brown sugar

Combine ingredients. Mix well.

COURTESY KRETSCHMER WHEAT GERM, A PRODUCT OF INTERNATIONAL MULTIFOODS.

Van Camp's Easy Bar-B-Que Chicken Casserole

1 can (1 lb) VAN CAMP'S® Pork and Beans
4 pieces of chicken (thighs, breasts, or legs)
¼ cup STOKELY'S Finest® Tomato Catsup
2 Tbsp peach preserves
2 tsp instant minced onion
¼ tsp soy sauce
¼ cup brown sugar

Place pork and beans in a 2-qt casserole. Top with chicken. Mix together the remaining ingredients and pour over chicken and VAN CAMP'S® Beans. Cover and bake at 325°F for 1 hour 45 minutes. Makes 4 servings.

COURTESY STOKELY-VAN CAMP, INC.

MOGEN DAVID®

Mogen David Light Puffs with Wine Sauce

- 3 *whole chicken breasts*
- 3 *Tbsp butter*
- 1 *cup fresh mushrooms, chopped*
- ½ *cup MOGEN DAVID White Wine*
- ½ *tsp dried tarragon leaves*
- ½ *tsp salt*
- *Dash of white pepper*
- 1 *pkg frozen patty shells, thawed*
- 1 *egg, beaten*
- 1 *Tbsp flour*
- 1 *cup half-and-half*
- ½ *cup sour cream*
- 1 *cup grated Parmesan cheese*

Bone, skin, and halve chicken breasts. Season underside of breasts with salt and pepper. Roll up, seasoned side in. Sauté in butter for about 4 minutes on each side. Remove from pan; drain well. Add mushrooms to pan drippings; cook for 1 minute. Stir in MOGEN DAVID Wine, tarragon, salt, and pepper. Add chicken, cover pan, and simmer 15 minutes. For each serving, roll out a patty shell on floured cloth until large enough to wrap around chicken breasts. Wrap and put seam-side-down in shallow baking pan. Repeat with remaining chicken. Brush each roll with beaten egg. Bake at 400°F 20–25 minutes, or until golden. For sauce, blend flour into cooled mushroom mixture until smooth. Stir in half-and-half; cook, stirring until thickened and smooth. Stir in sour cream and Parmesan. Heat gently until cheese is melted. Pour sauce over light puffs or serve separately.

COURTESY MOGEN DAVID WINE CORPORATION.

Pepperidge Farm Chicken Divan

- 1 *pkg PEPPERIDGE FARM Patty Shells*
- 1 *can cream of chicken soup*
- 1 *can cream of mushroom soup*
- 1½ *cups chicken; cut in bite-size pieces*
- ¾ *cup leftover broccoli; cut in bite-size pieces*

Bake patty shells as directed on package. Meanwhile, combine and heat condensed soups, undiluted. Add meat and vegetables. Warm until just heated through. Spoon into baked patty shells. Serves 4–6.

COURTESY PEPPERIDGE FARM, INC.

Mueller's® Golden Chicken 'n Noodles

2 to 2½ lb chicken parts
2 Tbsp butter or margarine
1 medium onion, sliced
1 clove garlic, mashed
⅛ tsp thyme leaves
1 can (10¾ oz) condensed golden mushroom soup
½ cup drained, diced, canned tomatoes
1 cup cooked, cut green beans, if desired
Salt and pepper
8 oz (7½ cups) MUELLER'S Hearty Egg Noodles

In a large skillet, brown chicken in butter; remove and set aside. Cook onion, garlic, and thyme in drippings a few minutes; stir in soup and tomatoes. Return chicken; cover and cook over low heat 30–45 minutes or until chicken is tender, adding beans during last 5 minutes of cooking. Season to taste with salt and pepper. Meanwhile, cook noodles as directed; drain. Serve chicken and sauce over noodles. Makes 4–6 servings.

COURTESY OF C.F. MUELLER COMPANY.

Del Monte Chicken Rice Bowl

1 cup uncooked rice
3 Tbsp salad oil
2 chicken bouillon cubes
1 tsp salt
2 cups hot water
2 cups uncooked chicken, boned and cut in thin strips
2 cups sliced celery
1 cup thinly sliced onion
½ cup chopped green pepper

1 can (15¼ oz) DEL MONTE Sliced Pineapple
1 Tbsp soy sauce

Brown rice in 1 Tbsp hot oil. Place in a 2-qt casserole. Dissolve bouillon cubes and salt in water; pour over rice. Cover and bake at 350°F, 20 minutes or until rice is tender. Brown chicken in 2 Tbsp hot oil. Stir in vegetables, pineapple syrup, and soy sauce. Simmer, covered, 10 minutes. Combine with rice; top with pineapple. Continue baking 10 minutes. Yield: 6–8 servings.

COURTESY DEL MONTE KITCHENS, DEL MONTE CORPORATION, P.O. BOX 3575, SAN FRANCISCO, CA 94119.

Campbell's Stuffed Chicken Roll-Ups

- *3 chicken breasts, split, skinned, and boned (about 1½ lb boneless)*
- *1 can (10¾ oz) CAMPBELL'S Condensed Cream of Onion Soup*
- *1 cup small bread cubes*
- *2 Tbsp chopped parsley*
- *½ tsp oregano leaves, crushed*
- *1 can (about 4 oz) sliced mushrooms, drained*
- *2 Tbsp butter or margarine*
- *¼ cup water*

Flatten chicken breasts with flat side of knife. To make stuffing, combine 3 Tbsp soup, bread cubes, parsley, and oregano. Place stuffing in center of each chicken breast. Roll up; tuck in ends. Secure with toothpicks. In skillet, brown chicken and mushrooms in butter. Add remaining soup and water. Cover; cook over low heat 20 minutes or until done. Stir occasionally. Makes 6 servings.

COURTESY CAMPBELL SOUP COMPANY.

Underwood Chicken Divan Roll-Ups

- *1 pkg (10 oz) buttermilk flaky biscuits*
- *2 cans (4¾ oz each) UNDERWOOD Chunky Chicken Spread*
- *1 pkg (10 oz) frozen broccoli spears, cooked according to package directions*
- *1 can (11 oz) condensed Cheddar cheese soup*
- *⅓ cup milk*

Preheat oven to 375°F. On a floured surface, roll each biscuit into an oval shape, 4 X 3 inches. Spread a scant 2 Tbsp chunky chicken spread over center of each biscuit. Arrange 2 broccoli spears on each biscuit so that flower ends extend beyond edge of roll. Fold ends of dough over broccoli so that they overlap; pinch to seal together. Place biscuits on ungreased baking sheet and bake 15 minutes, until golden brown. Meanwhile, in a small saucepan, mix soup and milk. Heat to boiling; simmer 2 minutes, stirring almost constantly. Serve sauce over biscuits. Makes 10 roll-ups.

REPRINTED WITH PERMISSION OF WM. UNDERWOOD CO., WESTWOOD, MA.

Swift's Turkey Paprika

- 2 cups sliced, cooked Butterball SWIFT'S Premium Turkey
- ½ stick (¼ cup) SWIFT'S Brookfield Butter
- 1 medium onion, sliced
- ¼ cup flour
- 1 tsp salt
- 2 cups milk
- 2 egg yolks, beaten
- 4 tsp paprika
- 1 4-oz can mushrooms, stems and pieces, drained
- 1 cup dairy sour cream
- 1 Tbsp poppy seed
- 2 Tbsp SWIFT'S Brookfield Butter
- 1 7-oz pkg noodles, cooked

Melt ½ stick butter in skillet. Add onion and cook until tender. Blend in flour and salt. Remove from heat. Gradually add milk. Stirring constantly, cook until mixture thickens. Stir ¼ cup white sauce into egg yolks; return to hot mixture. Bring to boil, stirring constantly. Reduce heat to low and stir in paprika. Add mushrooms and turkey slices. Simmer 5 minutes. Stir in sour cream and heat just until sauce is hot. Serve on poppy seed noodles. To make poppy seed noodles: Add poppy seed and butter to drained noodles. Toss together lightly. Yield: 6 servings.

COURTESY SWIFT & COMPANY.

Carnation Quick 'n Easy Turkey Pie

- 1 pkg (10 oz) refrigerator biscuits
- 3 cups cooked cubed turkey or chicken
- 1½ cups (10-oz pkg) cooked, drained frozen peas and carrots
- ½ cup chopped celery
- ⅓ cup chopped onion
- 1 tsp seasoned salt
- ½ tsp salt
- ¼ tsp crushed rosemary leaves
- ⅛ tsp white pepper
- ⅛ tsp poultry seasoning
- 1¼ cups (10¾-oz can) cream of mushroom soup
- ⅔ cup undiluted CARNATION® Evaporated Milk
- 2 Tbsp lemon juice

Roll out each biscuit to about 3½ inches in diameter and press around sides and bottom of buttered 10 X 6 X 2-inch baking dish. (Use 8 biscuits for sides and 2 for bottom.) Prick with fork. Bake in moderate oven (375°F) 5 minutes, or until partially baked. Combine remaining ingredients in large mixing bowl; mix well. Spoon turkey mixture into partially baked crust. Return to oven and bake an additional 25 minutes. Makes 6 servings.

LABEL ART AND RECIPE PROVIDED COURTESY CARNATION COMPANY.

Swift's Turkey Company Casserole

2 cups chopped cooked Butter Basted SWIFT'S Premium Turkey Roast
2 cans (8 oz each) tomato sauce
8 oz noodles
8 oz pkg cream cheese, softened
8 oz cottage cheese
⅓ cup chopped green onion
1 Tbsp chopped green pepper

Combine turkey and tomato sauce in saucepan; simmer 10 minutes. Cook noodles in boiling salted water for 10 minutes. Drain. Combine cream cheese, cottage cheese, onion, and pepper. In a buttered 2-qt shallow casserole, spread half the noodles. Cover with cheese mixture, then cover with remaining noodles. Spoon turkey mixture over noodles. Bake in 350°F oven 30 minutes. Yield: 8 servings, about 1 cup each.

COURTESY SWIFT & COMPANY.

Kellogg's® Orange-Stuffed Roast Duckling

1 duckling (4–5 lb), washed and patted dry
Salt
¼ cup regular margarine or butter
¾ cup finely chopped celery
1 can (11 oz) mandarin orange segments, drained, reserving syrup
½ pkg (3½ cups) KELLOGG'S® CROUTETTES Herb Seasoned Croutons
Orange-flavored liqueur
2 tsp cornstarch
2 tsp grated lemon peel
1 Tbsp lemon juice

Remove wing tips from duckling up to first joint. Sprinkle inside cavity with salt. Set aside. Melt margarine in small frypan. Add celery and cook over low heat until tender. Remove from heat. Stir in ¼ cup of the reserved orange syrup. (Save remaining syrup.) Set aside. Measure croutons into large mixing bowl. Add drained orange segments, mixing lightly. While tossing gently, add celery mixture. Lightly stuff duckling. Close opening with skewers and tie legs together with string. Prick skin several times with a fork to allow fat to drain slowly, self-basting the duckling. Place on rack, breast side up, in roasting pan. Roast duckling in oven at 325°F 2–2½ hours or until tender (about 30 minutes per lb). If necessary, cover duckling lightly with foil during last hour to prevent over-browning. For glaze, add orange-flavored liqueur to remaining syrup to measure ⅔ cup. In small saucepan, stir

together syrup mixture, cornstarch, lemon peel, and lemon juice. Cook over medium heat until thickened and clear, stirring frequently. Remove from heat. Brush over duckling several times during roasting. Yield: 4 servings.
COURTESY OF KELLOGG COMPANY.

Miller Skillet Duck

1 (4-lb) duck, cut in serving pieces
1½ cups MILLER High Life
4 carrots, sliced
1 large onion, chopped
3 large potatoes, peeled and sliced thin
2 large tomatoes, cored and chopped
1 tsp salt
Freshly ground pepper
1 tsp garlic powder
1 Tbsp minced parsley

Place duck in a large skillet over low heat. (As some of the duck fat will remain no matter how you attempt to cut it away, it is unnecessary to add butter or oil.) When skin is evenly brown and crisp, pour in MILLER High Life and add carrots, onion, potatoes, and tomatoes. Season with salt, pepper, and garlic. Sprinkle parsley over all. Cover and continue cooking over low heat for 50 minutes, or until duck is done. Juices run clear when fork-tested in thickest part of duck. Serves 4.
COURTESY MILLER BREWING COMPANY.

Seafood

Lea & Perrins Roasted Trout in Bacon

⅓ cup LEA & PERRINS Worcestershire Sauce
2 Tbsp onion powder
1 Tbsp lemon juice
2 tsp salt
¾ tsp garlic powder
3 (1½ lb each) dressed trout or other firm-fleshed fish
9 strips bacon

Combine all ingredients except fish and bacon; mix well. Brush LEA & PERRINS mixture inside and outside of fish. Place fish in a buttered baking pan. Score skin in 2 or 3 places and strip with bacon. Bake in a preheated moderate oven (350°F) 40–45 minutes or until fish flakes easily when tested with a fork. Baste often with pan juices during baking. Yield: 6 portions.

COURTESY LEA & PERRINS WORCESTERSHIRE SAUCE, A PRODUCT OF LEA & PERRINS, INC.

SeaPak Baked Flounder Deluxe

1 16-oz pkg SEAPAK Frozen, Skinless Flounder Fillets
½ cup dairy sour cream
2 Tbsp ReaLemon Juice
1 Tbsp milk or water
1 tsp salt
1 tsp chives
½ tsp white pepper

Coating

1½ cups corn flake crumbs
1 Tbsp Parmesan cheese
1 tsp salt

Partially thaw fillets and drain on paper towel. Combine the next 6 ingredients and dip each fillet to cover both sides. Mix corn flake crumbs, Parmesan cheese, and salt together. Bread fillets with corn flake mixture and place in a greased 15½ X 10½ X 1-inch shallow baking dish. Bake at 450°F for 12 minutes. Place under broiler 3–4 minutes. Garnish with parsley and slivered almonds. Serve warm. Makes 4–6 servings.

COURTESY RICH-SEAPAK CORPORATION.

Gorton's Fish Florentine

GORTON'S 18 Fish Portions or Fried Fish Fillets
1½ cups (1 pkg frozen) spinach
3 Tbsp butter
3 Tbsp flour
1 onion, chopped
1¾ cups milk
3 Tbsp parsley
¼ tsp garlic powder
¼ tsp Worcestershire sauce
1 tsp lemon juice
Salt and pepper
Dry bread crumbs

Saute onion in butter until tender. Stir in flour, parsley, and garlic powder. Slowly stir in milk. Add Worcestershire sauce, lemon juice, and salt and pepper to taste. Cook spinach in boiling water until done. Add to sauce and cook until thick. Place fish portions or fried fish fillets in shallow casserole and cover with sauce. Sprinkle with dry bread crumbs and dot with butter. Cook casserole at 425°F 15–18 minutes. Serves 6.

COURTESY GORTON'S OF GLOUCESTER.

Dole®

Dole® Fillets of Sole Cartagena

- *1/3 cup unblanched almonds*
- *3 Tbsp grated Parmesan cheese*
- *1/2 tsp salt*
- *1/4 tsp dill weed*
- *1/4 tsp paprika*
- *1 lb sole fillets*
- *1 Tbsp butter*
- *1 Tbsp oil*
- *2 medium Dole® Bananas*
- *1 Tbsp lemon juice*

Turn almonds into blender and blend fine (or grate, using Mouli grater). Mix with cheese, salt, dill, and paprika on sheet of waxed paper. Dip fillets one at a time in the mixture, coating both sides. Heat butter and oil in 10-inch skillet. Add sole in single layer and brown over moderate heat, turning once, and cooking each fillet about 5 minutes, just until fish is browned and flakes easily. Remove to heated serving platter. Peel DOLE® Bananas and halve crosswise. Add to skillet, along with lemon juice. Cook 1 minute, shaking skillet to turn DOLE® Bananas, so they cook on all sides. Arrange on serving platter with fish and serve at once. Makes 4 servings.

COURTESY OF CASTLE & COOKE FOODS (DOLE®).

Promise Savory Stuffed Fish Fillets

- *2 Tbsp PROMISE Sunflower Oil Margarine, divided*
- *1 carrot, shredded (1/2 cup)*
- *1 medium onion, chopped (1/2 cup)*
- *1 rib celery, chopped (1/4 cup)*
- *1/2 cup chopped mushrooms (2 oz)*
- *1/4 tsp dried leaf savory*
- *1 slice bread, cubed*
- *1 lb fresh* fish fillets (sole or flounder)*
- *2 Tbsp lemon juice*
- *1/8 tsp salt*

In medium saucepan, melt 2 Tbsp margarine; saute carrots, onion, and celery until crisp-tender. Add mushrooms and savory; cook 1 minute longer. Add bread cubes, toss lightly. Place half the fish fillets in shallow baking dish. Spoon vegetable stuffing over fish; cover with remaining fish fillets. Melt remaining 1 Tbsp margarine; stir in lemon juice; spoon over fish. Sprinkle lightly with salt. Bake in 350°F oven 20–25 minutes, basting several times with pan juices, until fish flakes easily with a fork. Yield: 4 servings.

*Note: To use packaged frozen fish fillets, partially thaw fish. Slice block in half lengthwise to make 2 rectangular pieces. Place stuffing between pieces and proceed as directed above.
COURTESY LEVER BROTHERS COMPANY.

Campbell's Stuffed Flounder Roll-Ups

- 2 *pkg (10 oz each) frozen broccoli spears, cooked and drained, or 4 medium cooked carrots, cut in thin sticks*
- 8 *fillets of flounder (2 lb)*
- 1 *can (10¾ oz) CAMPBELL'S Condensed Cream of Celery Soup*
- ¼ *cup mayonnaise*
- 1 *Tbsp lemon juice*

Divide broccoli among fillets; roll up. Secure with toothpicks. Arrange in 2-qt shallow baking dish (12 X 8 X 2 inches). Bake at 350°F for 20 minutes. Meanwhile, combine remaining ingredients; pour over fish, stirring into liquid around fish. Bake 15 minutes more or until done. Stir sauce before serving. Makes 6–8 servings.

COURTESY CAMPBELL SOUP COMPANY.

Booth's Haddock Oliviana

- 1 *(16 oz) pkg BOOTH'S Haddock Fillets*
- 2 *tsp olive oil*
- *Juice from ½ lemon*
- 1 *garlic clove, finely chopped*
- ¼ *tsp salt*
- 1 *tsp minced parsley*
- 1 *tsp oregano*
- 1 *Tbsp butter*
- *Mushrooms, sliced and sautéed*

Defrost fillets. Place in a single layer in a buttered baking dish. Brush fillets with a combination of olive oil and lemon juice. Combine finely chopped garlic clove, salt, minced parsley, and oregano and sprinkle over fish. Dot with butter and bake in a preheated 350°F oven 20–25 minutes until fish flakes easily with a fork. Garnish with sliced sautéed mushrooms. Note: You may add ¼ cup dry bread crumbs to the seasoning mixture for a golden brown appearance. Do not overcook.

COURTESY BOOTH FISHERIES CORPORATION.

Cheez-Ola® Broccoli Fish Casserole

- 1 *10-oz pkg frozen broccoli, thawed*
- 1 *to 1½ lb fish fillets, thawed*
- 6 *oz CHEEZ-OLA®, sliced*
- 1 *tsp oregano*
- ⅛ *tsp powdered thyme*
- ¼ *cup corn oil*
- 2 *medium onions, chopped*
- ½ *green pepper, chopped*
- 2 *Tbsp flour*
- ⅛ *tsp pepper*
- 1½ *cups skim milk*

Arrange broccoli in bottom of lightly oiled 13 X 8 X 2-inch baking dish. Top with layer of fish and layer of CHEEZ-OLA®. Sprinkle with oregano and thyme. Heat oil on low heat and cook onions and green pepper until tender. Stir in flour and pepper. Add milk and cook, stirring constantly until thickened. Pour over fish and CHEEZ-OLA® and bake at 400°F for 25 minutes or until fish flakes easily. Serves 4.

COURTESY FISHER CHEESE—AN AMFAC COMPANY.

King Oscar Royal Sardines Creole

- 1 *cup chopped green pepper*
- ¾ *cup chopped onion*
- ¾ *cup sliced celery*
- 1 *clove garlic, crushed*
- 3 *Tbsp cooking oil*
- 2 *cups canned tomatoes*
- 1 *can tomato paste mixed with 6 Tbsp water*
- ½ *tsp salt*
- ¼ *tsp thyme*
- 1 *bay leaf, crushed*
- *Dash of cayenne*
- 2 *cans KING OSCAR Sardines, drained*

Cook pepper, onions, celery, and garlic in the oil until tender. Add tomatoes, tomato paste, and seasonings. Simmer 25 minutes, stirring occasionally. Fold in sardines carefully to keep their shape. Serve over hot rice. Serves 6–8.

COURTESY KING OSCAR SARDINES.

Kikkoman Broiled Hawaiian Fish Fillets

⅓ *cup KIKKOMAN Soy Sauce*
1 *Tbsp brown sugar, packed*
2 *Tbsp salad oil*
1 *Tbsp cider vinegar*
½ *tsp ground ginger*
1 *clove garlic, crushed*
1½ *lb white fish fillets*
1 *Tbsp fresh parsley, minced*

Combine first 6 ingredients; marinate fish in sauce 20 minutes, turning once. Reserve sauce; broil fish 5 inches from heat 4 minutes. Turn, baste with sauce, and broil 4 minutes longer. Just before serving, sprinkle with parsley. Makes 4 servings.

COURTESY KIKKOMAN INTERNATIONAL INC.

Miller Crusty Baked Fillets

4 *fish fillets (flounder, whitefish, or carp)*
3 *Tbsp flour*
1 *tsp salt*
¼ *tsp white pepper*
1 *tsp onion powder*
¾ *tsp ground dill*
½ *cup MILLER High Life*
½ *cup heavy cream*
¼ *cup butter or margarine, melted*

1 *cup corn flake crumbs*
2 *Tbsp fresh chopped parsley*

Preheat oven to 350°F. Grease a 2-qt flat baking dish and place fillets, side by side, in a single layer. In a bowl combine flour, salt, pepper, onion powder, and dill. Dust over fish. In a separate bowl, blend MILLER High Life, cream, and butter. Stir in corn flake crumbs and moisten completely. Spoon crumb mixture over fish and sprinkle with parsley. Bake for 30 minutes, or until crust is well browned and fish flakes easily when tested with a fork. Serves 4.

COURTESY MILLER BREWING COMPANY.

Gorton's Cheese & Tomato Topped Fillets

1 pkg (16 oz) GORTON'S Ocean Perch, Sole, Haddock, Flounder or Cod Fillets, thawed
2 Tbsp butter or margarine
2 Tbsp flour
¼ tsp salt
¼ tsp dry mustard
⅛ tsp pepper
1 cup milk
½ cup shredded Cheddar cheese
2 tomatoes, thinly sliced
Paprika

Heat oven to 400°F. Lightly butter a square pan or baking dish, 9 X 9 X 2 inches. Arrange perch fillets in prepared pan. Bake 15 minutes. Melt butter in saucepan over low heat. Blend in flour, salt, mustard, and pepper. Cook over low heat, stirring until mixture is smooth and bubbly. Remove from heat. Stir in milk. Heat to boiling, stirring constantly. Boil and stir 1 minute. Stir in cheese. Cook over low heat, stirring constantly, until cheese is melted and sauce is smooth. Arrange tomato slices over fillets. Pour hot cheese sauce over all and sprinkle with paprika. Bake 10 minutes longer. Serves 4.
COURTESY GORTON'S OF GLOUCESTER.

Seven Seas Casserole

1½ cups water
1 can (10¾ oz) condensed cream of mushroom or celery soup
¼ cup finely chopped onion (optional)
1 tsp lemon juice (optional)
¼ tsp salt
Dash of pepper
1½ cups MINUTE® RICE
1 pkg (10 oz) BIRDS EYE® 5 Minute Sweet Green Peas, partially thawed

*1 can (7 oz) tuna, drained and flaked**
½ cup grated Cheddar cheese
Paprika

Combine water, soup, onion, lemon juice, salt, and pepper in a saucepan. Bring to a boil over medium heat, stirring occasionally. Pour about half of the soup mixture into a greased 1½-qt casserole. Then, in separate layers, add rice, peas, and tuna. Add remaining soup mixture. Sprinkle with cheese and paprika. Cover and bake at 375°F for 10 minutes. Stir; then cover and continue baking 10–15 minutes longer. Makes about 5½ cups, or 4 servings.

*Or use salmon, crabmeat, lobster, shrimp, or minced clams. With canned minced clams, drain and add water to liquid to make 1½ cups.

Chicken of the Sea® Tuna Florentine

- *2 pkg (10 oz each) frozen chopped spinach, thawed*
- *2 Tbsp instant minced onion*
- *1 can (12½ or 13 oz) CHICKEN OF THE SEA Brand Dinner Size Tuna*
- *6 hard-cooked eggs, sliced*
- *2 cans (10¾ oz) condensed cream of mushroom soup*
- *1 cup (½ pint) sour cream*
- *Salt and pepper*
- *¼ cup melted butter*
- *2 cups soft bread crumbs (about 4 slices)*

Squeeze spinach to remove excess liquid. Spread spinach evenly in a greased 3-qt casserole. Sprinkle with onion, tuna, and eggs. Mix mushroom soup and sour cream. Pour mixture evenly over eggs. Mix melted butter and crumbs and sprinkle evenly over top of casserole. Bake in preheated moderate oven (350°F) 30–35 minutes or until golden brown and bubbly. Casserole may be prepared ahead and refrigerated. Serves 6.

Bisquick® Patio Tuna Squares

- *2 cups BISQUICK® Baking Mix*
- *½ cup water*
- *2 cans (6½ oz each) tuna, drained, or 2 cans (7½ oz each) crabmeat, drained and cartilage removed*
- *1½ cups shredded Swiss cheese (about 6 oz)*
- *½ cup chopped celery*
- *⅓ cup sliced green onions*
- *⅓ cup mayonnaise or salad dressing*
- *1 tsp Worcestershire sauce*
- *¼ tsp salt*
- *⅛ tsp pepper*

Heat oven to 375°F. Grease baking pan, 9 X 9 X 2 inches. Mix baking mix and water until soft dough forms. Pat evenly in pan, pressing dough ½ inch up sides. Mix remaining ingredients; spread evenly over dough. Sprinkle with paprika if desired. Bake until edges are light brown, about 30 minutes. Yield: 9 servings.

COURTESY BETTY CROCKER FOOD & NUTRITION CENTER, GENERAL MILLS, INC. REGISTERED® TRADEMARK OF GENERAL MILLS, INC.

Bumble Bee® Caraway Cabbage Rolls

- *2 cans (6½ oz each) BUMBLE BEE® Chunk Light Tuna*
- *1 small cabbage (approx. 12 large leaves)*
- *Boiling water*
- *10 slices bacon*
- *½ cup chopped green pepper*
- *½ cup chopped onion*
- *1 cup cooked rice*
- *2 eggs, lightly beaten*
- *2½ tsp salt*
- *1 tsp sweet basil*
- *1 can (15 oz) tomato sauce*
- *1 can (16 oz) stewed tomatoes*
- *½ tsp caraway seeds*

Drain tuna. Remove entire core from cabbage with a sharp knife. Place cabbage, core side down, in boiling water. Remove and drain leaves as they begin to separate. Cook bacon until crisp. Remove; drain on absorbent paper and crumble. Sauté green pepper and onion in bacon drippings until pepper is soft. Combine bacon, sautéed vegetables, rice, eggs, salt, basil, and tuna. Spoon tuna mixture into cabbage leaves, rolling to secure filling by tucking in sides. Line a deep 3-qt casserole with extra cabbage leaves. Stack cabbage rolls on top. Pour tomato sauce, combined with undrained stewed tomatoes, over cabbage rolls. Sprinkle with caraway seeds. Cover and bake in a 350°F oven 45 minutes. Remove cover, bake 30 minutes longer. Makes 6 servings.

COURTESY OF CASTLE & COOKE FOODS (BUMBLE BEE®).

Chicken of the Sea® Tuna Wellington

1 pkg (6 oz) long grain and wild rice mix
1 pkg (10 oz) frozen mixed vegetables
1 can (12½ oz or 13 oz) CHICKEN OF THE SEA Brand Dinner Size Tuna
6 hard-cooked eggs, chopped
1 can (4 oz) mushrooms, drained and chopped
6 scallions, chopped
2 pkg (8 oz each) refrigerated crescent roll dough
1 can (10¾ oz) condensed cream of shrimp soup
½ cup sour cream

In a saucepan, combine rice mix (water and butter as directed on package) and frozen vegetables; simmer 20–25 minutes or until rice is tender and dry. Stir tuna, eggs, mushrooms, and scallions into rice mixture. Cover and chill. Unroll 1 pkg of dough on a heavily buttered cookie sheet, pinching seams to make a smooth sheet. Shape tuna mixture into a loaf 12 inches long, down center of dough, turning dough on tuna mixture. Unroll second sheet and pinch seams. Place dough over mixture and press firmly into place on all sides. Bake in a preheated moderate oven (350°F) 30–35 minutes or until richly browned. Heat soup and sour cream in a saucepan. Cut loaf with serrated knife into thick slices and serve with sauce. Filling may be prepared ahead and refrigerated.

USED WITH PERMISSION FROM VAN CAMP SEA FOOD COMPANY, A DIVISION OF RALSTON PURINA COMPANY. ®

Rice-A-Roni Clam Bake

2 Tbsp butter or margarine
1 pkg (7¼ oz) RICE-A-RONI Savory Rice Pilaf
4 strips diced bacon
1 cup chopped onion
½ cup chopped celery
½ cup chopped green pepper
2 (8 oz) cans clams
1 cup chopped tomatoes
1 (2½ oz) can sliced ripe olives

Sauté rice-macaroni in butter or margarine until brown; pour into 2-qt baking dish. In same frying pan, cook bacon; add onion, celery, green pepper; sauté until tender. Drain off excess fat; add to baking dish. Drain clams, reserving juice. Add clams, tomatoes, 1 (2½ oz) can olives (drained), and contents of flavor packet to rice mixture. Combine water and clam juice to measure 2½ cups liquid; stir into rice. Bake uncovered at 350°F 50–55 minutes or until water is absorbed and rice is tender. Makes six 1-cup servings.

COURTESY OF GOLDEN GRAIN MACARONI CO.

Gorton's Italian Baked Stuffed Clams

2 cans GORTON'S Clams, drained
¼ cup water
2 Tbsp parsley flakes
2 Tbsp instant minced onion
1 cup dry bread crumbs
¼ cup olive or salad oil
1 tsp salt
1 tsp oregano leaves
½ tsp garlic powder
½ tsp basil leaves
¼ tsp pepper

Heat oven to 450°F. Combine water, parsley, and onion; let stand 5 minutes. Stir in GORTON'S Clams and remaining ingredients. Spoon into individual baking dishes, clam shells, or shallow baking dish. Bake 8–10 minutes. Makes 6 servings.

COURTESY GORTON'S OF GLOUCESTER.

Wakefield Crabmeat Thermidor

1 (6 oz) pkg WAKEFIELD Alaska King Crabmeat
¼ cup butter or margarine
¼ cup flour
¼ tsp salt
¼ tsp paprika
2 cups milk
1 Tbsp chopped parsley
1 tsp Worcestershire sauce
¼ tsp dry mustard
¼ tsp Tabasco sauce
½ cup grated Cheddar cheese

Thaw crabmeat and retain liquid. Melt butter over medium heat; stir in flour, salt, and paprika until blended. Gradually stir in milk. Cook, stirring until mixture is thickened. Remove from heat. Stir in crab, liquid, parsley, Worcestershire, mustard, Tabasco, and ¼ cup cheese. Place in 1-qt casserole, top with remaining cheese and paprika. Bake 30 minutes at 350°F. Serve over hot, cooked rice or buttered noodles. Serves 3–4.

COURTESY PACIFIC PEARL SEAFOODS.

Wakefield Crab Au Gratin

1 (6 oz) pkg WAKEFIELD Alaska Snow Crabmeat
2 Tbsp butter or margarine
3 Tbsp flour
½ cup milk
½ cup half-and-half
¼ cup white wine
½ cup grated mild Cheddar cheese
½ tsp salt
⅛ tsp paprika
1 (2 oz) can sliced mushrooms, drained
1½ tsp chives or green onion, chopped
2½ Tbsp dry bread crumbs

Thaw crabmeat and retain liquid. Place butter in saucepan on medium heat. Stir in flour. Gradually stir in milk, half-and-half,

wine, and crab liquid. Cook, stirring constantly over medium heat until sauce is smooth and thick. Stir in cheese, salt, paprika, mushrooms, and chives. Stir until cheese is melted. Fold in crabmeat. Pour mixture into well-greased 1-qt casserole. Top with bread crumbs. Place in 400°F oven and bake 15 minutes or until top is golden brown. Serves 3–4.
COURTESY PACIFIC PEARL SEAFOODS.

Jos. Garneau Curried Scallops in a Ring of Rice

2 lb scallops
Seasoned flour
8 Tbsp butter
6 shallots, finely chopped
1½ Tbsp curry powder
⅓ cup ANHEUSER Laubenheimer
Rice
Watercress

Wash and dry scallops and dust them lightly with flour. Heat butter in a skillet and in it sauté shallots for 3 minutes. Add the scallops and cook them quickly, turning frequently to brown all sides, for about 3 minutes. Sprinkle the scallops with curry powder and add ANHEUSER Laubenheimer. Serve in a ring of rice and garnish with watercress.
COURTESY THE JOS. GARNEAU CO.

Holland House® Sherried Scallops

2 10-oz pkg frozen scallops or 1¼ lb fresh, shelled scallops
2 Tbsp melted butter or margarine
¼ cup HOLLAND HOUSE Sherry Cooking Wine
3 tsp lemon juice
Dash cayenne pepper
1 tsp minced onion
1 tsp sugar
1 Tbsp minced parsley

Thaw and rinse scallops or clean fresh scallops. Arrange on bottom of a lightly greased baking dish. Combine other ingredients, pour over top. Bake in 350°F oven for 30 minutes. Serves 4.
RECIPE SUPPLIED BY HOLLAND HOUSE BRANDS CO.

Kikkoman Far East Shrimp Kabobs

1 lb large shrimp (about 24 per lb)
¼ cup KIKKOMAN Soy Sauce
¼ cup white wine
1 Tbsp salad oil
2 tsp sugar
⅛ tsp cayenne pepper
1 clove garlic, crushed
1 can (13¼ oz) pineapple chunks, drained
1 green pepper, chunked
1 basket cherry tomatoes
Metal skewers

Shell and devein shrimp; put in shallow bowl. Combine soy sauce, white wine, salad oil, sugar, pepper, and garlic, stirring until sugar dissolves. Pour over shrimp and mix thoroughly. Marinate 30 minutes; stir several times. Remove shrimp from marinade; reserve marinade. Place pineapple chunk, green pepper piece, and cherry tomato alternately in curve of shrimp. Thread 4 shrimps on each metal skewer. Place kabobs on broiler pan; brush with marinade. Broil 3 inches from heat 2–3 minutes; turn, brush with marinade, and broil 2–3 minutes longer or until done. Makes about 6 kabobs.

COURTESY KIKKOMAN INTERNATIONAL INC.

Carolina Shrimp Commodore

1 small onion, chopped
2 Tbsp chopped green pepper
2 Tbsp butter or margarine
2 Tbsp flour
1 cup water
½ tsp salt
Dash of hot pepper sauce
1 tsp Worcestershire sauce
1 cup grated American cheese
¼ cup tomato juice
1 lb shrimp, cleaned, cooked, and peeled
3 cups hot cooked CAROLINA Extra Long Grain Rice

Sauté onion and green pepper in butter 2 minutes. Stir in flour, then water. Stir until mixture thickens, add seasonings. Add cheese and stir until melted. Blend in tomato juice, add shrimp, and heat thoroughly, about 5 minutes. Serve over hot cooked rice. Makes 4 servings (about ½ cup shrimp mixture and ⅔ cup rice).

COURTESY RIVIANA FOODS INC.

SeaPak Sweet and Sour Shrimp

- 1 cup pineapple cubes
- 1 green pepper, cut into strips
- ½ medium onion, cut into rings
- ⅓ cup cider vinegar
- ¼ cup firmly packed brown sugar
- ¾ cup water
- 1 Tbsp molasses
- 1 tsp soy sauce
- 2 Tbsp cornstarch
- ¼ cup water
- 1 lb SEAPAK Breaded Shrimp, cooked according to package directions

Combine first 8 ingredients in a saucepan and bring slowly to a boil, stirring constantly. Combine cornstarch and water. Pour into sauce, stirring constantly. Continue to cook over medium heat until sauce thickens and comes to a boil. Reduce heat to simmer. Cook shrimp and add to sauce. Serve with plain cooked rice or noodles. Serves 4.

COURTESY RICH-SEAPAK CORPORATION.

La Choy Shrimp Foo Young

Sauce

- ½ cup chicken broth
- 2 tsp sherry
- 1 Tbsp LA CHOY Soy Sauce
- 2 tsp cornstarch

Egg Mixture

- 3 eggs
- ¼ cup chopped onion
- ¼ cup green pepper
- ¼ cup celery
- ¾ cup rinsed, drained LA CHOY Bean Sprouts
- ¼ tsp salt
- Dash pepper
- 1 Tbsp cooking oil
- ½ cup chopped cooked shrimp*
- Hot cooked rice

In saucepan, combine ingredients for sauce; cook over low heat until thickened. Keep warm. Beat eggs lightly. Stir in vegetables, salt, and pepper. Heat oil in skillet until hot; fry ¼ cup mixture at a time. Place 2 Tbsp shrimp on pancake. When set and brown on edges, turn and brown other side. Keep warm until all mixture is cooked. Serve with heated sauce and rice. Makes 2 servings.

*Variations: shredded cooked pork, beef, chicken, or crabmeat may be substituted for shrimp.
COURTESY LA CHOY FOOD PRODUCTS.

Louisiana Baked Shrimp and Eggplant

1 can (4½ oz) LOUISIANA Shrimp
2 eggplants weighing about 1 lb each
1 cup chopped onion
2 garlic cloves, sliced
3 Tbsp butter or margarine
3 Tbsp flour
1 cup milk
1 tsp salt
¼ tsp cayenne pepper
¼ cup grated Parmesan cheese
1 cup seasoned bread crumbs

Drain shrimp. Preheat oven to 350°F; bake whole eggplants 40–45 minutes. In a saucepan saute onion and garlic in butter about 8 minutes. Blend and cook with flour, milk, and seasonings into a thick sauce. Add cheese and set aside. Cut eggplants in half. Holding stem ends, scoop out and chop pulp, reserving shells. Combine pulp, sauce, crumbs, and shrimp. Refill shells; sprinkle with *plain* buttered crumbs. Wrap skin area in aluminum foil; return to hot (425°F) oven about 15 minutes. Serve in foil. Yield: 4 servings.

COURTESY ROBINSON CANNING CO., INC.

SeaPak Shrimp Creole Elegante

2 Tbsp bacon drippings
½ cup chopped celery
½ cup finely chopped onion
3 cloves garlic, minced
¼ cup finely chopped green pepper
½ tsp dried thyme leaves, crushed
2 tsp salt
⅛ tsp cayenne pepper
1 crushed bay leaf
4 cups canned tomatoes with juice, cut up
¾ cup chili sauce
2 Tbsp beef consommé
½ cup tomato sauce
1 lb SEAPAK Frozen, Peeled and Deveined Shrimp
8 servings of cooked rice

In a large saucepan, sauté celery, onion, garlic, and green pepper in bacon drippings until tender but not browned; stir in thyme, salt, and pepper and blend well. Add bay leaf, tomatoes, chili sauce, consommé, and tomato sauce; bring to a boil, stirring constantly. Reduce heat, cover, and simmer 30 minutes. Stir in shrimp and continue simmering 5–10 minutes (depending on size of shrimp). Serve over cooked rice. Makes 8 servings.

COURTESY RICH-SEAPAK CORPORATION.

Pepperidge Farm Seashore Shells

- 1 pkg PEPPERIDGE FARM Patty Shells
- 1 can cream of celery soup
- 1 can tomato bisque soup
- 1½ cups fish fillets (halibut, cod, flounder, etc.; shrimp, crab)
- ½ cup peas, cooked
- ½ cup sliced celery, cooked

Bake PEPPERIDGE FARM Patty Shells as directed on package. Meanwhile, combine and heat condensed soups, undiluted. Add fish and vegetables. Warm until just heated through. Spoon into baked patty shells. Serves 4–6.

COURTESY PEPPERIDGE FARM, INC.

Wakefield Seafood Newburg

- 1 (6 oz) pkg WAKEFIELD Alaska Crabmeat & Shrimp
- ¼ cup butter or margarine
- 2 Tbsp flour
- ½ tsp salt
- ⅛ tsp nutmeg
- ⅛ tsp cayenne pepper
- 2 cups half-and-half
- 3 slightly beaten egg yolks
- 1½ Tbsp dry sherry
- Parsley (if desired)

Thaw crabmeat and shrimp and retain liquid. Melt butter in saucepan over medium heat. Add flour, salt, nutmeg, and cayenne. Stir until smooth. Gradually add half-and-half. Cook 8–10 minutes or until slightly thickened, stirring constantly. Gradually add ½ cup hot sauce mixture to egg yolks, beating to blend. Add egg yolk mixture to remaining sauce; mix well. Add crabmeat and shrimp and liquid. Cook 1–2 minutes or until thickened, stirring constantly. Remove from heat. Stir in sherry. Serve over hot, cooked rice. Garnish with parsley if desired. Serves 4–5.

COURTESY PACIFIC PEARL SEAFOODS.

Eggs and Cheese

Armour Quiche Lorraine

1½ cups milk
4 eggs, slightly beaten
½ tsp salt
Dash of ground red pepper
2 cups (8 oz) shredded Swiss cheese
2 Tbsp flour
½ lb ARMOUR Star Bacon, crisply cooked, crumbled
1 9-inch unbaked pastry shell
Bacon curls (below)
Parsley sprigs

Heat oven to 350°F. Combine milk, eggs, and seasonings; mix well. Toss cheese with flour; add cheese mixture and bacon to egg mixture. Pour into pastry shell. Bake at 350°F, 40–45 minutes. Garnish with bacon curls and parsley. Yield: 6 servings.

Bacon Curls

Cook slices of ARMOUR Star Bacon until almost crisp. Roll each slice around the tines of a fork to make a curl. Cook until crisp. Drain on absorbent paper.
COURTESY ARMOUR AND COMPANY.

Hunt-Wesson Foods Spinach Quiche

½ cup thinly sliced green onions
2 Tbsp butter
2 cups heavy cream
1 cup shredded Swiss cheese
4 eggs, slightly beaten
¾ tsp salt
⅛ tsp nutmeg
⅛ tsp pepper
1 (10 oz) pkg frozen chopped spinach, thawed and thoroughly drained
1 recipe STIR-N-ROLL Pastry for a 9-inch single crust pie, baked

In a small pan, sauté green onions in butter until onions are limp; set aside. In a bowl, combine cream, Swiss cheese, eggs, and seasonings; add spinach and onions. Pour into pastry shell.

Cover edge of pie crust with a strip of foil. Bake at 425°F 15 minutes; reduce heat to 325°F and bake 35 minutes longer.

Stir-N-Roll Pastry

1⅓ cups sifted all-purpose flour
1 tsp salt
⅓ cup Wesson® Oil
3 Tbsp cold milk

In a medium bowl, mix flour and salt. Pour oil and milk into 1 measuring cup (but don't stir); add all at once to flour. Stir until mixed. Press into smooth ball, flatten slightly. Place between 2 sheets of wax paper. Roll out gently to fit 9-inch pie pan. Peel off top paper. If dough tears, mend without moistening. Place paper side up in 9-inch pie pan. Peel off paper. Ease and fit pastry into pan. Flute edge. Prick thoroughly with fork. Bake at 475°F 8–10 minutes. Makes one 9-inch pie crust.

COURTESY HUNT-WESSON FOODS, INC.

Wyler's® Swiss Chicken Quiche

1 (9-inch) unbaked pastry shell
1 cup (4 oz) shredded Swiss cheese
2 Tbsp flour
1 Tbsp WYLER'S® Chicken-Flavor Instant Bouillon
2 cups cubed cooked chicken
1 cup milk
3 eggs, well beaten
¼ cup chopped onion
2 Tbsp chopped green pepper
2 Tbsp chopped pimiento

Preheat oven to 425°F. Bake pastry shell 8 minutes; remove from oven. Reduce oven temperature to 350°F. In medium bowl, toss cheese with flour and bouillon; add remaining ingredients. Mix well. Pour into prepared shell. Bake 40–45 minutes or until set. Let stand 10 minutes before serving. Refrigerate leftovers. Makes 6 servings.

A TESTED RECIPE DEVELOPED IN THE BORDEN KITCHENS. WYLER'S IS A REGISTERED TRADEMARK OF BORDEN, INC.

Wakefield Shrimp Mushroom Quiche Supreme

1 (6 oz) pkg WAKEFIELD Alaska Shrimp
1 9-inch pie shell
4 eggs
1 cup half-and-half
1 (4 oz) can sliced mushrooms, drained
½ tsp salt
Dash pepper
Dash nutmeg
½ cup grated Swiss cheese

Thaw and drain shrimp. Beat together lightly the eggs, half-and-half, and seasonings. Place mushrooms and shrimp in bottom of pie shell. Sprinkle with cheese. Add egg mixture and bake at 375°F 35–40 minutes or until center is firm.

To prepare a quiche ahead of time, bake 10 minutes less than directed, cool, then wrap and freeze. When ready to use, unwrap and bake at 325°F for 25 minutes.

COURTESY PACIFIC PEARL SEAFOODS.

California Avocado Mexican Cheese Pie

Butter
6 flour tortillas (small)
½ onion, thinly sliced
1 large tomato, chopped
1 (4 oz) can diced green chili peppers
3 eggs
1 tsp salt
3 Tbsp flour
½ tsp baking powder
½ cup milk
1 cup shredded Cheddar cheese
1 soft CALIFORNIA AVOCADO, peeled, seeded, and sliced lengthwise
Mild taco sauce

Butter a round baking dish, then line with tortillas, leaving ½ inch extending over top. Place onion, tomato, and chili peppers in bottom of dish on tortillas. In mixing bowl, beat eggs and mix with flour, salt, baking powder, and milk. Fold in cheese. Pour this mixture over ingredients in baking dish. Bake at 350°F 40–45 minutes. Before serving, place avocado slices on top of pie and cut into wedges. Spoon mild prepared taco sauce over the top of each serving. Makes 6 servings.

COURTESY CALIFORNIA AVOCADO COMMISSION.

Gerber Ham 'n Cheese Pie

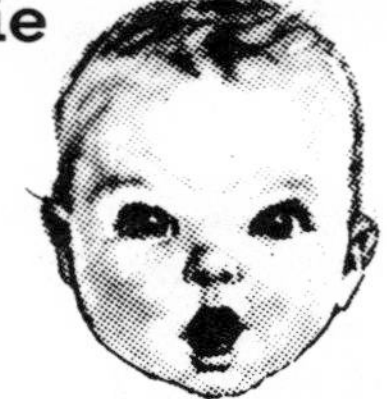

1 8-inch baked pie shell
1 jar (3½ oz) GERBER Junior Ham
1 small can (6 oz) evaporated milk (⅔ cup)
2 eggs, beaten
3 oz Cheddar cheese, grated (approx. 1 cup)
1 Tbsp dried minced onion
⅛ tsp salt (or more to taste)

Preheat oven to 325°F. Combine ingredients and mix well. Pour into pie shell. Bake in 325°F oven 30–40 minutes, or until set.
COURTESY GERBER PRODUCTS COMPANY.

Dorman's Eggplant-Provolone Quiche

Salt
1 medium-size eggplant, peeled and cut into ½-inch crosswise slices
Flour
Vegetable oil
¼ cup bread crumbs
3½ slices DORMAN'S Provolone
1 cup half-and-half
3 eggs
½ cup prepared spaghetti sauce
2 tsp vegetable oil

Sprinkle salt over eggplant. Place slices in a colander; weigh down with a heavy plate. Let drain 40 minutes. Dry slices with absorbent toweling. Coat slices with flour. Cook in hot oil until golden brown on both sides. Drain on absorbent toweling. Lightly oil a 10-inch-diameter quiche dish or shallow casserole. Sprinkle with bread crumbs. Stack eggplant slices around outer edge of dish. Cover top slices with a half slice of cheese. Grate remaining cheese in electric blender. Combine half-and-half, eggs, and grated cheese. Pour over eggplant. Spoon spaghetti sauce over eggplant. Sprinkle with oil. Bake at 375°F for 25 minutes or until lightly browned and puffed. Makes one 10-inch quiche.
COURTESY DORMAN CHEESE CO.

Lea & Perrins Eggs Foo Young

6 eggs
3 Tbsp water
1 Tbsp LEA & PERRINS Worcestershire Sauce
1/8 tsp salt
1 can (5 oz) water chestnuts, drained and coarsely chopped
1/4 cup thinly sliced scallions or green onions
1/4 cup diced green pepper
1 Tbsp butter or margarine

Preheat broiler. In a large bowl beat eggs, water, LEA & PERRINS, and salt. Stir in water chestnuts, scallions, and green pepper. In a 10-inch skillet with a heatproof handle, melt butter (or heat a nonstick skillet). Pour in egg mixture. As it cooks, lift up edges with a spatula to let uncooked portion run underneath. When surface is almost cooked, place skillet under the broiler. Broil until top is lightly browned, 3–4 minutes. With a spatula, loosen edges and slip omelet out onto a warm platter. Cut into wedges. Yield: 4 portions.

COURTESY LEA & PERRINS WORCESTERSHIRE SAUCE, A PRODUCT OF LEA & PERRINS, INC.

Francisco French Omelette

1/2 cup FRANCISCO Cheese Garlic Crispy Croutons
3 eggs
2 Tbsp water or milk
3 Tbsp butter or margarine
Parsley, finely chopped (optional)

Beat eggs. Heat butter in a 7-inch skillet until sizzling. Fold croutons into egg mixture and pour into skillet. Cook without stirring over low heat or until underside of omelette is brown and top is slightly moist. Lift edges of omelette from time to time to allow uncooked portion to run underneath. Fold omelette in skillet and slide out onto serving plate. Garnish with parsley.

COURTESY ARNOLD BAKERS, INC./OROWEAT FOODS COMPANY.

Dole®

Dole® Garden Fresh Omelets

2 cups sliced DOLE® Fresh Mushrooms
2 Tbsp chopped green onion
3 Tbsp butter
1 small tomato
½ tsp onion salt
½ tsp dried sweet basil, crumbled
6 eggs
2 Tbsp water
½ tsp salt
Dash Tabasco
Dash pepper

In a large skillet, sauté mushrooms and green onion in 1 Tbsp butter. Chop tomato and add to mushrooms, along with onion salt and basil. Simmer while making omelets. Lightly beat together 3 eggs, water, salt, Tabasco, and pepper. Melt 1 Tbsp butter in a 7-inch omelet pan or skillet, until bubbly. Add egg mixture and cook until firm, lifting edges slightly to let uncooked egg run under. Spoon half the mushroom mixture down center. Fold sides over, remove from pan, and keep warm. Repeat with remaining half. Makes 2 large servings.

COURTESY OF CASTLE & COOKE FOODS (DOLE®).

Ore Ida

Ore-Ida Huevos California

1 Tbsp butter or margarine
½ cup frozen ORE-IDA Potatoes O'Brien
¼ tsp salt
¼ tsp chili powder
2 eggs, beaten
2 Tbsp sour cream
1 Tbsp taco sauce (optional)
1 tsp chopped green onions
1 large (9 inch) flour tortilla

In skillet over medium heat (350°F) melt butter, add potatoes, salt, and chili powder; cook until potatoes are tender. Stir occasionally. Add eggs, scramble with potatoes until set. Briefly warm tortilla in dry frying pan over very low heat, turning often. Place egg mixture on tortilla; top with sour cream, taco sauce, and sprinkling of green onions. Fold the two sides envelope fashion and roll up; garnish with additional sour cream and green onions. Yield: 1 serving.

COURTESY FAMILY FAVORITES FROM ORE-IDA.

Okray's® Fry-n-Egg

Butter or margarine
OKRAY'S® Hash Brown Potato Patties
Salt and pepper to taste
1 egg for each potato patty

Cover bottom of skillet with butter or margarine and add desired number of OKRAY'S® Hash Brown Potato Patties. Cook for 10 minutes at medium heat. Turn patties and, with the back of a spoon, make a depression in the browned patties. Salt and pepper to taste. Slip a cracked egg onto each patty, continue frying 5–6 minutes; cover skillet and cook an additional 2–4 minutes (depending on the desired firmness of the eggs). Serve immediately.

OKRAY'S FROZEN HASH BROWNS AND FRENCH FRIES ARE MANUFACTURED AND SOLD BY INTERNATIONAL CO-OP OF GRAND FORKS, NORTH DAKOTA. IT'S O.K. IF IT'S OKRAY'S.

Oroweat Eggs Béarnaise

Sauce

3 egg yolks
2 tsp tarragon vinegar
¼ tsp onion salt
¼ tsp dried tarragon
½ cup butter, melted

Place egg yolks in blender, along with vinegar, salt, and tarragon. Cover the jar and blend this mixture at top speed for 2 seconds. Uncover and, still blending at top speed, slowly dribble in the hot butter (do not pour quickly, as the sauce will not thicken) until all of the butter is blended with the egg mixture. Keep sauce warm by placing blender jar in a pan of warm (not hot) water.

Muffins

6 presplit OROWEAT Honey Wheat Berry English Muffins
12 slices Canadian bacon
12 eggs
Paprika
Black olive slices

Bake muffin halves in a 350°F oven for 1 minute. Top each half with a slice of Canadian bacon and return to oven until bacon is warm and muffins begin to brown around the edges. Just before serving, poach eggs 2–4 minutes. Place on Canadian bacon.

Spoon warm Béarnaise sauce over each serving. Garnish with paprika and black olive slices.
FROM OROWEAT, "ONE OF THE WORLD'S MOST RESPECTED BAKERS".

Campbell's Swiss Fondue

- *1 can (11 oz) CAMPBELL'S Condensed Cheddar Cheese Soup*
- *1 pkg (8 oz) rectangular slices natural Swiss cheese, cut or torn in pieces*
- *¼ tsp prepared mustard*
- *¼ tsp Worcestershire sauce*
- *¼ tsp hot pepper sauce*
- *French or Italian bread cubes*

In saucepan, combine soup, cheese, mustard, Worcestershire sauce, and pepper sauce. Heat until cheese melts. Stir occasionally. Spear bread with fork or toothpick and dip into hot cheese. Makes about 2 cups.
COURTESY CAMPBELL SOUP COMPANY.

Dorman's Danish Fondue

- *4 slices DORMAN'S Tilsiter*
- *4 tsp vegetable oil*
- *Cooked bacon slices*

In the top of a double boiler, over hot water, melt cheese and oil together, stirring frequently, until well blended. Serve immediately with bacon slices. Serves 4.
COURTESY DORMAN CHEESE CO.

Miller Stewed Cheese 'n Beer

- *4 Tbsp flour*
- *2 eggs, well beaten*
- *½ tsp salt*
- *Freshly ground pepper*
- *1 tsp onion powder*
- *⅛ tsp dried tarragon*
- *1½ cups MILLER High Life*
- *2 Tbsp butter or margarine*
- *1¾ lb Gouda cheese, sliced ¼ inch thick*
- *6 large slices rye bread*

In a mixing bowl blend together flour, eggs, salt, pepper, onion powder, and tarragon. Beat in MILLER High Life. Melt butter in

a skillet. Dip cheese slices into egg mixture to coat thoroughly. Sauté cheese slices until lightly browned on one side. Turn and pour remaining batter over. Cook for 2 minutes longer. Divide into 6 equal portions and serve on slices of rye bread. Serves 6.
COURTESY MILLER BREWING COMPANY.

Budweiser Classic Rarebit

2 *cups (8 oz) shredded natural Cheddar cheese*
½ *cup BUDWEISER Beer*
1 *Tbsp butter or margarine*
¼ *tsp dry mustard*
¼ *tsp paprika*
1 *egg, slightly beaten*
Toast triangles

Heat cheese, beer, butter or margarine, and seasonings in double boiler. Keep heat low, stirring until smooth. Blend in egg. Stir until thickened. Serve over toast triangles. Serves 4.
REPRINTED BY PERMISSION, ANHEUSER-BUSCH, INC., ST. LOUIS, MO.

French's Pizza Pick-Ups

2 *loaves frozen bread dough, thawed in refrigerator overnight*
½ *lb ground beef*
1 *envelope (1½ oz) FRENCH'S Spaghetti Sauce Mix*
1 *can (6 oz) tomato paste*
1 *cup water*
1 *cup shredded mozzarella cheese*

Brown ground beef in skillet, stirring to crumble; pour off excess fat. Stir in contents of spaghetti sauce mix envelope, tomato paste, and water. Simmer 10 minutes, stirring occasionally; cool slightly. Roll out 1 loaf of dough on floured surface to 16 X 8-inch rectangle; spread with half the meat sauce and sprinkle with half the cheese. Roll up, starting with 16-inch side; pinch edges together to seal. Cut into 4 rolls. Repeat with remaining dough and filling. Arrange on well-greased cookie sheet. Bake in 400°F oven 15–20 minutes, until golden brown. Serve hot. Yield: 8 servings.

Note: wrap and freeze leftovers in individual servings. To serve, unwrap and reheat without thawing in 350°F oven 15–20 minutes.
COURTESY THE R.T. FRENCH COMPANY.

Pillsbury Hot Roll Pizza

- *1 pkg PILLSBURY Hot Roll Mix*
- *1 cup very warm water (105°–115°F)*
- *2 cups (8 oz) pizza cheese, shredded or sliced thin (provolone, mozzarella, or other cheese)*

Pizza Sauce

- *½ cup chopped onion*
- *1 Tbsp salad oil*
- *1 8-oz can (1 cup) tomato sauce*
- *1 6-oz can (¾ cup) tomato paste*
- *1 tsp salt*
- *½ tsp oregano*
- *¼ tsp garlic salt*
- *¼ tsp pepper*

To prepare sauce, cook onion in oil until golden brown. Stir in remaining ingredients. Heat oven to 450°F. Grease two 14-inch pizza pans or four 9-inch pie pans. Prepare hot roll mix as directed on package, using 1 cup warm water and omitting egg. *Do not let rise.* With greased fingers, pat out dough in prepared pans. Brush with oil, cover with half of pizza cheese and all of pizza sauce. Top with remaining cheese. Bake 15–20 minutes. Makes 2 large or 4 small pizzas.

COURTESY OF THE PILLSBURY COMPANY.

Ragu´ Mexican Pizza

- *1 jar (14 oz) RAGU´ Pizza Quick Sauce (any variety)*
- *3 English muffins, split and toasted*
- *6 Tbsp finely chopped onion*
- *1 to 2 Tbsp finely chopped jalapenos (optional)*
- *1 cup shredded Monterey Jack cheese*
- *⅓ cup shredded lettuce*
- *½ cup crushed corn chips*
- *½ cup sliced black olives (optional)*

Preheat oven to 350°F. Spoon 1½ Tbsp RAGU´ Pizza Quick Sauce on each muffin half. Evenly top with onions, jalapenos and cheese. Place pizzas on baking sheet and bake 15–20 minutes or until cheese melts. Top with lettuce, corn chips, and black olives before serving. Makes 6 pizzas.

COURTESY RAGU´ FOODS, INC.

Pasta

Even in translation, the names are as romantic and varied as Italy itself: butterflies and angel's hair, cartwheels and roller coasters, stars and seashells. These imaginative names all describe members of a family that ranges from "little strings" (spaghetti) to large hollow "muffs" (manicotti) and includes more than 500 different shapes in all.

Some of the many pasta varieties probably originated outside of Italy, but the Italians deserve credit for inventing pasta itself. Despite all the stories about Marco Polo's discovering spaghetti in China, scholars have found references to pasta in Italian manuscripts that were written before Marco Polo was born.

Italians are still the authorities on pasta, and they claim that all varieties—spaghetti, noodles, and macaroni, as well as the more exotic pastas—should be cooked in the traditional Italian way. This means that the final product should be *al dente* or "to the tooth"—firm and just bitable, never soft or mushy.

At first glance, it may seem that cooking pasta to the desired consistency is as easy as boiling water. Pasta professionals, however, often differ in their preferred cooking methods. Most say that you should cook the pasta in salted, vigorously boiling water, test it until it is cooked to the proper consistency, drain it, and then serve. That is simple enough, but other cooks say it is even simpler if you boil the pasta for only a few minutes, then turn down the heat and allow the pasta to stand in the water until it is cooked to the desired texture. Still other good cooks advise that you should cook pasta in boiling water until it is almost done, then drain it, add a little sauce or a pat of butter, and continue cooking over low heat for a few more minutes or just until the spaghetti is *al dente*.

Fortunately for the confused, most pasta manufacturers give specific directions on their packages about how their products should be prepared. Because the cooking qualities of pastas may vary from brand to brand, we recommend that you follow the manufacturers recipes as closely as possible.

Enrico's Lasagne

½ lb ground beef
½ lb sausage
1 clove garlic, mashed
½ cup chopped celery
½ cup chopped onion
3 cups hot water
2 tsp sugar
2 tsp salt
½ tsp sage
1 lb lasagne noodles, cooked
½ lb ricotta cheese
½ lb mozzarella cheese, sliced thin
12 oz ENRICO'S Spaghetti Sauce

Cook ground beef with sausage until meat is crumbly. Add celery, garlic, and onion and cook until tender. Stir in ENRICO'S Spaghetti Sauce, water, and seasonings. Blend. Cover, simmer for 50 minutes. Drain excess fat. Place alternate layers of noodles, sauce, and cheese in shallow, greased dish 13 X 9 inches. Make top layer of mozzarella. Bake in oven at 375°F for 25 minutes or until cheese melts. Five minutes after removing from oven, cut into squares. Yield: 6–8 servings.
COURTESY VENTRE PACKING COMPANY, INC.

Ronzoni

Ronzoni Baked Manicotti with Cheese Filling

1 pkg RONZONI Manicotti
2 lb ricotta cheese (or cottage cheese)
½ lb mozzarella cheese, diced (or muenster cheese)
2 eggs
½ cup RONZONI Grated Parmesan Cheese
1 Tbsp chopped parsley (season with salt, pepper, and nutmeg and add chopped nuts and raisins, if desired)
2 small jars (or 1 large) RONZONI Prepared Sauce (meat or meatless)

Mix ricotta, mozzarella, eggs, grated cheese, and chopped parsley. Season with salt, pepper, and nutmeg. Mix until well blended. Parboil manicotti as directed on box. Fill immediately with cheese filling, using butter knife or teaspoon. Cover bottom of baking dish with sauce. Arrange filled manicotti side by side in a single layer in baking dish. Cover with remainder of sauce and bake in moderate oven (350°F) for 20 minutes. Sprinkle with RONZONI Grated Cheese. Serve piping hot. Serves 6–8.
THIS RECIPE IS COURTESY OF RONZONI MACARONI CO., INC.

Buitoni Meat-Filled Macaroni Columns

- *1 pkg BUITONI Rigatoni No. 31*
- *1 lb ground beef*
- *1 Tbsp chopped parsley*
- *½ tsp nutmeg*
- *1 egg*
- *1 3-oz jar BUITONI Grated Parmesan Cheese*
- *1 15-oz jar BUITONI Marinara Sauce*

Preheat oven to 425°F. Cook rigatoni 12 minutes *(al dente),* according to package directions. Drain and rinse with cold water through colander. Mix well beef, parsley, nutmeg, egg, and half the Parmesan cheese and salt and pepper to taste. Using very small spoon, fill each rigatoni with meat mixture. Pour half the sauce in bottom of baking dish and lay stuffed rigatoni side by side on top. Pour over remaining sauce, sprinkle with remaining Parmesan, and bake 25 minutes, until bubbly. Serve piping hot.

COURTESY BUITONI FOODS CORP.

Hunt's®

Hunt's® Tangy Pasta Florentine

- *1 lb ground beef*
- *1 onion, chopped*
- *1 (12-oz) can HUNT'S® Tomato Paste*
- *1 (10½-oz) can condensed beef broth*
- *¼ cup water*
- *½ tsp basil leaves*
- *½ tsp oregano leaves*
- *½ tsp garlic salt*
- *¼ tsp pepper*
- *1 cup small-curd cottage cheese*
- *1 egg*
- *1 (10-oz) pkg frozen chopped spinach, thawed and pressed dry*
- *4 cups cooked elbow macaroni*
- *1 cup shredded Cheddar cheese*

In a large skillet, cook beef and onion until beef loses redness; drain. Add HUNT'S Tomato Paste, beef broth, water, basil, oregano, garlic salt, and pepper; mix well. Simmer, covered, 10 minutes. In small bowl, combine cottage cheese, egg, and spinach. Grease 2½-qt casserole, layer mixtures as follows: *half* of macaroni, *half* of meat sauce, *all* of cottage cheese-spinach mixture, *remaining* macaroni, *remaining* meat sauce. Top with cheese. Bake, uncovered, at 350°F 40 minutes. Allow to stand 10 minutes before serving. Makes 6–8 servings.

COURTESY HUNT-WESSON FOODS, INC.

TRIBUNO

Tribuno Bolognese Sauce

- 1/3 cup butter
- 1/4 cup minced lean ham
- 1/4 cup finely chopped carrot
- 1/4 cup finely chopped onion
- 1 cup chopped lean beef
- 2 Tbsp tomato paste
- 1 strip lemon peel
- Pinch of nutmeg
- 1 cup beef stock
- 1/2 cup TRIBUNO Dry Vermouth
- 1/4 cup whipping cream

Melt butter in a large saucepan. Add ham, carrot, and onion. Stir and cook for 1 or 2 minutes. Add chopped beef and brown over medium heat. Add tomato paste, lemon peel, nutmeg, beef stock, and vermouth. Partially cover and simmer slowly for 1 hour. Remove from heat, take out lemon peel, and stir in whipping cream. Serve over green noodles. Yield: 2 cups.

COURTESY MOGEN DAVID WINE CORPORATION.

Pompeian Spaghetti Meat Sauce

- 1/4 cup POMPEIAN Olive Oil
- 1 cup chopped onions (2 large)
- 2 garlic cloves, minced
- 1 lb ground beef
- 2 1-lb cans whole peeled tomatoes
- 2 6-oz cans tomato paste
- 1/2 cup water
- 1/2 cup chopped celery
- 2 Tbsp chopped parsley
- 1 Tbsp salt
- 1 tsp sugar
- 1 bay leaf

- 1 tsp oregano
- 1/2 tsp marjoram
- 1/4 tsp pepper

Heat olive oil in a large saucepan. Add onions and garlic and cook until soft, about 5 minutes. Add ground beef and fry until brown. Add remaining ingredients and simmer 2½–3 hours, stirring occasionally, until sauce thickens. Makes 3½ pints.

COURTESY OF POMPEIAN OLIVE OIL.

Hunt's® 10-Minute "Real" Spaghetti Sauce

- 1 lb ground beef
- ⅓ cup chopped onion
- 1 clove garlic, minced
- 1 (15-oz) can HUNT'S® Tomato Herb Sauce (generic term: tomato herb sauce)
- 1 cup water or red wine
- 1 Tbsp Worcestershire sauce
- ½ tsp salt
- ½ tsp oregano
- ½ tsp sugar
- ⅛ tsp pepper
- 1 Tbsp grated Parmesan cheese
- 4 oz spaghetti, cooked and drained

Brown ground beef in 10-inch skillet, drain. Add onion and garlic; cook until soft. Add remaining ingredients, except spaghetti. Bring to boil; simmer over medium heat 5 minutes, stirring occasionally. Serve over spaghetti. Makes 4 servings.

COURTESY HUNT-WESSON FOODS, INC.

Progresso White Clam Sauce

- 1 minced garlic clove
- ½ cup olive oil
- 2 Tbsp parsley, chopped
- ¼ tsp crushed red peppers
- 1 10¼-oz can (net weight) PROGRESSO Whole Baby Clams, partially drained

Lightly brown minced garlic in ½ cup olive oil. Add remaining ingredients and simmer 3 minutes. Pour over spaghetti.

Red Clam Sauce

Drain clams, add to PROGRESSO Marinara Sauce, heat, and serve.

COURTESY PROGRESSO QUALITY FOODS.

San Giorgio Savory Spaghetti and Meatballs

- 1 lb ground meat
- 3 Tbsp chopped parsley
- ½ clove garlic, crushed
- ¼ cup Parmesan or Romano cheese
- 1 egg, beaten
- Salt and pepper to taste
- 1 slice bread, soaked in water
- 2 Tbsp salad oil
- 4 cups (32-oz jar) spaghetti sauce
- ½ lb SAN GIORGIO Spaghetti No. 8

Combine meat with parsley, garlic, cheese, beaten egg, salt, and pepper. Add soaked bread, which has been squeezed dry

and crumbled. Blend thoroughly and shape into small balls. Brown well on all sides in oil. Add sauce; simmer for ½ hour in covered pan. Prepare SAN GIORGIO Spaghetti according to package directions; drain well. Serve sauce and meatballs over spaghetti and top with grated cheese. Serves 3–4.
COURTESY SAN GIORGIO-SKINNER, INC.

Prince Chicken Liver Sauce with Non-Skid Spaghetti

- *1 small onion, minced*
- *2 Tbsp olive or salad oil*
- *1 lb chicken livers—sprinkled with salt and pepper*
- *2 Tbsp flour*
- *¼ tsp salt*
- *Dash pepper*
- *1 4-oz can sliced mushrooms*
- *1 cup mushroom liquid (liquid from can with water)*
- *1 lb PRINCE Non-Skid Spaghetti (No. 80)*
- *PRINCE Romano Grated Cheese*

Sauté onion in oil until soft; do not allow to brown. Add seasoned chicken livers and cook slowly for 5 minutes. Blend in flour, seasonings, and liquid and cook, stirring constantly, until gravy is thick and smooth. Stir in mushrooms and let simmer for 5 minutes. Pour over cooked PRINCE Non-Skid Spaghetti. Serve with PRINCE Grated Cheese. If desired, stir in 1¼ cups of sherry just before serving. Serves 4–6.
COURTESY THE PRINCE COMPANY, INC.

La Rosa Vermicelli al Pesto

- *8 oz (½ pkg) LA ROSA Vermicelli*
- *1 clove garlic, minced*
- *⅓ cup olive oil*
- *1 cup firmly packed fresh basil leaves or parsley sprigs*
- *½ cup grated Parmesan cheese*
- *2 Tbsp pine nuts or coarsely chopped walnuts*
- *1 Tbsp butter*
- *½ tsp salt*
- *⅛ tsp pepper*
- *Additional grated Parmesan cheese*

Cook garlic in olive oil until lightly browned. Combine with remaining ingredients in electric blender; blend at high speed to a pastelike consistency, about 1 minute. Cook LA ROSA Vermicelli as directed on package; drain. Serve sauce over cooked vermicelli with additional Parmesan cheese. Serves 4.

Note: to prepare Al Pesto by hand, crush basil or parsley with a mortar and pestle until pastelike. Work in salt and pepper, garlic, nuts, and butter. Add olive oil a little at a time. Mix in the ½ cup grated Parmesan cheese.

COURTESY V. LA ROSA & SONS, INC.

Ragu´ Linguine with Julienne Zucchini

- 1 *jar (15½ oz) RAGU´ Old World Style Spaghetti Sauce, any flavor*
- 2 *medium zucchini, sliced into julienne strips*
- 2 *cloves garlic, minced*
- 1 *medium onion, finely chopped*
- 3 *Tbsp butter or margarine*
- ½ *tsp basil*
- *Salt and pepper to taste*
- ½ *pkg (16 oz) linguine, cooked and drained*
- 1 *cup shredded Provolone cheese*
- ⅓ *cup grated Parmesan cheese*

In a saucepan, simmer sauce 5 minutes or until heated through. Set aside and keep warm. In large skillet, sauté zucchini, garlic, and onion in butter until zucchini is almost tender. Add basil, salt, and pepper. Top linguine with sauce, zucchini mixture, Provolone, and Parmesan cheese. Toss well and serve immediately. Serves 4.

COURTESY RAGU´ FOODS, INC.

San Giorgio Fettucini Carbonara

- ¼ *lb bacon*
- 1 *box (12 oz) SAN GIORGIO Fettucini*
- ¼ *cup butter or margarine, softened*
- ½ *cup heavy cream, at room temperature*
- ½ *cup grated Parmesan cheese*
- 2 *eggs, slightly beaten*
- 2 *Tbsp snipped parsley*

Sauté bacon until crisp; drain well and crumble. Cook SAN GIORGIO Fettucini according to package directions. Drain well and place in warm serving dish large enough for tossing. Add crumbled bacon, butter, heavy cream, grated cheese, eggs, and snipped parsley; toss until fettucini is well coated. Serve.

COURTESY SAN GIORGIO-SKINNER, INC.

Prince Superoni Linguine Spaghetti with Lobster Sauce

1 large broiled lobster
1 pint jar PRINCE Marinara Spaghetti Sauce
1 pkg PRINCE Superoni
Spaghetti
PRINCE Romano Grated Cheese

Remove shell from lobster and cut lobster meat in large pieces. Add to PRINCE Marinara sauce and simmer for 10 minutes. Cook PRINCE Spaghetti according to package directions. Drain. Pour lobster sauce on top and serve with PRINCE Grated Cheese. Serves 4–6.

COURTESY THE PRINCE COMPANY, INC.

Bumble Bee® Salmon Fettucini in Caper Sauce

1 can (15½ oz) BUMBLE BEE® Pink Salmon
1 pkg (8 oz) fettucini (or spaghetti)
Boiling salted water
2 cloves garlic, minced
1 medium green pepper, diced
2 cups fresh DOLE® Mushrooms
1 cup diced green onion
½ tsp oregano, crumbled
½ tsp sweet basil, crumbled
¼ tsp rosemary, crumbled
½ cup butter
½ cup olive oil
⅓ cup dry white wine
1 medium zucchini, julienne cut
2 Tbsp capers
Chopped parsley
Grated Parmesan cheese

Drain BUMBLE BEE® Pink Salmon. Remove skin, if desired. Mash bones. Cook fettucini in water 5–7 minutes until just tender. Sauté garlic, green pepper, mushrooms, onion, oregano, basil, and rosemary in butter and olive oil until green pepper is tender-crisp. Stir in wine, zucchini, and capers. Simmer 1 minute until zucchini is tender-crisp. Remove from heat. Gently fold in salmon and mashed bones. Toss with cooked fettucini. Top with chopped parsley. Serve with generous amounts of Parmesan cheese. Makes 4–6 servings.

COURTESY OF CASTLE & COOKE FOODS (BUMBLE BEE® AND DOLE®).

Buitoni Macaroni and Cheese Italian Style

- *1 pkg BUITONI Mezzani No. 28*
- *4 Tbsp melted butter or margarine*
- *1 15-oz jar BUITONI Spaghetti Sauce*
- *3 oz mozzarella cheese, finely diced*
- *1 3-oz jar BUITONI Grated Parmesan Cheese*

Preheat oven to 425°F. Cook BUITONI Mezzani for 9 minutes *(al dente)* according to package directions, drain well, and place in large baking dish. Add the butter or margarine, half of the sauce, and about ⅔ of mozzarella and Parmesan cheeses. Blend well. Pour over remaining sauce, dot with remaining mozzarella and sprinkle over the rest of the Parmesan. Bake about 20 minutes until golden and bubbly.

COURTESY BUITONI FOODS CORP.

Creamettes Cheese Bake

- *2 cups uncooked CREAMETTES*
- *½ cup butter or margarine*
- *2 Tbsp flour*
- *1½ cups milk*
- *1 tsp salt*
- *¼ tsp pepper*
- *1 cup grated process Cheddar cheese*
- *Paprika*

Prepare CREAMETTES according to general directions on package. Drain. Melt butter. Add flour and cook, stirring constantly, for 2 minutes. Do not brown. Stir in milk, salt, and pepper. Cook until smooth and thickened. Combine macaroni with white sauce. Pour into an 11 X 7-inch casserole. Top with cheese. Sprinkle with paprika. Bake in a 350°F oven 25–30 minutes. Yield: 4–6 servings.

COURTESY THE CREAMETTE COMPANY.

La Rosa Skillet Beef Macaroni

- *3 Tbsp butter*
- *¼ cup chopped onions*
- *¼ cup chopped green peppers*
- *1 lb ground beef*
- *½ Tbsp salt*
- *½ Tbsp freshly ground pepper*
- *2 Tbsp paprika*
- *1 15-oz jar LA ROSA Marinara Sauce*
- *1 lb LA ROSA Jumbo Elbows*

Using a large skillet on a burner over a steady even heat, melt butter, then sauté chopped onions and chopped green peppers for 5 minutes. Add ground beef and crumble it with a fork; cook until browned, stirring constantly. Sprinkle with salt, freshly ground pepper, and paprika; stir in LA ROSA Marinara Sauce, mixing and blending well; heat thoroughly. Meanwhile, cook LA ROSA Jumbo Elbows according to directions on package; drain and turn into skillet, blending well with sauce mixture, and cook 5 minutes.

COURTESY V. LA ROSA & SONS, INC.

Prince Eggplant Sauce with Shells

- 2 *small cloves garlic, mashed*
- ¼ *cup olive or vegetable oil*
- 1 *large eggplant, peeled and cubed*
- 1 *can (1 lb 12 oz) whole tomatoes*
- 2 *cans (8 oz each) tomato sauce*
- ½ *cup water*
- 1 *tsp salt*
- 1 *tsp sugar*
- ¼ *tsp pepper*
- ¼ *tsp basil leaves*
- 12 *oz PRINCE Superoni Medium Shells*
- *Parmesan cheese*

In large skillet, sauté garlic in oil a few minutes. Add eggplant cubes, sauté until lightly browned. Stir in tomatoes, tomato sauce, water, salt, sugar, pepper, and basil leaves. Cover. Simmer 45 minutes or until eggplant is tender. Cook PRINCE Shells according to package directions. Drain. Combine shells and sauce. Heat. Serve with Parmesan cheese sprinkled on top. Yield: 6 servings.

COURTESY THE PRINCE COMPANY, INC.

San Giorgio Rotini with Meatballs

- 1 *lb chopped meat*
- 1 *cup bread crumbs*
- 1 *clove chopped garlic*
- 1 *small chopped onion*
- 1 *can tomato paste*
- 1 *can tomatoes*
- 2 *eggs*
- 1½ *tsp salt*
- ½ *tsp pepper*
- ½ *cup grated Parmesan or Romano cheese*
- 4 *Tbsp olive oil*
- 1 *lb SAN GIORGIO Rotini*

Mix meat with crumbs, cheese, eggs, garlic, and seasoning and add a little water. Shape into balls and fry in olive oil. Remove from frying pan and sauté chopped onion in same pan. Add tomato paste, ½ cup water, and tomatoes; after mixture comes

to a boil, add meatballs. Simmer for 1 hour. Cook SAN GIORGIO Rotini according to package directions. Serve with sauce and meatballs. Serves 4–6.
COURTESY SAN GIORGIO-SKINNER, INC.

La Rosa Macaroni with Sausage Sauce, Calabria

- *3 Tbsp water*
- *1 lb sweet or hot Italian sausage*
- *½ cup chopped onions*
- *½ cup chopped celery*
- *2 Tbsp olive oil*
- *1 16-oz can tomatoes, strained*
- *1 Tbsp chopped parsley*
- *½ can tomato paste, dissolved in 1 cup water*
- *1 bay leaf*
- *Salt and pepper to taste*
- *1 lb LA ROSA Macaroni*
- *LA ROSA Grated Cheese*

Place sausages in saucepan with water; cook gently until water evaporates and sausages begin to brown slightly. Remove from pan. Brown onion and celery in olive oil in pan where sausages were browned. Slice sausages and add to vegetables; also add tomatoes, tomato paste, parsley, bay leaf, and salt and pepper to taste, and simmer gently 30–45 minutes. Cook LA ROSA Macaroni according to package directions; drain and put into warm serving dish. Top with sauce, mix gently, and sprinkle generously with LA ROSA Grated Cheese. For a delicious quick substitute, use LA ROSA Spaghetti Sauce without Meat, to which may be added cooked and sliced sausages.
COURTESY V. LA ROSA & SONS, INC.

San Giorgio

San Giorgio Seashells in the Sunset

- *¼ cup minced onion*
- *¼ cup butter or margarine*
- *⅓ cup unsifted all-purpose flour*
- *3 cups milk*
- *1 cup shredded sharp cheese*
- *1 tsp salt*
- *Dash pepper*
- *Dash nutmeg*
- *1 can (7 oz) tuna, drained and flaked*
- *¼ cup chopped fresh parsley*
- *2 Tbsp chopped pimiento*
- *⅓ cup bread crumbs*
- *½ lb SAN GIORGIO Shell Macaroni*

Sauté onion in butter or margarine until soft, but not brown; blend in flour. Gradually add milk. Cook and stir constantly over

medium heat until mixture begins to boil; boil and stir 1 minute. Remove from heat. Add sharp cheese, salt, pepper, and nutmeg; blend well until cheese is melted. Stir in tuna, parsley, and pimiento; keep warm over heat. Cook SAN GIORGIO Shells according to package directions; drain. Toss with warm sauce mixture; serve immediately. Or: turn shell mixture into a buttered 2-qt casserole. Sprinkle with bread crumbs; bake at 350°F for 25 minutes. Yield: 4–6 servings.
COURTESY SAN GIORGIO-SKINNER, INC.

Buitoni Macaroni with Chicken

1 5- to 6-lb chicken
2 tsp salt
¼ tsp pepper
1 pkg Enriched BUITONI Pasta Romana (Ditali)
6 slices bacon, shredded
2 large sweet onions, chopped

1 1½-oz shaker BUITONI Grated Cheese
1 8-oz can mushrooms

Cut chicken into pieces, cover with water, add salt and pepper, and cook slowly until meat loosens from bones. Remove meat from bones and cut into small pieces. Cook macaroni in boiling chicken broth until tender, and drain. Brown bacon in large pot, add onion, brown lightly, add mushrooms, and mix thoroughly. Add chicken and macaroni and keep over low flame until thoroughly heated. Add cheese and mix thoroughly. If needed, moisten with a little chicken broth. Yield: 7–8 servings.
COURTESY BUITONI FOODS CORP.

La Rosa Shell and Cheese Puff

8 oz LA ROSA Maruzzelle Shells, cooked and drained (½ pkg)
6 Tbsp butter or margarine
¼ cup flour
1½ tsp salt
1½ tsp dry mustard
½ tsp paprika
2 cups milk

½ lb Cheddar cheese, shredded (2 cups)
6 eggs, separated
Sesame seeds

Melt butter in a saucepan and blend in flour, salt, mustard, and paprika. Cook, stirring constantly. Add milk and continue stirring until sauce thickens. Add cheese, stir until it melts, and remove from heat. Beat egg whites until they form soft peaks. In a separate bowl, beat egg yolks until creamy and thick. Gradually add cooked cheese sauce, stirring until well blended. Add cooked, drained shells and lightly stir in egg whites. Pour into an ungreased 8-cup soufflé dish. To give a tiered top, gently cut a deep circle in the mixture about 1 inch in from the outside edge. Sprinkle with sesame seeds and bake in a 350°F oven for 1 hour or until puffed and golden brown.

COURTESY V. LA ROSA & SONS, INC.

Eveready® New Age Italian Noodles

1 pkg (12 oz) spinach noodles
Boiling salted water
3 Tbsp HOLLYWOOD Safflower Oil
1 cup chopped fresh onion
2 cloves garlic, mashed
3 Tbsp unbleached white flour
1 can (12 oz) EVEREADY® Carrot Juice
1 can (16 oz) tomato sauce
1½ tsp Italian herbs
2 Tbsp chopped parsley
¼ tsp sea salt
1 can (9¼ oz) chunk light tuna
Grated Parmesan cheese

Cook noodles in boiling salted water until tender. Drain; toss lightly in 1 Tbsp safflower oil and keep warm. Sauté onion and garlic in 2 Tbsp safflower oil until translucent. Stir in flour until blended. Add carrot juice, tomato sauce, Italian herbs, parsley, and salt, stirring until thickened. Drain tuna; add to sauce. Serve over noodles topped with Parmesan cheese. Makes 6 servings.

COURTESY H. & J. FOODS.

Herb-Ox Noodles and Cottage Cheese

½ lb egg noodles
3 qt boiling salted water
1 lb cottage cheese or ricotta cheese
2 Tbsp parsley flakes
½ cup grated Parmesan cheese
2 packets HERB-OX Onion Flavored Instant Broth and Seasoning
2 Tbsp butter or margarine
½ cup sliced black olives

Cook noodles in boiling salted water until tender yet firm, about 10 minutes. Drain. Blend cottage cheese, parsley flakes, grated cheese, instant broth, and butter. Add to drained noodles, toss, top with sliced olives. Makes 4–6 servings.

COURTESY THE PURE FOOD COMPANY, INC.

Dole® Mushroom Noodles Monterey

3 cups uncooked egg noodles
Salted water
2 cups quartered DOLE® Fresh Mushrooms
½ cup julienne-cut green pepper
¼ cup chopped green onion
3 Tbsp butter
½ tsp garlic salt
1 Tbsp flour
⅔ cup milk
½ tsp seasoned salt
⅓ cup dry white wine
2 cups shredded Monterey Jack cheese

Cook noodles in boiling, salted water until just tender; drain. In a large skillet, sauté quartered DOLE® Mushrooms, green pepper, and green onion in 2 Tbsp butter. Sprinkle vegetables with garlic salt as they cook; remove from pan. Melt remaining butter in skillet; blend in flour. Gradually add milk, stirring until smooth and thickened. Blend in seasoned salt, wine, and 1 cup shredded cheese. Cook and stir until cheese melts. Mix together noodles, cheese sauce, and vegetables. Turn into 1½-qt casserole dish. Top with remaining shredded cheese. Bake in a 350°F oven 20 minutes until bubbly. Makes 4–6 servings.

COURTESY OF CASTLE & COOKE FOODS (DOLE®).

Friendship Spinach Noodle Casserole

1 pkg (8 oz) medium egg noodles
½ cup butter
½ cup chopped onions
1 clove garlic, minced
1 pkg (10 oz) frozen chopped spinach, slightly defrosted
¾ tsp salt
¼ tsp black pepper
¼ tsp leaf tarragon, crumbled
⅛ tsp ground nutmeg
1 container FRIENDSHIP Cottage Cheese (8 oz)
¾ cup FRIENDSHIP Sour Cream
2 Tbsp bread crumbs

Cook noodles, following label directions; drain; return to kettle. Toss with 2 Tbsp of the butter. Sauté onion and garlic in 4 Tbsp of the butter in a large skillet until softened and golden. Add spinach, salt, pepper, tarragon, and nutmeg. Cover; cook over moderate heat 5 minutes. Uncover, continue to cook until liquid is evaporated. Add spinach mixture to noodles. Add cottage cheese and sour cream; blend thoroughly. Turn mixture into a greased 8-cup casserole. Melt remaining butter in a small skillet; add bread crumbs; blend with a fork until thoroughly coated with butter. Sprinkle over top of casserole. Bake at 375°F for 30 minutes or until bubbly and lightly browned. Makes 4–6 servings.

RECIPE COURTESY OF FRIENDSHIP FOOD'S HOME ECONOMIST, HELEN SCHWARTZ.

Side Dishes

Deep purple eggplants surrounded by melted cheese, crunchy yellow corn in a smooth cream sauce, piping hot rice blended with savory seasonings—many side dishes are so delectable that they can stand on their own apart from the meat or other main dish.

In fact, with the growing popularity of low-meat and meatless dinners, side dishes have taken on much greater importance. Vegetables and vegetarian casseroles that once were considered only side dishes now may be the center of a meal—and why not? We always knew that vegetables were low in cost, low in calories, and high in nutrition. Now we are learning that they can taste great, too.

The key to preparing great vegetables is to begin with good raw ingredients and then use the natural flavors to the best advantage. Whether you buy canned, fresh, or frozen vegetables, shop carefully for the crispest, most succulent varieties. Combine flavors to accent each vegetable's unique color, taste, and texture: mild beans with pungent onions, bright green broccoli with golden corn, subtle squash with tart fruit.

When it is time to cook your vegetables, remember that less is usually more. A few varieties, such as cabbage, turnips, and beets, profit by being cooked uncovered for a long period over low heat. Most vegetables, however, will turn gray and lose flavor if subjected to this kind of treatment. Probably the easiest way to get good nutrition and taste out of your peas, crisp carrots, and green beans is to cook them quickly in a small amount of water. You may want to add salt to taste, or throw in a dash of lemon juice or vinegar to help maintain the bright colors. Whatever you do, however, do not overcook.

For your convenience, the vegetable recipes in this chapter are arranged alphabetically by vegetable. Following the vegetables, there are stuffings, rice dishes, and other casseroles. Many of these dishes can be served either alone or as accompaniments to your main dishes. Experiment—you may find that your side dishes become a main attraction.

Vegetables

Berio Artichokes Greek Style

4 artichokes, medium size
1 qt water
2 Tbsp FILIPPO BERIO Olive Oil
1 Tbsp cider vinegar
1 Tbsp salt

Put artichokes in a pan of briskly boiling water to which salt and cider vinegar have been added. Cook for about 20–30 minutes or until outer leaves of artichoke pull out easily. Take out artichokes and allow to cool. Serve with a dressing of 2 parts FILIPPO BERIO Olive Oil and 1 part lemon juice, well mixed.

COURTESY BERIO IMPORTING CORP.

MUSSELMAN'S®

Musselman's Asparagus Parmesano

1 can (14½ oz) MUSSELMAN'S Asparagus
¼ to ⅓ cup milk
1 Tbsp butter or margarine
2 Tbsp finely chopped onion
½ tsp salt
1 Tbsp flour
2 Tbsp grated Parmesan cheese
2 Tbsp fine bread crumbs

Drain asparagus, saving liquid. Add milk to liquid to make 1 cup. Spread drained asparagus in 1-qt casserole. Melt butter in saucepan. Add onion. Cook until limp. Stir in salt and flour. Gradually stir in asparagus liquid until smooth. Heat to boiling. Boil 1 minute or until slightly thickened. Pour over asparagus. Combine cheese and bread crumbs. Sprinkle over asparagus. Bake at 425°F for 15 minutes or until lightly browned and bubbly. Serve hot. Makes 4 servings, ½ cup each.

PET, AN IC INDUSTRIES COMPANY, HOME ECONOMICS DEPT., P.O. BOX 392, ST. LOUIS, MO 63166.

Durkee Green Bean Casserole

- 1 *pkg (10 oz) frozen green beans, cooked, or 1 can (1 lb) green beans*
- 1 *can (10¾ oz) condensed cream of mushroom soup*
- *Dash DURKEE Black Pepper*
- 1 *can (3 oz) DURKEE French Fried Onions*
- 2 *Tbsp diced pimiento (optional)*

Drain beans; combine with soup, pepper, and ½ can onions. Pour into greased 1-qt casserole. Bake at 350°F for 20 minutes. Garnish with mixture of remaining onions and pimiento; bake 5 minutes longer. Makes 4 servings.

COURTESY DURKEE FAMOUS FOODS, DIV. SCM CORPORATION.

Sizzlean Southern Green Beans

- 6 *to 8 slices SIZZLEAN Pork Breakfast Strips, cut into ½-inch pieces*
- ½ *cup chopped onion*
- 2 *cups cooked French-style green beans*
- ⅓ *cup chili sauce*

Panfry pork breakfast strips in skillet until browned. Drain. Brown onion in drippings. Add green beans, chili sauce, and pork breakfast strips. Combine well. Heat thoroughly before serving. Yield: 4–5 servings (2½ cups).

COURTESY SWIFT & COMPANY.

La Choy Green Beans with Water Chestnuts

- 1 *Tbsp cooking oil*
- 3 *Tbsp water*
- ½ *tsp salt*
- 1 *pkg (9 oz) frozen cut green beans*
- ½ *cup sliced LA CHOY Water Chestnuts*
- 2 *Tbsp finely chopped green onion*
- 2 *Tbsp chopped pimiento*
- 1 *Tbsp cider vinegar*
- ½ *tsp dill weed*
- ⅛ *tsp pepper*

Combine oil, water, and salt in saucepan; add frozen beans. Cook over low heat, stirring often to separate beans. Cover and cook until tender. Add remaining ingredients; toss lightly and heat. Makes 4 servings.

COURTESY LA CHOY FOOD PRODUCTS.

Campbell's Big Bean Bonanza

1 can (16 oz) tomatoes, chopped
1 cup sliced onion
1 medium clove garlic, minced
1 Tbsp chili powder
2 Tbsp butter or margarine
1 can (11¼ oz) CAMPBELL'S Condensed Green Pea Soup
1 can (about 16 oz) lima beans, drained
1 can (15½ oz) kidney beans, undrained
1 can (8½ oz) butter beans, drained
4 slices (about 4 oz) mild process cheese, cut in half diagonally

In skillet, simmer tomatoes and onion with garlic and chili in butter about 15 minutes or until tender. Stir in soup. Add remaining ingredients except cheese. Heat; stir occasionally. Top with cheese. Cover; heat until cheese melts. Makes about 5½ cups.

COURTESY CAMPBELL SOUP COMPANY.

B&M Apple-Topped Baked Beans

1 28-oz can B&M Baked Beans
1 large apple, pared and shredded
1 Tbsp butter
¼ cup packed brown sugar
3 slices bacon, diced and partially cooked

Place beans in a 1½-qt casserole. Sprinkle with apple; dot with butter. Sprinkle with brown sugar; top with bacon pieces. Bake at 350°F for 30 minutes or until mixture bubbles. Makes 4–5 servings.

REPRINTED WITH PERMISSION OF WM. UNDERWOOD CO., WESTWOOD, MA.

MICHELOB®

Michelob Baked Beans

1 lb navy beans
Water
½ lb salt pork, cut into chunks
1 medium onion, chopped
¾ cup dark molasses
1 12-oz MICHELOB Beer
¼ cup light brown sugar
1 Tbsp prepared mustard
2 tsp salt
¼ tsp pepper

Put beans in large kettle, cover with cold water, and soak overnight. Next day, drain beans and cover with 2 qt fresh water. Bring to a boil, cover, and simmer 30 minutes. Drain. Place beans in a 3-qt casserole, fold in salt pork and onions. Combine molasses, beer, brown sugar, mustard, salt, and pepper. Pour over beans and mix well. Cover and bake at 325°F for about 6 hours. Stir once every hour so beans cook evenly. If beans seem dry, add water during cooking. Makes 8 servings.

REPRINTED BY PERMISSION, ANHEUSER-BUSCH, INC., ST. LOUIS, MO.

Chefs Best Swiss Cheese Sauced Beans

1 Tbsp butter or margarine
1 Tbsp flour
¾ tsp salt
½ cup milk
1 cup shredded Swiss cheese
3 or 4 drops hot sauce
½ cup dairy sour cream
1 No. 303 can (approx. 2 cups) CHEFS BEST French Style Green Beans, drained

Melt butter in small saucepan. Blend in flour, salt, and milk. Cook and stir over low temperature until sauce is smooth. Stir in cheese and hot sauce. Heat until cheese is melted. (Sauce will not be smooth.) Remove from heat and stir in sour cream. Arrange drained beans in a buttered 1-qt casserole. Pour over sauce and bake uncovered at 350°F 25–30 minutes.

COURTESY OCONOMOWOC CANNING CO.

IGA Pinto Surprise

- 1 No. 300 can IGA Pinto Beans
- 2 slices bacon
- 3 Tbsp finely chopped onion
- 1 Tbsp molasses
- 1½ Tbsp IGA Tomato Catsup
- ¼ tsp IGA Salt
- ¼ tsp IGA Powdered Dry Mustard
- ½ tsp Worcestershire sauce, if desired

Fry bacon, remove from pan, and cook onion for a few minutes in bacon fat. Add molasses, catsup, salt, mustard, and Worcestershire sauce. Add beans and mix lightly. Pour into baking dish. Crumble bacon and sprinkle over top. Bake 20 minutes at 350°F.

COURTESY OF IGA, INC.

Stokely's Orange Glazed Beets

- 1 can (1 lb) STOKELY'S Finest® Cut Beets
- 1 Tbsp butter or margarine
- 2 tsps flour
- 2 Tbsps brown sugar
- ½ cup orange juice

Heat beets in their own liquid. In small saucepan, melt butter. Remove from heat; add flour, brown sugar, and orange juice. Return to heat, stirring constantly until thickened. Drain beets; add sauce to STOKELY'S Beets. Makes 4–5 servings.

COURTESY STOKELY-VAN CAMP, INC.

Boggs Rosy-Red Beets

- ½ cup BOGGS Cranberry Liqueur
- 2 tsp cornstarch
- 1 can (16 oz) sliced beets, drained
- 1 small onion, sliced and separated into rings
- ½ tsp salt
- ¼ cup sour cream

In small saucepan mix BOGGS and cornstarch. Cook over medium heat until clear and slightly thickened. Mix in beets, onion and salt. Heat thoroughly. Remove from heat and stir in sour cream. Serve immediately. Serves 4.

COURTESY BOGGS CRANBERRY LIQUEUR.

Wesson®
Broccoli Marinade

- *½ cup WESSON Oil*
- *¼ cup vinegar*
- *1 tsp salt*
- *¼ tsp pepper*
- *2 cups broccoli flowerets*
- *1 cup coarsely chopped red onion*
- *1 cup shredded Cheddar cheese*
- *1 cucumber, peeled and coarsely chopped*
- *1 tomato, coarsely chopped*

In a small bowl, combine WESSON Oil, vinegar, salt, and pepper. Pour over remaining ingredients in a large bowl. Toss to mix well. Marinate 3–4 hours, stirring occasionally. Makes 4–6 servings.

COURTESY HUNT-WESSON FOODS, INC.

Campbell's Cheese Divan

- *2 pkg (10 oz each) frozen broccoli spears, cooked and drained*
- *1 can (11 oz) CAMPBELL'S Condensed Cheddar Cheese Soup*
- *¼ cup sour cream*
- *2 Tbsp milk*
- *1 can (about 8 oz) whole-kernel corn, drained*
- *¼ tsp curry powder*

In a 1½-qt shallow baking dish (10 X 6 X 2 inches), arrange broccoli. Blend soup, sour cream, milk, corn, and curry; pour over broccoli. Bake at 400°F for 20 minutes or until hot. Garnish with pimiento if desired. Makes 4–6 servings.

COURTESY CAMPBELL SOUP COMPANY.

Stokely's Broccoli Corn Casserole

- 1 *pkg (10 oz) Frozen STOKELY'S Chopped Broccoli, thawed*
- 1 *can (1 lb 1 oz) STOKELY'S Finest® Cream Style Golden Corn*
- ½ *cup chopped onion*
- ¼ *cup plus 2 Tbsp coarsely crushed saltine crackers, divided*
- 1 *egg, well beaten*
- 3 *Tbsps butter or margarine, melted and divided*
- ½ *tsp salt*
- ⅛ *tsp pepper*

Completely thaw STOKELY'S Broccoli. Mix broccoli with STOKELY'S Corn, onion, ¼ cup crushed crackers, egg, 2 Tbsp butter, salt, and pepper. Pour into a 1½-qt casserole. Mix together the remaining 2 Tbsp crushed crackers and 1 Tbsp butter, sprinkle over casserole. Bake uncovered at 350°F for 1 hour. Makes 6 servings.

COURTESY STOKELY-VAN CAMP, INC.

Imperial Country-Style Cabbage

- ¼ *cup IMPERIAL Margarine*
- 1 *small head cabbage, shredded*
- ½ *cup chicken broth*
- 1 *tsp salt*
- ¼ *tsp pepper*
- 2 *pimentos, chopped*

Melt margarine in large skillet. Add cabbage; stir until cabbage is well coated with margarine. Add broth, salt, and pepper; cover. Cook over medium heat 5–6 minutes. Stir in pimentos. Makes 6 servings.

COURTESY LEVER BROTHERS COMPANY.

Campbell's Sweet-and-Sour Cabbage

- *3 slices bacon*
- *½ cup chopped onion*
- *1 can (10¾ oz) CAMPBELL'S Condensed Chicken Broth*
- *¼ cup red wine vinegar*
- *2 Tbsp sugar*
- *¼ tsp salt*
- *Generous dash pepper*
- *1 medium bay leaf*
- *7 cups shredded red cabbage, 1 small head (about 1½ lb)*
- *3 cups sliced apples, 2 medium*
- *4 tsp cornstarch*
- *2 Tbsp water*

In skillet, cook bacon until crisp; remove and crumble. Cook onion in drippings until tender. Stir in chicken broth, vinegar, sugar, salt, pepper, and bay leaf. Bring to boil; add cabbage. Reduce heat; simmer 10 minutes. Arrange apples on cabbage; cook 10 minutes more or until done. Stir occasionally. Combine cornstarch and water; stir into sauce. Cook, stirring until thickened. Remove bay leaf. Garnish with bacon. Makes about 4 cups.

COURTESY CAMPBELL SOUP COMPANY.

Stokely's Apple Kraut Bavarian

- *1 pkg (10 oz) brown and serve sausages*
- *1 can (16½ oz) STOKELY'S Finest® Applesauce*
- *1 can (1 lb) STOKELY'S Finest® Bavarian Style Sauerkraut, slightly drained*

Brown sausage; stir in STOKELY'S Applesauce and Sauerkraut. Heat to serving temperature. Serve with mashed potatoes. Makes 4 servings.

COURTESY STOKELY-VAN CAMP, INC.

Sunkist® California Orange Carrots

1 lb carrots, cut in ¼-inch slices (about 3 cups)
½ tsp salt
¾ cup water
½ tsp fresh grated orange peel
1 SUNKIST® Orange, peeled, cut in bite-size pieces
2 Tbsp butter or margarine, softened
1 Tbsp chopped green onion

In covered saucepan, cook carrots with salt in water until just tender (10–15 minutes); drain. Add remaining ingredients; heat, stirring occasionally. Makes 4 servings (about 3 cups).

Variation: Omit green onion; stir in 2 Tbsp brown sugar or 1 Tbsp honey with remaining ingredients.

COURTESY SUNKIST GROWERS, INC.

La Choy Sweet Sour Carrots

1 lb carrots, pared
1 cup water
¼ tsp salt
2 Tbsp butter
¼ cup LA CHOY Sweet & Sour Sauce
1 Tbsp LA CHOY Teriyaki Sauce
¼ cup buttered dry bread crumbs
2 Tbsp chopped parsley

Cut carrots into narrow strips about 2 inches long. Place carrots in saucepan; add water and salt. Cover and cook 15 minutes or until just tender; drain well. Add butter. Combine sauces and pour over carrots, stirring gently. Spoon into serving dish. Sprinkle with bread crumbs and parsley. Makes 4–5 servings.

COURTESY LA CHOY FOOD PRODUCTS.

Lea & Perrins Heavenly Carrots

4 cups cooked sliced carrots
1½ cups plain croutons
1 cup grated, sharp Cheddar cheese
2 eggs, beaten
¼ cup light cream
¼ cup butter or margarine, melted
1½ tsp LEA & PERRINS Worcestershire Sauce
1 tsp salt

Place carrots in a buttered 1½-qt casserole. Stir in croutons and cheese. Mix remaining ingredients. Pour over carrot mixture.

Bake, uncovered, in a preheated hot oven (400°F) 20 minutes or until brown. Yield: 6 portions.

COURTESY LEA & PERRINS WORCESTERSHIRE SAUCE, A PRODUCT OF LEA & PERRINS, INC.

Minute Maid®

Copper Carrot Pennies

2 lb medium carrots
1 small green pepper, chopped
1 medium onion, thinly sliced
¼ cup MINUTE MAID® 100% Pure Lemon Juice
1 cup sugar
½ cup vinegar
½ cup salad oil
1 10-oz can condensed tomato soup
1 tsp salt
1 tsp prepared mustard
1 tsp Worcestershire sauce
¾ tsp pepper

Peel and slice carrots. Cook in a little salted water in a pan with a tight cover until just fork tender; then cool quickly in cold water. Arrange in a glass container in layers with the pepper and onion. Make a marinade of the remaining ingredients, beaten to blend well. Pour marinade over vegetables, cover, and refrigerate for several hours before using. To use, remove vegetables from marinade with a slotted spoon to a serving dish. This will keep for up to a week in the refrigerator, and the marinade may be saved to use a second time.

 COURTESY THE COCA-COLA COMPANY FOODS DIVISION.

Land O'Lakes Herbutter Corn-on-the-Cob

8 ears corn, fresh or frozen and thawed
1 cup LAND O LAKES® Sweet Cream Butter, softened
2 tsp salt
1 tsp marjoram leaves
1 tsp parsley, flakes or chopped
¼ to ½ tsp rosemary

Preheat oven or grill: 425°F. Husk fresh corn or thaw frozen ears. Have ready 8 squares of heavy-duty foil. (If desired, 2–4 ears may be wrapped together.) In small bowl, combine butter and seasonings until light and fluffy. Spread about 2 Tbsp butter mixture evenly over each ear. Wrap tightly in heavy-duty foil, sealing well. Bake at 425°F or place on grill over hot coals 25–35 minutes, turning frequently until tender. Serve hot with additional butter and salt. This butter mixture can also be served with fresh corn that has been boiled 4–10 minutes or until tender. Yield: 8 ears.

COURTESY OF THE LAND O'LAKES KITCHENS, MINNEAPOLIS, MN.

Stokely's Spanish Corn and Zucchini

½ cup chopped onion
½ cup chopped green pepper
1 clove garlic, minced
3 Tbsps butter or margarine, melted
1 lb zucchini squash, thinly sliced (unpeeled)
1 can (1 lb 1 oz) STOKELY'S Finest® Whole Kernel Golden Corn, drained
1 can (8 oz) STOKELY'S Finest® Tomato Sauce
1 tsp Worcestershire sauce

1 tsp sugar
½ tsp salt
½ tsp chili powder
⅛ tsp dry mustard
Dash pepper

Sauté onion, green pepper, and garlic in butter until tender. Add squash and heat for 10 minutes over low heat. Add remaining ingredients and cook for 20 minutes, stirring occasionally, being careful not to break squash slices. Makes 6 servings.

COURTESY STOKELY-VAN CAMP, INC.

Dairymate Scalloped Corn

2 cans (12 oz each) corn
1 cup DAIRYMATE
½ cup chopped onion
1 tsp salt
⅛ tsp pepper
25 unsalted plain crackers, crushed to make 1 cup crumbs
5 unsalted plain crackers
1 Tbsp margarine

Combine all ingredients except 5 crackers and margarine. Pour into 1½-qt casserole dish. Crush 5 crackers over mixture. Dot with margarine. Bake in 375°F oven for 40 minutes or until mixture puffs up. Serve hot. Makes 8 servings, ½ cup each.

PET, AN IC INDUSTRIES COMPANY, HOME ECONOMICS DEPT., P.O. BOX 392, ST. LOUIS, MO 63166.

Enrico's®

Enrico's Eggplant Parmesan

- *1 eggplant*
- *1 onion, chopped fine*
- *½ green pepper, chopped*
- *¾ cup grated Parmesan cheese (or any Italian-style cheese)*
- *1½ tsp salt*
- *⅛ tsp pepper*
- *2 cups soft bread crumbs*
- *1 egg*
- *1 cup ENRICO'S Spaghetti Sauce*
- *3 Tbsp fat*

Slice eggplant in ¼-inch slices, peel, and dip in crumbs, in egg that has been mixed with water, and again in crumbs. Fry in hot deep fat until brown. Sauté onion and pepper in fat and add seasonings. Place in casserole in layers, adding cheese, onion, green pepper, and ENRICO'S Spaghetti Sauce with each layer. Bake in moderate oven—350°F, about 30 minutes.

COURTESY VENTRE PACKING COMPANY, INC.

Berio Eggplant (Caponata)

- *1 medium eggplant*
- *6 Tbsp FILIPPO BERIO Olive Oil*
- *1 sliced onion*
- *3 Tbsp tomato sauce*
- *2 stalks celery, diced*
- *2 Tbsp FILIPPO BERIO Wine Vinegar*
- *1 Tbsp sugar*
- *1 Tbsp capers*
- *4 green olives stuffed with red peppers*
- *¼ tsp salt*
- *⅛ tsp pepper*

Peel eggplant and dice and fry in 5 Tbsp of FILIPPO BERIO Olive Oil. Remove eggplant from pan, add 1 Tbsp olive oil. Fry onions until brown. Add tomato sauce and celery—cook until celery is tender. If needed, add 1 Tbsp water. Put back into pan, sliced eggplant, capers, and chopped olives. Heat FILIPPO BERIO Wine Vinegar with sugar and pour over eggplant. Salt and pepper to taste. Simmer 10–15 minutes, stirring frequently.

Serve cool on toasted squares of bread. Leftover can be put into refrigerator for later use.
COURTESY BERIO IMPORTING CORP.

Green Giant® Marinated Mushrooms

3 Tbsp salad oil or olive oil
2 Tbsp lemon juice
1 Tbsp chopped onion
1 tsp parsley flakes
½ tsp salt
½ tsp prepared mustard
4 2½-oz or two 4½-oz jars GREEN GIANT® Whole Mushrooms, drained

In small saucepan, combine all ingredients except mushrooms. Bring to a boil; add mushrooms. Simmer 5 minutes. Cool; then chill, stirring occasionally. Makes about 1½ cups.
COURTESY THE GREEN GIANT COMPANY.

Colonna Mushrooms au Gratin

12 large mushrooms
2 Tbsp butter
1 small onion, chopped
½ tsp salt
½ tsp pepper
½ Tbsp parsley
2 Tbsp water
2 Tbsp COLONNA Flavored Bread Crumbs
2 Tbsp butter
1 Tbsp COLONNA Parmesan Cheese

Remove stems from mushrooms and wash well. Chop stems and fry in 2 Tbsp butter with onion. Brown lightly, add salt, pepper, parsley, and water, and cook 5 minutes longer. Remove from fire and mix well. Fill mushroom caps with the stuffing, top with COLONNA Flavored Bread Crumbs and Grated Cheese, dot with butter, and place in well-greased baking dish in moderate oven (375°F) for 15 minutes. Serves 4.
COURTESY COLONNA BROTHERS.

Oscar Mayer Bacon-Stuffed Mushrooms

1 lb fresh mushrooms
2 Tbsp chopped onion
2 Tbsp butter
1 slice bread, torn into small pieces
1 cup (4 oz) shredded Cheddar cheese
1 can (3 oz) OSCAR MAYER Real Bacon Bits

Remove stems from mushrooms and set aside caps; chop stems. Cook onions and chopped mushroom stems in butter until tender; add bread pieces. Remove from heat; stir in bacon bits and cheese. Mound filling in caps; place in shallow baking pan. Bake in 400°F oven 15 minutes until cheese is melted. Serve warm. Makes 15–20 appetizers.

COURTESY OSCAR MAYER & CO.

MICHELOB®

Michelob French Fried Beerings

1 large Bermuda onion
1 12-oz can MICHELOB Beer
1 cup sifted flour
2 tsp salt
1½ tsp baking powder
1 egg, separated
1 Tbsp salad oil
Cooking oil

Cut peeled onion into ¼-inch slices, separate into rings, and place in deep bowl. Cover with beer. Let stand 30 minutes, stirring once or twice. Drain, reserving ⅔ cup beer. Sift together flour, salt, and baking powder. Beat egg yolk slightly, stir in beer and salad oil. Add this mixture to flour, stir until smooth. Beat egg white until it holds a peak, then fold into batter. Heat 1 inch cooking oil in skillet to 375°F, dip onion rings in batter (let excess drip into bowl) and drop several at a time into hot oil. Fry until golden. Drain on paper towels.

REPRINTED BY PERMISSION, ANHEUSER-BUSCH, INC., ST. LOUIS, MO.

McCormick/Schilling French Onion Casserole

- 4 *cups thinly sliced onions*
- 2 *Tbsp margarine, melted*
- 1 *pkg MCCORMICK/ SCHILLING Brown Gravy Mix*
- ¾ *cup water*
- ¼ *cup white wine*
- 1½ *cups croutons*
- 1 *cup chopped tomatoes*
- 1 *cup shredded Swiss cheese*

In a shallow 2-qt baking dish, combine onions and margarine. Blend gravy mix and water; pour over onions and stir in wine. Bake in 350°F oven 30 minutes. Mix in croutons and tomatoes; sprinkle cheese over all. Bake 5 more minutes or until cheese melts. Makes 6 servings.

Campbell's Minted Peas and Mushrooms

- ½ *lb fresh mushrooms, cut in half (about 2 cups)*
- ¼ *cup sliced almonds*
- 2 *Tbsp butter or margarine*
- 1 *can (10¾ oz) CAMPBELL'S Condensed Cream of Celery Soup*
- ¼ *cup water*
- 2 *Tbsp chopped pimiento*
- ½ *tsp dried mint leaves, crushed*
- 1 *pkg (10 oz) frozen peas, cooked and drained*

In saucepan, brown mushrooms and almonds in butter. Add remaining ingredients. Heat; stir occasionally. Makes about 3 cups.

COURTESY CAMPBELL SOUP COMPANY.

Chefs Best Oriental Peas

1 5-oz can water chestnuts, drained
2 Tbsp butter or margarine
1 tsp lemon juice
1 tsp soy sauce
¼ tsp onion salt
¼ tsp monosodium glutamate
1 No. 303 can CHEFS BEST Sweet Peas, drained

Slice water chestnuts. Sauté in butter, lemon juice, soy sauce, onion salt, and monosodium glutamate, 3–4 minutes. Stir in drained peas. Cover and heat over low temperature 5–8 minutes, occasionally stirring.

COURTESY OCONOMOWOC CANNING CO.

Stokely's Pea Casserole

2 cans (1 lb 1 oz each) STOKELY'S Finest® Peas, drained
1 can (10¾ oz) cream of mushroom soup
1 can (8 oz) water chestnuts, sliced and drained
1 jar (2 oz) STOKELY'S Finest® Sliced Pimientos, drained
2 Tbsps instant minced onion
1 cup fresh bread crumbs
¼ cup butter or margarine, melted

Combine first 5 ingredients in a 1½-qt casserole. Stir together bread crumbs and butter and sprinkle over casserole. Bake at 350°F for 30 minutes. Makes 8 servings.

COURTESY STOKELY-VAN CAMP, INC.

Land O'Lakes Zesty Baked Potatoes

6 baking potatoes
½ cup LAND O LAKES® Sweet Cream Butter, softened
2 Tbsp sloppy joe or chili seasoning mix
1 tsp salt

Preheat oven or grill: 375°F. Scrub and dry potatoes; *do not peel.* Cut each in 3 or 4 lengthwise slices. In small bowl, blend butter and seasonings. Spread on slices and reassemble each potato. Wrap each securely in 10- to 12-inch square of double thickness heavy-duty foil. Place on baking sheet in 375°F oven or on grill 3–4 inches from hot coals 55–70 minutes, or until potatoes are soft when pinched. Turn potatoes occasionally to

disperse seasoning. To serve, turn down foil to make a serving dish. Season with salt and pepper, if desired. Yield: 6 servings.
COURTESY OF THE LAND O'LAKES KITCHENS, MINNEAPOLIS, MN.

College Inn Scalloped Potatoes and Onions

- 5 *large potatoes, pared and thinly sliced (1 qt)*
- ¾ *cup chopped onion*
- 3 *Tbsp butter or margarine*
- ¼ *cup all-purpose flour*
- 1¾ *cups COLLEGE INN Chicken Broth*
- ¼ *cup mayonnaise*
- ¾ *tsp salt*
- ⅛ *tsp white pepper*
- *Paprika*

In round 1½-qt casserole, layer potatoes and onion. In medium saucepan, melt butter or margarine and stir in flour; cook until frothy. Gradually stir in broth, mayonnaise, salt, and pepper. Cook, stirring frequently, until sauce bubbles and thickens. Pour over potatoes. Sprinkle generously with paprika. Bake in a preheated moderate oven (350°F) for 1¼ hours or until potatoes are fork-tender and top is browned. Serves 4.
COURTESY PREPARED FOOD AND BEVERAGE PRODUCTS GROUP OF DEL MONTE CORPORATION.

Betty Crocker® Pizza Potatoes

- 1 *pkg BETTY CROCKER® Scalloped Potatoes*
- 1 *can (16 oz) tomatoes*
- 1½ *cups water*
- ¼ *tsp dried oregano leaves, crushed*
- 1 *pkg (4 oz) sliced pepperoni*
- 1 *pkg (4 oz) shredded mozzarella cheese*

Heat oven to 400°F. Empty potato slices and Sauce Mix into ungreased 2-qt casserole. Heat tomatoes (with liquid), water, and oregano to boiling; stir into potatoes. Arrange pepperoni on top; sprinkle with cheese. Bake until potatoes are tender, 30–35 minutes. Yield: 4 servings.
COURTESY BETTY CROCKER FOOD & NUTRITION CENTER, GENERAL MILLS, INC. REGISTERED® TRADEMARK OF GENERAL MILLS, INC.

Campbell's

Campbell's Scalloped Potatoes

- 1 can (10¾ oz) *CAMPBELL'S Condensed Cream of Celery or Mushroom Soup*
- ⅓ *to* ½ *cup milk*
- ¼ *cup chopped parsley*
- *Dash pepper*
- 4 *cups thinly sliced potatoes*
- 1 *small onion, thinly sliced*
- 1 *Tbsp butter or margarine*
- *Dash paprika*

Combine soup, milk, parsley, and pepper. In 1½-qt casserole, arrange alternate layers of potatoes, onion, and sauce. Dot top with butter; sprinkle with paprika. Cover; bake at 375°F for 1 hour. Uncover; bake 15 minutes more or until potatoes are done. Makes about 3½ cups.

COURTESY CAMPBELL SOUP COMPANY.

Ore-Ida Gourmet Potato Patties

- 1 *pkg (3 oz) cream cheese, softened*
- 1 *Tbsp flour*
- ½ *tsp salt*
- ½ *tsp paprika*
- 1 *Tbsp snipped parsley*
- 6 *Tbsp shredded extra-sharp Cheddar cheese*
- 2 *Tbsp evaporated milk*
- 1 *Tbsp frozen ORE-IDA Chopped Onions, minced*

- 1 *egg, beaten until thick*
- 2 *bricks ORE-IDA Shredded Hash Browns, defrosted and separated*
- *Butter or margarine*

With electric mixer, mix cream cheese, flour, salt, paprika, parsley, and shredded cheese. Add milk and onion; mix until smooth. Gently fold in well-beaten egg and separated ORE-IDA Shredded Hash Browns. Lightly grease medium skillet; place over medium heat. Pour ¼ cup batter onto hot skillet for each pancake. Spread batter to make thin pancakes about 3 inches in diameter. Fry pancake until golden and crisp; brown other side, adding more oil as needed. Drain on paper towels. Serve hot. Yield: about 10 3-inch pancakes.

COURTESY "FAMILY FAVORITES" FROM ORE-IDA.

Colonna Potatoes Parmigiana

- *4 medium potatoes, peeled and diced fine*
- *2 Tbsp butter*
- *1 tsp meat extract, blended in 1 Tbsp water*
- *½ tsp salt*
- *¼ tsp pepper*
- *2 Tbsp butter, melted*
- *3 Tbsp Grated COLONNA Cheese*

Cook potatoes in butter 7 minutes, or until tender. Add meat extract and water. Place potatoes and gravy in greased baking dish, sprinkle with salt, pepper, melted butter, and cheese, and bake in hot oven (400°F) 10 minutes. Serves 4.

COURTESY COLONNA BROTHERS.

McCormick/Schilling Cook-Out Potatoes

- *¼ cup oil*
- *2 tsp MCCORMICK/ SCHILLING Season-All® Seasoned Salt*
- *⅛ tsp MCCORMICK/ SCHILLING Garlic Powder*
- *4 potatoes*

Combine oil, MCCORMICK/SCHILLING Season-All®, and garlic powder in a bowl. Pare potatoes, slice ½ inch thick. Toss in seasoned oil. Portion slices between 4 squares of heavy foil. Wrap securely, place on grill, and cook until done, about 15–20 minutes.

Miller Pocabsca

- 2 *lb potatoes, peeled and quartered*
- 2 *cups MILLER High Life*
- 2 *tsp salt*
- 3 *cups coarsely chopped cabbage*
- 1 *cup sliced scallions (including green tops)*
- ¼ *cup milk*
- *Freshly ground pepper*
- 2 *tsp minced parsley*
- 3 *Tbsp butter or margarine*

In a heavy saucepan, combine potatoes, MILLER High Life, and salt. Add enough water to fill saucepan to ⅔ of capacity. Cook, covered, over medium heat for 15 minutes. Then add cabbage, cover again, and continue to cook for 12 minutes longer. In a separate saucepan, simmer scallions in milk for 10 minutes, then add to cabbage-potato mixture. Season with pepper, add parsley, and stir in butter, breaking up potato pieces into uneven sizes as you stir. Continue cooking over low heat for 3 minutes longer. Drain and serve immediately. An excellent vegetable dish with corned beef or braised beef. Serves 6.

COURTESY MILLER BREWING COMPANY.

Friendship Fritada de Espinaca (Spinach Side Dish)

- 12 *cups fresh spinach, chopped very fine*
- 8 *eggs, yolks and whites beaten separately*
- 8 *oz FRIENDSHIP Cottage Cheese*
- 4 *oz grated Parmesan cheese*
- 2 *medium potatoes, boiled and grated (or ¼ cup potato flakes)*
- 1½ *tsp salt*
- *Oil*

In a large bowl, thoroughly mix spinach, beaten egg yolks, both cheeses, potatoes, and salt. Fold in egg whites, beaten until stiff. Pour oil in bottom of baking pan and heat it in oven. When oil is hot, pour spinach mixture in baking pan and bake in a 350°F oven for approximately 1 hour, or until spinach is golden brown and firm. Allow spinach to cool slightly; then cut it into serving squares. Spinach can be frozen and reheated in a 350°F oven for serving. Serves 10.

RECIPE COURTESY OF FRIENDSHIP FOODS' HOME ECONOMIST, HELEN SCHWARTZ.

Berio Spinach and Rice

- 1 *lb spinach*
- 1 *cup rice*
- 2 *cups chicken broth*
- 2 *medium-size onions minced*
- ¼ *cup FILIPPO BERIO Olive Oil*
- *Salt and pepper*

Sauté onion in the FILIPPO BERIO Olive Oil. Wash spinach thoroughly 3 or 4 times and drain well. Put spinach, broth, and the onions and olive oil in the pot and bring to a boil. Add rice that has been previously washed. Stir the complete mixture and add salt and pepper. Allow to simmer for 25 minutes.

COURTESY BERIO IMPORTING CORP.

Ocean Spray's Baked Cranberry-Acorn Squash Recipe

- 4 *small acorn squash*
- 1 *cup chopped unpared apple*
- 1 *cup OCEAN SPRAY® Fresh or Frozen Cranberries, chopped*
- ½ *tsp grated orange peel*
- ½ *cup brown sugar*
- 2 *Tbsp butter or margarine, melted*

Cut squash in half lengthwise; remove seeds. Place cut side down in 13 X 9 X 2-inch baking dish. Bake in 350°F oven for 35 minutes. Turn cut side up. Combine remaining ingredients; fill squash with fruit mixture. Continue baking for 25 minutes or until squash is tender. Makes 8 servings.

COURTESY OCEAN SPRAY CRANBERRIES, INC.

Sizzlean Summer Squash Casserole

- 8 *slices SIZZLEAN Pork Breakfast Strips, cut into ½-inch pieces*
- 1 *lb yellow crookneck squash*
- 5 *slices American process cheese*
- 1 *Tbsp flour*

Wash but do not pare squash. Cut into thin slices, then cut larger slices into halves. Panfry pork breakfast strips until

browned. Drain. In a 1-qt casserole, arrange layers of squash, cheese, then pork breakfast strips. Sprinkle flour over pork breakfast strips. Top with remaining squash and cheese with pork breakfast strips over all. Bake uncovered in a 325°F oven 35–40 minutes or until done. May also be enclosed in heavy-duty foil and cooked on an outdoor grill. Yield: 5–6 servings.
COURTESY SWIFT & COMPANY.

Land O'Lakes Butterstuff Tomatoes

- *6 firm ripe tomatoes (2½-inch diameter)*
- *¼ cup LAND O LAKES® Sweet Cream Butter*
- *2 cups thinly sliced zucchini*
- *2 Tbsp finely chopped onion*
- *1½ tsp garlic salt*
- *½ tsp dill weed*
- *1 Tbsp all-purpose flour*
- *1 7-oz can whole kernel corn, drained (1 cup)*

Preheat oven: 350°F. Wash and dry tomatoes, cut about ¼ inch off stem end. Cut around pulp and remove gently with spoon into small bowl. In large skillet, melt butter. Stir in next 4 ingredients. Sautē uncovered over low heat 5 minutes or until zucchini is tender yet firm. Stir in flour, corn, and ½ cup tomato pulp. Cook over low heat, stirring frequently 3–5 minutes or until mixture thickens. Lightly salt tomato shells and fill each with about ⅓ cup filling. Place in pan; bake at 350°F 12–15 minutes or until tomatoes are hot yet firm. Yield: 4–6 servings.
COURTESY OF THE LAND O'LAKES KITCHENS, MINNEAPOLIS, MN.

Berio Stuffed Tomatoes

- *6 to 8 medium-sized firm tomatoes*
- *1 lb chopped meat*
- *2 Tbsp minced onion*
- *½ cup parsley leaves, cut fine*
- *1 Tbsp small-grained rice, washed*
- *3 Tbsp FILIPPO BERIO Olive Oil*
- *¾ tsp salt*
- *Pepper*
- *½ cup FILIPPO BERIO Olive Oil*
- *½ cup grated Parmesan cheese*

Wash tomatoes, cut top back to permit scooping out pulp with a small spoon. Mix meat with other ingredients in a bowl by kneading or with a fork, to keep light. One-third of the tomato pulp may be added to the mixture. Fill tomatoes, using fingers or small spoon. Place in shallow pan with balance of pulp. Pour over FILIPPO BERIO Olive Oil, cover tightly, and let simmer for 40 minutes. Serve hot. Dish can be reheated on a very low flame.

COURTESY BERIO IMPORTING CORP.

Sunkist® Evergreen Zucchini

1 lb zucchini, cut in ½-inch slices
½ tsp salt
Boiling water
2 Tbsp chopped parsley
½ tsp fresh grated SUNKIST® Lemon peel
1 Tbsp fresh squeezed lemon juice
1 Tbsp butter or margarine, softened
2 tsp instant minced onion

In covered saucepan, cook zucchini with salt in 1 inch boiling water until tender (about 6–8 minutes); drain. Add remaining ingredients; heat, stirring occasionally. Makes 3–4 servings.

COURTESY SUNKIST GROWERS, INC.

Friendship Zucchini Casserole

4 cups sliced zucchini (about 4 medium)
1 tsp salt
½ cup chopped onion
1 medium clove garlic, chopped or crushed
½ tsp oregano
¼ tsp pepper
2 cups cooked rice
1 can (8 oz) tomato sauce
1 cup FRIENDSHIP Cottage Cheese
¾ cup shredded, sharp Cheddar cheese
1 egg

Toss zucchini with salt. Place ½ zucchini in a greased 2-qt casserole. In a medium skillet, sauté the onion, garlic, oregano, and pepper in oil until lightly browned. Stir in the rice and sauce. Spread mixture over zucchini. Mix together cottage cheese, ½ cup Cheddar cheese, and the egg. Spoon over the rice mixture. Layer with remaining zucchini and sprinkle with remaining Cheddar cheese. Bake at 350°F 30–40 minutes or until lightly browned and bubbly. Yield: 6 servings.

RECIPE COURTESY OF FRIENDSHIP FOODS' HOME ECONOMIST, HELEN SCHWARTZ.

Heinz French-Style Vegetable Stew

- 1 *cup chopped onions*
- 2 *cloves garlic, minced*
- 2 *small zucchini, thinly sliced*
- 1 *medium green pepper, cut into thin strips*
- ½ *cup olive or salad oil*
- 1 *medium eggplant, pared, cut into 2-inch X ½-inch strips*
- 3 *Tbsp flour*
- 4 *medium tomatoes, peeled, cut into eighths*
- ¼ *cup HEINZ Tomato Ketchup*
- 1 *Tbsp salt*
- 1 *tsp HEINZ Apple Cider Vinegar*
- ½ *tsp crushed oregano leaves*
- ¼ *tsp pepper*

In Dutch oven, sauté first 4 ingredients in oil until onion is transparent. Coat eggplant with flour; add with tomatoes to sautéed vegetables. Combine ketchup and remaining ingredients; pour over vegetables. Cover; simmer 30–35 minutes; stir occasionally, or until vegetables are tender. Makes 8–10 servings (about 7 cups). Note: Zucchini can be peeled if skin is tough.

COURTESY OF HEINZ U.S.A., DIVISION OF H.J. HEINZ COMPANY.

Sunkist® Vegetables à la Bacon 'n Mushrooms

- 3 *slices bacon, cut in 1-inch pieces*
- 1 *can (about 2 oz) sliced mushrooms, drained*
- *Juice of ½ SUNKIST® Lemon*
- 1 *Tbsp sugar*
- 2 *tsp instant minced onion*
- ½ *tsp salt*
- 1 *pkg (9 oz) frozen cut green beans, cooked, drained, or 1 can (16 oz) cut green beans, drained*

In skillet, cook bacon until crisp; remove. To drippings, add mushrooms, lemon juice, sugar, onion, and salt. Stir in green beans; heat. Garnish with cooked bacon. Makes 3–4 servings.

Variation

Substitute 1 pkg (10 oz) frozen peas, cooked and drained, or 2 pkg (10 oz each) frozen leaf spinach, cooked and well drained, or 1 can (17 oz) whole kernel corn, drained—for green beans.

COURTESY SUNKIST GROWERS, INC.

Wesson® Dressed-Up Vegetables

- *2 medium carrots, cut into julienne strips 2 inches long*
- *1 medium onion, sliced ¼ inch thick and separated into rings*
- *1 cup sliced mushrooms*
- *1 cup broccoli flowerets*
- *WESSON Oil*
- *2 cups ice water*
- *2½ cups all-purpose flour*
- *2 egg yolks*
- *1½ Tbsp sugar*
- *1½ tsp salt*
- *½ tsp baking soda*

Wash vegetables and pat dry. Fill deep fryer or heavy kettle to ⅓ its depth with WESSON Oil, heat to 375°F, using a frying thermometer to check temperature. Combine 2 tsp oil and remaining ingredients. Mix until smooth. Dip vegetables into batter a few at a time. Fry until golden. Drain on paper towels. Dip in ketchup, soy sauce, hot mustard, or other dipping sauce, if desired. Makes 6–8 servings.

COURTESY HUNT-WESSON FOODS, INC.

Rice and Other Side Dishes

Arnold Country Casserole

- 1 cup ARNOLD All-Purpose Bread Crumbs
- 1 can (1 lb) creamed-style corn
- ¼ lb grated Cheddar cheese
- 4 slices Canadian bacon
- 1 cup milk
- 2 whole eggs, beaten
- 2 egg whites, beaten
- 2 Tbsp chopped green pepper
- 1 tsp salt
- ¼ tsp pepper

Combine corn, bread crumbs, eggs, egg whites, milk, green pepper, and spices. Pour into a 1-qt casserole and sprinkle with grated cheese. Cook bacon until half done and place on top. Bake in moderate oven (325°F) 1 hour 15 minutes. Serves 4–6.

COURTESY ARNOLD BAKERS, INC./OROWEAT FOODS COMPANY.

Doritos® Brand Tortilla Chips Tomato Sour Cream Casserole

- 1 medium onion, chopped
- 2 Tbsp salad oil
- 1 1-lb 12-oz can tomatoes
- 1 pkg Mexican style "sloppy joe" seasoning mix
- 1 4-oz can green chilies, chopped
- 1 5½-oz pkg nacho cheese flavor DORITOS® Brand Tortilla Chips
- ¾ lb Monterey Jack cheese, grated
- 1 cup sour cream
- ½ cup grated Cheddar cheese

Sauté onion in oil; add tomatoes, seasoning mix, and green chilies. Simmer, uncovered, 10–15 minutes. In a greased, deep 2-qt baking dish, layer ingredients in order: sauce, crushed nacho cheese flavor DORITOS® Brand Tortilla Chips, Monterey Jack cheese, sauce, and Monterey Jack cheese. Top with sour cream. Bake at 325°F for 30 minutes. Sprinkle with Cheddar cheese; bake 10 minutes longer. Makes 8 servings.

COURTESY FRITO-LAY, INC. DORITOS® IS A REGISTERED TRADEMARK OF FRITO-LAY, INC.

Uncle Ben's® Red Beans and Brown Rice

- 1 cup UNCLE BEN'S® Brown Rice
- 4 slices bacon, cut into 1-inch pieces
- ½ small onion, coarsely chopped
- 1 Tbsp flour
- 1 can (about 15 oz) red beans or kidney beans
- 1 Tbsp chopped parsley
- ½ tsp salt
- ¼ tsp chili powder
- ¼ tsp minced garlic
- ⅛ tsp pepper
- Dash of Tabasco sauce

Cook rice according to package directions. While rice is cooking, fry bacon in another pan, add onions, and sauté until tender. Remove bacon and onions from pan and blend flour into bacon drippings. Cook over low heat, stirring constantly, until flour is lightly browned. Add juice from beans and enough water to make 1 cup liquid. Cook until slightly thickened; add beans, bacon, onion, and other seasonings. Simmer for 10 minutes to blend flavors. Serve over cooked rice. Makes 6–8 servings.

COURTESY UNCLE BEN'S FOODS.

Old El Paso Mexican Green Rice

- 3 cups cooked rice
- 2 eggs, beaten
- 1 cup milk
- 1 4-oz can OLD EL PASO Chopped Green Chili
- 1 cup finely chopped parsley
- 1 small onion, chopped, or ¼ cup dry onion flakes
- 1 tsp salt
- ¼ tsp black pepper
- 2 cups grated cheese
- ½ cup melted butter

Combine all ingredients and pour into 9 X 13-inch baking dish. Bake, uncovered, at 350°F for 30 minutes. Uncover and bake 10 minutes longer. Serves 10.

PET, AN IC INDUSTRIES COMPANY, HOME ECONOMICS DEPARTMENT, P.O. BOX 392, ST. LOUIS, MO 63166.

Dromedary Savory Stuffing

½ cup butter or margarine
1 cup chopped onion
1 cup chopped celery
½ cup chopped green pepper
*8 cups crumbled DROMEDARY Corn Bread**
1 lb sausage meat, cooked, drained
2 tsp poultry seasoning
1 tsp salt
¼ tsp ground black pepper
¼ cup water
1 egg, beaten
1 (12–15 lb) turkey

Melt butter or margarine; add next 3 ingredients; sauté until golden. Toss together next 5 ingredients. Blend in onion mixture, water, and egg. Use to stuff neck and body cavity of turkey. Roast turkey according to directions. Makes 20 servings, each about 6 oz of turkey and ½ cup stuffing.

*Prepare 1 (15-oz) pkg DROMEDARY Corn Bread Mix according to package directions, using 1 cup milk and 1 egg. Cool. Crumble. Makes 8 cups crumbled corn bread.

COURTESY NABISCO, INC.

Arnold/Francisco Whole Wheat Savory Stuffing

1 pkg (6 oz) ARNOLD/FRANCISCO Whole Wheat Crispy Croutons
1½ cups beef broth
1 small onion, chopped
½ cup chopped celery
1 egg
6 thick pork chops

In a bowl, mix ARNOLD/FRANCISCO Whole Wheat Crispy Croutons, beef broth, onion, celery, and egg. Mix well and let stand for 10 minutes. Put into a 1-qt casserole and bake in a preheated oven (350°F) 35–40 minutes. This mixture can also be used unbaked to stuff pork chops, game hens, chicken, breast of veal, ducks, small turkeys, or fish.

COURTESY ARNOLD BAKERS, INC./OROWEAT FOODS COMPANY.

Quaker® Country Corn Bread Dressing

- *1 cup chopped nuts*
- *1 cup celery slices*
- *½ cup green onion slices*
- *¾ cup butter or margarine, melted*
- *6 cups crumbled corn bread (see below)*
- *6 cups dry bread cubes*
- *1½ tsp poultry seasoning*
- *1½ tsp salt*
- *¼ tsp pepper*
- *2 eggs, beaten*
- *1¼ cups water*

Sauté nuts, celery, and onion in ¼ cup butter. Add to combined corn bread, bread cubes, poultry seasoning, salt, and pepper; mix well. Gradually add remaining ½ cup butter, eggs, and water; toss lightly. Lightly stuff dressing into 12-lb turkey. Roast according to standard directions. Makes about 2½ qt dressing. *Note*: one 8- or 9-inch square baking pan of corn bread yields about 6 cups crumbled corn bread.

Corn Bread

- *1 cup QUAKER® or AUNT JEMIMA® Enriched Corn Meal*
- *1 cup all-purpose flour*
- *¼ cup sugar, if desired*
- *4 tsp baking powder*
- *½ tsp salt*
- *1 cup milk*
- *1 egg*
- *¼ cup vegetable shortening*

Combine corn meal, flour, sugar, baking powder, and salt. Add milk, egg, and shortening. Beat until fairly smooth, about 1 minute. Bake in greased 8-inch square baking pan in preheated hot oven (425°F) 20–25 minutes. Makes one 8-inch square corn bread.

Wheat Chex Holiday Casserole Stuffing

3 cups WHEAT CHEX® Cereal
1 pkg (7 oz) cube stuffing mix (herb-seasoned)
1 cup diced celery with leaves
½ cup diced onion
¼ cup and ½ cup butter or margarine
2 cups chicken bouillon
½ tsp salt
¾ tsp thyme
¼ tsp sage

Combine Chex and stuffing mix in large bowl. Set aside. Sauté celery and onion in ¼ cup butter until tender. Stir in remaining ingredients. Pour over Chex mixture. Toss lightly to combine. Turn into 2-qt casserole. Bake covered at 350°F 25–30 minutes. Makes about 6 cups.

CREATED AND TESTED AT CHECKERBOARD KITCHENS. REPRINTED COURTESY OF RALSTON PURINA COMPANY.

Mrs. Cubbison's

Mrs. Cubbison's Tomato Sausage Stuffing Ole

½ lb pork sausage
1 bag (6 oz) MRS. CUBBISON'S Corn Bread Stuffin' Mix
¼ cup diced celery
½ cup minced onion
1 Tbsp minced parsley
½ cup (1 stick) butter or margarine
½ cup diced California fresh tomatoes with juice (about 2 medium)
1 tsp instant chicken bouillon and seasoning
1 4-oz can diced green chilies

Saute pork, stirring to break up until cooked thoroughly. Drain. Mix together pork sausage, MRS. CUBBISON'S Corn Bread Stuffin' Mix, celery, onion, and parsley. Stir in melted butter or margarine, tomatoes, instant chicken bouillon, and chilies. Blend lightly until evenly moistened, enough for up to one 12-lb turkey or enough to stuff 3½-lb roasting chicken. Bake any leftover dressing in covered casserole last 45 minutes while roasting poultry.

COURTESY MRS. CUBBISON'S FOODS, INC.

Rice-A-Roni Sour Cream Pilaff

1 pkg (8 oz) RICE-A-RONI Chicken Flavor and Other Natural Flavors
Chopped chives
1 bay leaf
1 4-oz can mushrooms
½ pint cultured sour cream

Cook RICE-A-RONI as directed on package, adding 1 bay leaf to chicken broth. Remove bay leaf from cooked RICE-A-RONI. Add one 4-oz can mushrooms (drained) and ½ pint cultured sour cream. Stir and heat through. Garnish with chopped chives. Season to taste.

COURTESY OF GOLDEN GRAIN MACARONI CO.

Carolina Swiss Rice Amandine

3 cups hot, cooked CAROLINA Extra Long Grain Rice
2 Tbsp butter or margarine
2 Tbsp minced pimiento
2 packets MBT Instant Chicken Flavored Broth
1 cup shredded Swiss cheese
½ cup soft bread crumbs
¼ cup slivered almonds, toasted

Combine rice, butter, pimiento, and instant chicken broth. Spoon into a buttered shallow 1-qt casserole. Combine cheese, bread crumbs, and almonds. Sprinkle over rice. Bake at 400°F for 15 minutes. Makes 6 servings (about ½ cup each).

COURTESY RIVIANA FOODS INC.

Stokely's Beefy Baked Rice

¾ cup long-grain rice
¼ cup chopped onion
3 Tbsp butter or margarine, melted
1 can (10½ oz) condensed beef broth
¾ cup STOKELY'S Finest® Tomato Juice

In a skillet with heat-proof handle, sauté rice and onion in butter until onion is tender and rice is slightly golden. Add beef broth and STOKELY'S Tomato Juice; cover and bake at

350°F for 30 minutes. Stir rice and bake an additional 15 minutes. Makes 6 servings.
COURTESY STOKELY-VAN CAMP, INC.

River Brown Rice Supreme

12 slices bacon
½ cup chopped onion
1 jar (2½ oz) sliced mushrooms, drained
1 garlic clove, minced
3 cups cooked RIVER Brand Brown Rice
1½ cups shredded Cheddar cheese
1 cup dairy sour cream
½ tsp salt

In a skillet, cook bacon until crisp. Remove and crumble. Drain off all but 1 Tbsp bacon drippings. In this, saute onion, mushrooms, and garlic until tender. Add rice, 1 cup cheese, sour cream, and salt. Mix well. Pour into lightly buttered 2-qt casserole. Sprinkle with remaining cheese and crumbled bacon. Bake at 350°F for 5 minutes. Makes 8 servings (about ½ cup each).
COURTESY RIVIANA FOODS INC.

Uncle Ben's®

Uncle Ben's® Sesame Fried Rice

1 can (13¾ oz) chicken broth
2 cups diced cooked meat (ham, pork, chicken, or beef)
2 Tbsp cooking oil
1 cup UNCLE BEN'S® CONVERTED® Brand Rice
¼ cup soy sauce
¼ cup sesame seeds, plain or toasted (see below)
4 green onions, cut in ¼-inch slices

Add water to chicken broth to make 2¼ cups liquid. Set aside. Lightly brown meat in cooking oil in 10-inch skillet over moderate heat. Reduce heat to low. Remove skillet from heat and stir in rice. Cook rice over low heat, stirring constantly, until golden. Stir in liquid, soy sauce, and sesame seeds. Bring to boil. Reduce heat, cover, and simmer until liquid is absorbed, about 25 minutes. Stir in green onion. To toast sesame seeds, spread on a baking sheet and place in a 350°F oven until golden, about 10–15 minutes. Makes 4–6 servings.

COURTESY UNCLE BEN'S FOODS.

Sunkist® East-West Orange Rice

- *¼ cup chopped onion*
- *¼ cup chopped green pepper*
- *2 Tbsp butter or margarine*
- *1 cup raw regular rice*
- *Juice of 3 SUNKIST® Oranges (1 cup)*
- *1 cup water*
- *½ tsp salt*
- *¼ tsp oregano leaves, crushed*
- *2 SUNKIST® Oranges, peeled, cut in bite-size pieces*

In large saucepan, sauté onion and green pepper in butter until just tender. Add rice, orange juice, water, salt, and oregano; bring to boil. Reduce heat. Cover; simmer 25 minutes or until liquid is absorbed. Stir in orange pieces. Makes 6 servings (about 4 cups).

COURTESY SUNKIST GROWERS, INC.

Sauces

No wonder the saucemaker was once the most important of all cooks. Before the days of refrigeration, foods were frequently a little "off." Unrefrigerated meats and poultry did not immediately spoil, but they did not stay at the peak of flavor, either. Who wouldn't welcome a tasty sauce that masked the flavor of poorly preserved meat?

Thanks to advances in canning, freezing, and other methods of preservation, we no longer need to use sauces to conceal the natural flavor of our foods. Yet we still appreciate how sauces can make good foods taste even better. As every food lover knows, delicate sauces can enhance fresh fish and vegetables, spicy sauces can add zip to plain meats, and piquant relishes can liven up any meal.

What's more, smooth, perfectly flavored sauces are now far easier to prepare than they ever were in the past. In the 1700s, for example, a French nobleman's personal saucemaker might spend hours preparing a specialty such as Hollandaise sauce. Today that same Hollandaise sauce, a blend of egg yolks, butter, and lemon juice that turns a dish of broccoli into a culinary classic, can be made at home in minutes.

Because French cooks concentrated so much effort on perfecting and refining their sauces, many of the sauces we enjoy today are French in origin. Our basic white sauce, for example, can be traced back to the labors of the French *saucier.*

As the following recipes illustrate, however, great sauces and relishes have come from every part of the world. There is tomato sauce from Italy (see also the Pasta chapter), chutney from India, sweet and sour sauce from China, and barbecue sauce from backyards all over America. Many of the recipes are simplified by the use of prepared soups, salad dressings, and other shortcuts. All are delicious, and all can help you to enhance the flavors of your already good foods.

Cream Corn Starch Thin, Medium, and Thick White Sauces

Thin White Sauce

1 Tbsp butter or margarine
2 tsp CREAM Corn Starch
½ tsp salt
⅛ tsp pepper
1 cup milk

Melt butter in saucepan. Blend in CREAM Corn Starch, salt, and pepper. Gradually add milk. Heat to boiling over direct heat and then boil gently 2 minutes, stirring constantly. Makes 1 cup sauce.

For cream soups, heat with 1½ cups cooked or canned strained vegetables. Serves 4.

Medium White Sauce

1½ Tbsp butter or margarine
1 Tbsp CREAM Corn Starch
½ tsp salt
⅛ tsp pepper
1 cup milk

Melt butter in saucepan. Blend in CREAM Corn Starch, salt, and pepper. Gradually add milk. Heat to boiling over direct heat and then boil gently 2 minutes, stirring constantly. Makes 1 cup sauce. Combine 2 cups drained, cooked, or canned vegetables, diced meat, flaked fish, or 4 hard-cooked, sliced eggs. Serves 4.

For scalloped dishes, place creamed vegetable in greased baking dish. Sprinkle with ½ cup soft bread crumbs mixed with 1 Tbsp melted butter or margarine. Bake in moderately hot oven (375°F) 20 minutes or until crumbs are browned. Serves 4.

Thick White Sauce

2 Tbsp butter or margarine
2½ Tbsp CREAM Corn Starch
½ tsp salt
⅛ tsp pepper
1 cup milk

Melt butter in saucepan. Blend in CREAM Corn Starch, salt, and pepper. Gradually add milk. Heat to boiling over direct heat and then boil gently 2 minutes, stirring constantly. Makes 1 cup sauce.

For croquettes, combine with 2 cups cooked or canned chopped meat, vegetables, eggs or flaked fish. Chill. Shape into 8 croquettes. Roll in fine bread crumbs and brown in 2–3 inches of hot fat. Drain on absorbent paper. Serve hot. Serves 4.

For soufflés, combine with 1½ cups (¼ lb) grated cheese, flaked fish, cooked or canned chopped vegetables or meat. Add 2 slightly beaten egg yolks. Fold in 2 stiffly beaten egg whites. Pour into greased casserole. Bake in slow oven (325°F)

50 minutes or until knife inserted in center comes out clean. Serves 4.

COURTESY OF A.E. STALEY MANUFACTURING COMPANY, CONSUMER PRODUCTS GROUP, OAK BROOK, ILLINOIS.

Grandma's® Basic Barbecue Sauce

- *1 cup GRANDMA'S® Molasses*
- *1 cup vinegar*
- *1 cup prepared mustard*

Mix molasses and mustard; stir in vinegar. Cover and refrigerate. Yield: 3 cups.

COURTESY GRANDMA'S UNSULPHURED MOLASSES, A REGISTERED TRADEMARK OF DUFFY-MOTT COMPANY, INC., NEW YORK 10017.

A.1.® Original Barbecue Sauce

- *¼ cup A.1. Steak Sauce*
- *½ cup catsup*
- *2 Tbsp brown sugar (or ⅓ cup orange juice concentrate)*

Mix A.1. Steak Sauce with catsup and brown sugar (or orange juice). Bring to boil. Simmer 5 minutes. Makes ¾–1cup.

COURTESY OF HEUBLEIN, INC.

Del Monte Sweet-Sour Sauce

- *4 tsp cornstarch*
- *¾ cup vinegar*
- *1 cup firmly packed brown sugar*
- *½ cup DEL MONTE Tomato Catsup*
- *½ cup DEL MONTE Pineapple Juice*
- *1 tsp soy sauce*

Blend cornstarch with vinegar in saucepan. Add remaining ingredients. Cook, stirring constantly, until thickened. Yield: 3 cups sauce.

COURTESY DEL MONTE KITCHENS, DEL MONTE CORPORATION, P.O. BOX 3575, SAN FRANCISCO, CA 94119.

Wish-Bone Onion Glaze

1 cup (8 oz) WISH-BONE Russian Dressing
1 envelope LIPTON Onion Soup Mix
1 jar (12 oz) apricot preserves

In small bowl, combine all ingredients. Use as marinade or glaze for chicken, spareribs, and other meats. Makes about 2½ cups.
COURTESY OF THE LIPTON KITCHENS.

Cream Corn Starch for Better Gravies

3 Tbsp bacon fat or meat drippings
2 Tbsp CREAM Corn Starch
1½ cups water
¾ tsp salt
⅛ tsp pepper

Blend fat and CREAM Corn Starch over low heat until it is a rich brown color, stirring constantly. Gradually add water, salt, and pepper. Heat to boiling over direct heat and then boil gently 2 minutes, stirring constantly. For cream gravy, use milk or cream instead of water. Makes 1½ cups.
COURTESY OF A.E. STALEY MANUFACTURING COMPANY, CONSUMER PRODUCTS GROUP, OAK BROOK, ILLINOIS.

Blue Diamond® Almond Lemon Sauce

⅓ cup BLUE DIAMOND® Blanched Slivered Almonds
½ cup butter or margarine
3 Tbsp lemon juice
¼ tsp salt

In saucepan, sauté almonds in butter over medium-low heat until lightly browned, stirring constantly. Stir in lemon juice and salt. Serve hot over vegetables, fish, or broiled or roasted fowl. Makes 4 servings. *Variation*: Substitute 3 Tbsp orange juice and 1 tsp grated orange rind for lemon juice.
COURTESY CALIFORNIA ALMOND GROWERS EXCHANGE.

Campbell's Tangy Fish Sauce

¼ cup chopped celery
1 small clove garlic, minced
⅛ tsp dry mustard
2 Tbsp butter or margarine
1 can (11 oz) CAMPBELL'S Condensed Cheddar Cheese Soup
⅓ cup milk
1 Tbsp chopped dill pickle

In saucepan, cook celery with garlic and mustard in butter until tender. Add remaining ingredients. Heat; stir occasionally.

Makes about 1½ cups. Serve over cooked white fish.
COURTESY CAMPBELL SOUP COMPANY.

Minute Maid®

Blender Hollandaise

- 4 egg yolks
- 2 to 3 Tbsp MINUTE MAID® 100% Pure Lemon Juice
- ¼ tsp salt
- Dash of pepper
- ½ cup melted butter or margarine

Place egg yolks, lemon juice, salt, and pepper in an electric blender. Turn to high speed and slowly pour melted butter into egg yolk mixture. Continue blending for 60 seconds. Serve immediately. Serves 4.

MINUTE MAID IS A REGISTERED TRADEMARK OF THE COCA-COLA COMPANY. COURTESY THE COCA-COLA COMPANY FOODS DIVISION.

Campbell's Mornay Sauce

- 1 can (10¾ oz) CAMPBELL'S Condensed Cream of Mushroom Soup
- ½ cup shredded natural Swiss cheese
- ⅓ cup light cream or milk
- 2 Tbsp grated Parmesan cheese

In saucepan, combine ingredients. Heat until cheese melts; stir often. Serve over cooked meats, poultry, fish, vegetables, or poached eggs. Makes about 1½ cups.
COURTESY CAMPBELL SOUP COMPANY.

Progresso Fave and Tomato Sauce

- 1 15-oz can PROGRESSO Fave
- 1 8-oz can PROGRESSO Peeled Tomatoes
- 3 Tbsp PROGRESSO Olive Oil
- 1 small onion, chopped
- ½ cup celery, chopped fine
- Salt and pepper

Brown 1 small chopped onion in PROGRESSO Olive Oil. Add finely chopped celery and one 8-oz can PROGRESSO Peeled Tomatoes. Simmer for 20 minutes. Add 1 can drained PROGRESSO Fave and simmer 10 minutes longer. Season to

taste. Serve hot. (This may be added to cut up spaghetti that has been cooked and drained.)
COURTESY PROGRESSO QUALITY FOODS.

Heinz Creole Sauce

1 large onion, thinly sliced
¼ cup chopped green pepper
2 Tbsp butter or margarine
½ cup HEINZ Tomato Ketchup
½ cup water
1 Tbsp HEINZ Worcestershire Sauce
½ tsp salt
Dash pepper

In saucepan, sauté onion and green pepper in butter until tender. Stir in ketchup, water, Worcestershire sauce, salt, and pepper. Simmer, uncovered, 10 minutes, stirring occasionally. Makes 1½ cups sauce. Serve over baked, broiled or fried fish, omelets, or other meat or chicken dishes.
COURTESY OF HEINZ U.S.A., DIVISION OF H.J. HEINZ COMPANY.

DANNON® YOGURT

Dannon Yogurt–Mustard–Horseradish Dip or Dressing

2 cups DANNON Plain Yogurt
1 Tbsp mustard
1 Tbsp horseradish
Salt to taste

Mix all ingredients until blended. Use as a dip for vegetables or as a spread with cold meats.
COURTESY THE DANNON COMPANY.

California Dried Fig Golden State Chutney

- 2 cups chopped CALIFORNIA Dried Figs
- 1 apple, peeled and diced
- 1 lemon, sliced paper thin
- ½ cup brown sugar
- ½ cup molasses
- ½ cup vinegar
- ½ tsp ground cloves
- ½ tsp ground ginger
- ½ tsp ground cinnamon

In large saucepan, combine dried figs and apple. Add remaining ingredients. Bring to a boil; simmer, uncovered, 30 minutes. Makes about 4 cups. Serve as an accompaniment to pork, lamb, or chicken.

COURTESY CALIFORNIA DRIED FIG ADVISORY BOARD.

Dole® Yogurt Relish Dressing

- ¼ cup finely diced celery
- ¼ cup finely diced carrot
- ¼ cup finely diced zucchini
- 1 Tbsp finely diced radish
- 1 Tbsp thinly sliced green onion
- ½ cup plain low-fat yogurt
- ¼ tsp salt
- 1 medium DOLE® Banana

Combine vegetables, yogurt, and salt; mix well. Dice DOLE® Banana to make ½ cup. Fold into other ingredients. Serve with broiled or poached fish. Makes 1⅓ cups relish.

COURTESY OF CASTLE & COOKE FOODS (DOLE®).

Gerber Dutch Apple–Cranberry Relish

- 1–lb bag cranberries
- 1 jar (7¾ oz) GERBER Junior Dutch Apple Dessert
- 1 cup sugar
- 1 cup chopped walnuts
- 2 Tbsp orange peel

Grind cranberries in food grinder or chop at low speed in blender. Add remaining ingredients and mix well. Yield: 4 cups.

COURTESY GERBER PRODUCTS COMPANY.

Libby's Pantry Peach Relish

Libby's
Libby's
Libby's

1 can (16 oz) LIBBY'S CHUNKY Peaches
Water
¼ cup raisins
1 cinnamon stick, broken
¼ tsp whole cloves or allspice
1 Tbsp cornstarch
2 tsp lemon juice
¼ cup slivered almonds

Drain LIBBY'S CHUNKY Peaches, reserving syrup. Add enough water to syrup to equal 1½ cups. In medium saucepan, combine syrup-water mixture, raisins, cinnamon, and cloves; simmer 10 minutes. Stir in cornstarch, blended with ¼ cup additional water and lemon juice, and heat until sauce is thickened. If desired, remove spices; stir in peaches and almonds. Spoon into covered container; chill. (Relish may be served warm.) Yields 2½ cups. *Variation*: For spicy walnut relish, increase whole cloves to ½ tsp and substitute chopped walnuts for almonds.

COURTESY, LIBBY'S.

MCP Ripe Tomato Preserves

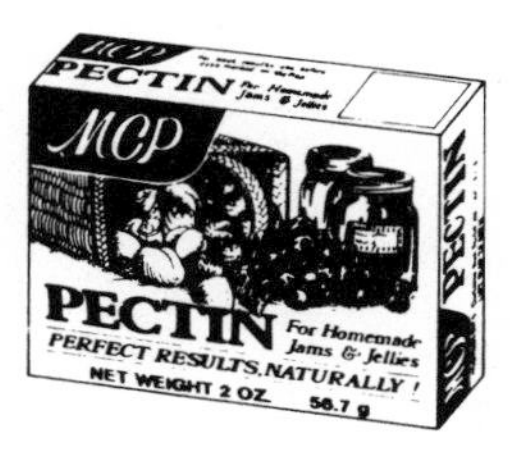

2¼ cups ground ripe tomatoes
4 Tbsp lemon juice
¼ cup boiling water
3½ level cups sugar
⅛ tsp salt
1 pkg MCP Pectin
Grated rind of 1 lemon

Wash tomatoes, pour boiling water over and slip off skins. Cut out stems and hard cores, put through grinder. Measure the pulp, lemon juice and ¼ cup boiling water, salt, and grated rind of lemon into a large kettle; add MPC Pectin, bring to a boil. Now add sugar and bring back to a full rolling boil. Boil 4 minutes, skim and pour into sterilized jars. This makes a firm preserve the consistency of jelly.

COURTESY MCP FOODS, INC.

Beverages

Whether it is coffee, tea, or something stronger, nothing expresses hospitality as easily and graciously as beverages. Frosty iced tea makes a perfect welcome in the summer; steaming cocoa warms guests throughout the winter; refreshing punches bring life to any party; mellow cappuccino rounds out elegant dinners.

Even more than most foods, beverages seem to enjoy fads in society. One year it may be chic to drink martinis, another year everyone may ask for bottled water. Yet some drinks never seem to go out of fashion. In this chapter, you will find perennial favorites, such as fresh lemonade and homemade egg nog, as well as more recent innovations, such as low calorie shakes and blender fruit drinks.

Most of the following recipes can be adapted to quantities suitable for serving the crowd at your next party. Delicious party punches may range from discreet lemonade to fire on ice, but all should be made with special care. For example, if your tap-water quality is uncertain, you may want to invest in bottled water to dilute the ingredients or to make the ice cubes.

Most punches improve by ripening, so mix your ingredients in advance and allow time for them to blend before the party. Also, be sure to prepare more punch than you think you will need. It is always better to have leftovers than it is to run out of punch in the middle of the party. Besides, haphazardly mixing refills during the party can be disastrous—especially if you are serving an alcoholic punch.

Before the guests arrive, garnish the punch with the freshest, most attractive fruits you can find. Then you will be prepared to greet your friends with a welcome drink.

Hershey's Favorite Hot Cocoa

¼ cup plus 1 Tbsp HERSHEY'S Cocoa
½ cup sugar
Dash salt
⅓ cup hot water
1 qt milk
¾ tsp vanilla

Combine dry ingredients in saucepan; blend in water. Bring to boil over medium heat, stirring constantly; boil and stir 2 minutes. Add milk; stir and heat. *Do not boil.* Remove from heat; add vanilla. Beat with rotary beater until foamy. Yield: about 1 qt. *Single serving:* Use 1 Tbsp HERSHEY'S Cocoa, 2 Tbsp sugar, dash salt, and 1 Tbsp water; boil and stir 1 minute. Add 1 cup milk and ⅛ tsp vanilla.
THIS RECIPE HAS BEEN DEVELOPED, TESTED AND APPROVED BY HERSHEY FOODS CORPORATION'S TEST KITCHEN.

Medaglia d'Oro Modern Cappuccino

2 coffee measures (4 Tbsp) MEDAGLIA D'ORO Ground Espresso Coffee
1½ cups water
1½ cups milk
¼ cup heavy cream, whipped (optional)
Sugar (optional)
Nutmeg
Cinnamon or cinnamon stick

Use ground espresso coffee and water to prepare hot espresso, utilizing a macchinetta or regular coffee maker. Just before espresso is ready to serve, heat milk to just below simmering point. Pour in hot espresso gradually while beating at high speed with portable mixer. Continue beating until froth forms. Pour into 4 cups. If whipped cream topping is used, add ¼ whipped cream to each cup and stir gently, to begin blending. Add sugar to taste, if desired. Sprinkle with nutmeg and/or cinnamon or place a cinnamon stick stirrer in each cup. Makes 4 servings.

Caffé Chocolaccino

Top the whipped cream with shaved semisweet chocolate.
COURTESY MEDAGLIA D'ORO, S.A. SCHONBRUNN & CO., INC.

Faygo Low-Calorie Cola Coffee Shake

1 qt (32 oz) diet FAYGO Cola
3 diet FAYGO Cola ice cubes
⅓ cup instant nonfat dry milk powder
½ tsp instant coffee powder
1 tsp vanilla
2 tsp artificial sweetener

Fill ice cube tray with diet FAYGO Cola and freeze solid. Place ¾ cup chilled cola in blender. Add 3 frozen cola cubes, nonfat dry milk, coffee powder, vanilla, and sweetener. Blend at high speed about 1½ minutes or until mixture thickens. Pour over additional cola cubes in tall glass and serve immediately. Serves 1.

THIS RECIPE BY MRS. MARGARETHA STRAMECKI OF RIVER ROUGE, MICHIGAN IS REPRINTED COURTESY OF FAYGO BEVERAGES, INC.

Minute Maid®

Old-Fashioned Lemonade

1 bottle (7½ oz) MINUTE MAID® 100% Pure Lemon Juice
1 cup sugar
6 cups water
Ice

Mix MINUTE MAID® 100% Pure Lemon Juice, sugar, and water in a ½-gallon glass or plastic container until sugar is dissolved; then add ice to fill.

MINUTE MAID IS A REGISTERED TRADEMARK OF THE COCA-COLA COMPANY. COURTESY THE COCA-COLA COMPANY FOODS DIVISION.

Lipton®

Lipton Cape Cod Cooler

3 cups boiling water
3 LIPTON Flo-Thru Tea Bags
⅓ cup sugar
1 cup cranberry juice cocktail
1 Tbsp lemon juice

In teapot, pour water over tea bags; brew 3–5 minutes. Remove tea bags; stir in sugar and cool. Pour into pitcher; stir in cranberry juice cocktail and lemon juice. Serve over ice in tall glasses. Makes 4–6 servings.

COURTESY OF THE LIPTON KITCHENS.

Celestial Seasonings® Lemon Mist Iced Herb Tea Recipe

1 part CELESTIAL SEASONINGS® Lemon Mist Tea (Medium Brew)
1 part black Ceylon tea (medium brew) or Darjeeling tea
Honey to taste (optional)

First measure 1½ to 1¾ tsp for each 8-oz glass. Pour fresh boiling water over the herbs and let them steep 3–6 minutes. The longer it steeps, the stronger it gets, and remember it's going to be iced, so make your tea stronger than usual. Strain into an iced tea pitcher and add honey while the tea is hot. Add the other ingredients and set aside to cool. Pour over ice and serve with a sprig of fresh mint.

Dole® Breakfast-in-a-Glass

1 medium DOLE® Banana
1 large egg
⅓ cup water
1½ Tbsp frozen orange juice concentrate
1 tsp wheat germ
1 tsp honey
Dash salt

Slice banana into blender jar. Add all remaining ingredients and blend at high speed 1 minute. Makes 1⅓ cups.

COURTESY OF CASTLE & COOKE FOODS (DOLE®).

Faygo Berry Delite

1 cup chilled diet FAYGO Black Raspberry
5 cracked ice cubes
1 tsp vanilla extract
1 cup frozen strawberries
⅓ cup nonfat dry milk powder
2 tsp artificial sweetener

In blender jar, place diet FAYGO Black Raspberry, ice cubes, vanilla extract, strawberries, dry milk powder, and sweetener. Stir mixture with a spoon, then blend slowly to mix well. Blender may be stopped from time to time to free mixture with spoon. Pour into tall glass and serve with spoon. Thin with more diet FAYGO if desired. Serves 1.

THIS RECIPE BY CAROL RYNER OF ANN ARBOR, MICHIGAN IS REPRINTED COURTESY OF FAYGO BEVERAGES, INC.

Crush® Tropics Fizz

4 scoops vanilla ice cream (about ½ pint)
¼ cup drained crushed pineapple
¼ cup papaya nectar
1 bottle (10 oz) chilled Orange CRUSH®
Flaked coconut (optional)
Orange slices (optional)
Fresh mint (optional)

Combine 1 scoop vanilla ice cream, 2 Tbsp crushed pineapple and 2 Tbsp papaya nectar in bottoms of 2 tall (10–12 oz) soda glasses; mix well. Fill glasses with Orange CRUSH®. Top sodas with a scoop of vanilla ice cream and sprinkle with coconut. Garnish with pineapple chunks, orange slices on pick, and fresh mint.

THIS RECIPE HAS BEEN PROVIDED AND IS PUBLISHED WITH PERMISSION OF CRUSH INTERNATIONAL INC., EVANSTON, ILLINOIS, MANUFACTURER OF THE FAMOUS CRUSH® SOFT DRINK PRODUCTS. ORANGE CRUSH IS A REGISTERED TRADEMARK OF CRUSH INTERNATIONAL INC., EVANSTON, IL 60202.

Friendship Strawberry-Banana Yogurt Cooler

½ cup FRIENDSHIP Plain Yogurt
½ cup skim milk
½ cup fresh strawberries
½ banana
1 raw egg (optional)
1 Tbsp sugar (optional)

Mix ingredients together in blender and blend for 30 seconds.

RECIPE COURTESY OF FRIENDSHIP FOODS' HOME ECONOMIST, HELEN SCHWARTZ.

Canada Dry Banana Cream

2 cups whole milk, chilled
1 cup mashed bananas
4 ice cubes
¼ to ½ tsp leaf mint, crumbled
7 oz CANADA DRY Club Soda

Mix milk, banana, ice cubes, and mint in electric blender for 30 seconds at medium speed. Pour in CANADA DRY Club Soda just before serving. Garnish with banana slices or leaf mint. for *lime cream,* substitute ¾ cup freshly squeezed lime juice for the bananas and ¼ cup honey for the leaf mint. For *tomato cream,* substitute 1 cup tomato juice, chilled, for the bananas and 2 oz lemon juice for the mint. Salt to taste.

COURTESY OF CANADA DRY CORPORATION.

Welch's Purple Cow

2 scoops vanilla ice cream
Chilled WELCH'S Grape Juice

In a 12-oz glass, add ice cream and fill with WELCH'S Grape Juice.

COURTESY WELCH FOODS INC.

DANNON® YOGURT

Dannon Yogurt Nog

1 cup DANNON Vanilla Yogurt
1 egg
2 Tbsp honey
Nutmeg or cinnamon to taste

Put yogurt, egg, and honey in a blender. Blend at high speed until frothy. Pour into a tall glass and sprinkle with nutmeg or cinnamon to taste. Serve immediately. Makes 1 serving.

COURTESY THE DANNON COMPANY.

Land O'Lakes Hot Buttered Tomato Juice

1 46-oz can tomato juice (6 cups)
1½ tsp Worcestershire sauce
½ tsp salt
½ tsp oregano leaves
¼ cup LAND O LAKES® Sweet Cream Butter

In 3-qt saucepan, combine all ingredients. Cook over medium heat, stirring occasionally, until heated through, about 10–15 minutes. Serve piping hot. Tip: Garnish with celery sticks, or chunks of cheese pierced with long pretzel sticks. Yield: eight 6-oz servings.

COURTESY OF THE LAND O'LAKES KITCHENS, MINNEAPOLIS, MN.

Welch's White Grape Juice Punch

- 2 *bottles (24 fluid oz each) WELCH'S White Grape Juice, chilled*
- 1 *qt ginger ale, chilled*
- 1 *ring ice mold (made with WELCH'S White Grape Juice and cubed fruit)*

When ready to serve the punch, empty white grape juice and ginger ale into cold punch bowl. Carefully unmold ice ring and add to punch. Makes about twenty-six 3-oz servings. Keep additional chilled white grape juice ready to add to the punch.

COURTESY WELCH FOODS INC.

PET®

Pet Creamy Eggnog

- 6 *eggs*
- ⅔ *cup sugar*
- ¼ *tsp salt*
- 2 *tall cans (13 fluid oz each) PET Evaporated Milk*
- 2 *cups heavy cream*
- 4 *Tbsp vanilla*
- 2 *to 3 Tbsp rum flavoring or ½ cup rum*
- *Nutmeg or cinnamon*

Beat eggs, sugar, and salt in 3-qt mixing bowl. Mix in evaporated milk, cream, vanilla, and rum. Chill. Pour into punch bowl. Sprinkle with nutmeg or cinnamon. Makes 2 qt.

PET, AN IC INDUSTRIES COMPANY, HOME ECONOMICS DEPT., P.O. BOX 392, ST. LOUIS, MO 63166.

Dole® Banana Frappe Punch

- 1 *cup water*
- ½ *cup sugar*
- 2 *medium ripe DOLE® Bananas*
- 2 *cans (6 oz each) DOLE® Unsweetened Pineapple Juice*
- ½ *cup orange juice*
- 1½ *Tbsp lemon juice*
- 1 *can (12 oz) lemon-lime soda, chilled*

Stir water and sugar together in small saucepan over low heat until sugar dissolves. Remove from heat. Mash DOLE® Bananas to make 1 cup. Add bananas, DOLE® Pineapple Juice, and orange and lemon juices; mix well. Turn into a 9 X 5 X 2¾-inch loaf pan and place in freezer. Freeze about 3 hours, or until icy. Remove from freezer, stir well, and blend in soda. Serve at once. Makes 1½ generous qt.

COURTESY OF CASTLE & COOKE FOODS (DOLE®).

Crush® Bubbling Fruit Cocktail

- ⅔ cup cold water
- ⅔ cup crystal sugar
- ⅔ cup lemon juice
- ⅔ cup Orange CRUSH®
- 2 Tbsp lemon juice
- 2 egg whites
- 4 cups crushed ice, fine

Mix cold water and crystal sugar with fruit juices, egg whites, and crushed ice. Place in a cocktail shaker or a tightly closed jar and shake until mixture becomes light and bubbly. Yield: 8 servings.

THIS RECIPE HAS BEEN PROVIDED AND IS PUBLISHED WITH PERMISSION OF CRUSH INTERNATIONAL INC., EVANSTON, ILLINOIS, MANUFACTURERER OF THE FAMOUS CRUSH® SOFT DRINK PRODUCTS. ORANGE CRUSH IS A REGISTERED TRADEMARK OF CRUSH INTERNATIONAL INC., EVANSTON, IL 60202.

Gallo Rosé Punch

- 1 gallon GALLO Vin Rosé
- 1 16-oz pkg frozen strawberries in syrup, thawed but cold
- 2 cups 7-Up
- Fresh strawberries (optional)

Chill wine. Just before serving, add strawberries and 7-Up; stir gently. Serve over ice. If desired, a garnish of fresh strawberries may be used.

COURTESY E. & J. GALLO WINERY.

Christian Brothers Glögg

- 3 bottles CHRISTIAN BROTHERS Burgundy
- 1 cup raisins
- ½ cup CHRISTIAN BROTHERS Sweet Vermouth
- 6 whole cardamom pods, crushed slightly
- 5 whole cloves
- 2 sticks cinnamon
- Peel from 1 orange
- 1 cup sugar
- 1 cup whole blanched almonds

In saucepan, mix 1 bottle wine, raisins, and vermouth. Place cardamom, cloves, and cinnamon in cheesecloth bag; add to wine. Simmer, covered, 15 minutes; remove spices. Stir in remaining wine, orange peel, and sugar; bring to boil, stirring

to dissolve sugar. Add almonds. Serve hot with spoons to scoop up raisins and almonds. Yield: twelve 8-oz servings.
FROM THE CHRISTIAN BROTHERS OF NAPA VALLEY, CALIFORNIA.

Ocean Spray's Cranapple® Snowblower Recipe

1 qt (32 oz) CRANAPPLE® Cranberry Apple Drink
2 Tbsp lemon juice
¼ tsp ground cloves
⅓ cup rum (optional)
6 slices lemon

In a large saucepan, mix together CRANAPPLE® Cranberry Apple Drink, lemon juice, and cloves. Heat and simmer for 10 minutes. Stir in rum. Serve in mugs with lemon slices. Makes 6 servings.
COURTESY OCEAN SPRAY CRANBERRIES, INC.

Desserts

It happens all the time. Shopping with a particular dessert recipe in mind, you pick up a container of cocoa, a bag of nuts, or a box of sugar. When you look at the package, though, you notice that the manufacturer's product recipe looks even more appealing than your cookbook's recipe. You try the new recipe once. It's so good that you make it again—and again. After awhile, you wouldn't think of making the dessert any other way.

When planning the dessert for your next meal, remember that tempting desserts don't have to be too rich to eat or too time consuming to fix. In this chapter, there are luscious cakes to savor on special occasions, but there are also light fruit desserts to enjoy any day of the week. There are irresistible cookies to serve as snacks, as well as satisfying puddings to round out light meals. To make these recipes even more attractive, many of the following desserts can be prepared quickly and easily with the help of mixes, packaged puddings and gelatins, ready-made crusts, and other conveniences.

Because there are so many delicious recipes to choose from, the desserts are divided into four sections:

Pies: Pies are always special, but they don't have to be a lot of trouble. This section offers ideas for pies and pastries that can be "cooked" by baking, refrigerating, or even freezing.

Cakes: Elegant cheese cakes, easy snack cakes, special birthday cakes, holiday fruit cakes—there are cake and frosting recipes for every occasion, but with such good recipes you won't want to wait for a special occasion.

Custards and Other Desserts: Puddings and custards have always been after-dinner favorites, but there are also other special desserts, such as homemade ice cream, chocolate fondue, and baked Alaska, that make easy but impressive finales for your menu.

Cookies and Candies: Cookies and candies are ideal for gift giving, but these recipes are so delicious you may want to keep the results all to yourself. Some of America's all-time favorites are included in this section along with some new recipes that are bound to become your future favorites.

Pies and Pastries

Amazing Coconut Pie

- 2 cups milk
- ¾ cup sugar
- ½ cup biscuit mix
- 4 eggs
- ¼ cup butter or margarine
- 1½ tsp vanilla
- 1⅓ cups BAKER'S® ANGEL FLAKE® Coconut

Combine milk, sugar, biscuit mix, eggs, butter, and vanilla in electric blender container. Cover and blend at low speed for 3 minutes. Pour into greased 9-inch pie pan. Let stand about 5 minutes; then sprinkle with coconut. Bake at 350°F for 40 minutes. Serve warm or cool.

REPRODUCED COURTESY OF GENERAL FOODS CORP., OWNER OF THE REGISTERED TRADEMARKS BAKER'S AND ANGEL FLAKE.

Karo Pecan Pie

- 3 eggs
- 1 cup KARO Light or Dark Corn Syrup
- 1 cup sugar
- 2 Tbsp corn oil margarine, melted
- 1 tsp vanilla
- ⅛ tsp salt
- 1 cup pecans
- 1 unbaked (9-inch) pastry shell

In medium bowl with mixer at medium speed, beat eggs slightly. Beat in corn syrup, sugar, margarine, vanilla, and salt. Stir in pecans. Pour filling into pastry shell. Bake in 350°F oven 55–65 minutes or until knife inserted halfway between center and edge comes out clean. Cool. If desired, serve with whipped cream.

COURTESY KARO CORN SYRUP.

Mazola Corn Oil Pastry for a Single Crust Pie

- ⅓ cup MAZOLA Corn Oil
- 2 Tbsp skim milk
- 1¼ cups unsifted flour
- ½ tsp salt

In measuring cup, stir together corn oil and milk. In medium bowl, stir together flour and salt. Add corn oil mixture, stirring constantly with fork. With hands, form into ball. Roll out to

12-inch circle between 2 sheets of waxed paper. Peel off top paper. Turn into 9-inch pie plate, paper side up. Peel off paper; fit pastry loosely into pan. Roll sides to form edge; flute. If shell is to be baked before filling, prick thoroughly and bake in 450°F oven 10–12 minutes, or until golden brown. If shell and filling are to be used together, do not prick shell; bake pie according to filling used.

COURTESY MAZOLA CORN OIL.

Ocean Spray's Cranberry-Apple Pie Recipe

Pastry for 9-inch 2-crust pie
1¾ to 2 cups sugar
⅓ cup all-purpose flour
1 tsp apple pie spice
4 cups sliced pared tart apples
2 cups OCEAN SPRAY® Fresh or Frozen Cranberries
2 Tbsp butter or margarine

Preheat oven to 425°F. Prepare pastry. Stir together sugar, flour, and spice. In pastry-lined pie pan, alternate layers of apples, cranberries, and sugar mixture, beginning and ending with apples. Dot with butter. Cover with top crust. Cut slits in crust, and seal and flute edges. Bake 40–50 minutes. Cool.

COURTESY OCEAN SPRAY CRANBERRIES, INC.

Ritz Mock Apple Pie

Pastry for 2-crust 9-inch pie
36 RITZ Crackers
2 cups water
2 cups sugar
2 tsp cream of tartar
2 Tbsp lemon juice
Grated rind of 1 lemon
Butter or margarine
Cinnamon

Roll out bottom crust of pastry and fit into 9-inch pie plate. Break RITZ Crackers coarsely into pastry-lined plate. Combine water, sugar and cream of tartar in saucepan; boil gently for 15 minutes. Add lemon juice and rind; cool. Pour syrup over crackers; dot generously with butter or margarine and sprinkle with cinnamon. Cover with top crust; trim and flute edges together; cut slits in top crust to let steam escape. Bake in a preheated hot oven (425°F) 30–35 minutes, until crust is crisp and golden. Serve warm, with a garnish of cheese apples if desired. (Cheese apples: roll small balls of cheese in paprika for a rosy glow and insert a whole clove in each for the stem.)

COURTESY NABISCO, INC.

MUSSELMAN'S®

Musselman's Cherry Pie

- 2 *PET-RITZ "Regular" Pie Crust Shells*
- 2 *cans (16 oz each) MUSSELMAN'S Red Tart Pitted Cherries*
- 1 *cup sugar*
- 3 *Tbsp cornstarch*
- 1 *Tbsp butter or margarine*
- *Few drops red food coloring, if desired*

Invert 1 pie shell onto waxed paper. Thaw until flattened. Meanwhile, drain cherries, reserving 1 cup liquid. Mix sugar and cornstarch in a small heavy saucepan. Gradually stir in reserved liquid until smooth. Cook and stir over medium heat until mixture bubbles. Cook 1 minute more until thick and clear. Remove from heat. Stir in butter, cherries, and food coloring. Pour into bottom crust. Cover with flattened top crust. Seal and crimp edge. Cut air vents in top crust. Bake at 425°F 40–45 minutes or until browned and bubbly. Cool. Makes 6–8 servings.

PET, AN IC INDUSTRIES COMPANY, HOME ECONOMICS DEPT., P.O. BOX 392, ST. LOUIS, MO 63166.

Mrs. Smith's® Peach Crumb Pie

- 1 *9- or 9⅝-inch MRS. SMITH'S® Pie Crust Shells*
- 2 *1-lb 5-oz cans peach pie filling*
- ½ *cup flaked coconut*
- ⅓ *cup flour*
- ⅓ *cup firmly packed brown sugar*
- ½ *tsp cinnamon*

- ⅓ *cup butter or margarine*
- ¾ *cup chopped salted nuts*

Preheat oven to 350°F. Thaw shell at room temperature for 20 minutes. Spread pie filling evenly in shell. Mix remaining ingredients with the fingers until well blended. Sprinkle evenly over pie. Bake 30–35 minutes. Cool thoroughly before serving.

COURTESY MRS. SMITH'S FROZEN FOODS CO.

Wilderness French Blueberry Pie

Crust

- 1¼ cups graham cracker crumbs
- ¼ cup sugar
- ¼ cup butter or margarine (melted)

Combine and press into 9-inch pie pan. Bake at 375°F 7–8 minutes. Cool.

Filling

- 1 cup dairy sour cream
- 1 pkg (3¾ oz) instant vanilla pudding
- 1 cup milk
- 1 tsp almond flavoring
- 1 can (21 oz) WILDERNESS Blueberry Fruit Filling
- Whipped cream

Beat sour cream, milk, pudding, and flavoring together until stiff. Pour into cooled graham cracker crust. Spread blueberry fruit filling over pudding mixture. Refrigerate a few hours. When ready to serve, garnish with whipped cream.

COURTESY OF WILDERNESS FOODS.

Argo Lemon Meringue Pie

- 1 cup sugar
- 3 Tbsp ARGO or KINGSFORD'S Corn Starch
- 1½ cups cold water
- 3 egg yolks, slightly beaten
- Grated rind of 1 lemon
- ¼ cup lemon juice
- 1 Tbsp corn oil margarine
- 1 baked (9-inch) pastry shell
- 3 egg whites
- ⅓ cup sugar

In 2-qt saucepan, stir together 1 cup sugar and corn starch. Gradually stir in water until smooth. Stir in egg yolks. Stirring constantly, bring to boil over medium heat and boil 1 minute. Remove from heat. Stir in lemon rind, lemon juice, and margarine. Cool. Turn into pastry shell. In small bowl with mixer at high speed, beat egg whites until foamy. Add ⅓ cup sugar, 1 Tbsp at a time, beating well after each addition. Continue beating until stiff peaks form. Spread some meringue around edge of filling, first touching crust all around; then fill in center.

Bake in 350°F oven 15–20 minutes or until lightly browned. Cool at room temperature away from drafts. Makes 6–8 servings.

COURTESY ARGO CORN STARCH.

Calavo Lime Meringue Pie

Filling

1½ cups sugar
7 Tbsp cornstarch
Dash salt
1½ cups water
3 beaten egg yolks
1 tsp grated lime peel
2 Tbsp butter or margarine
½ cup fresh CALAVO Lime Juice
Crushed vanilla wafer crust
Freshly grated CALAVO Coconut

In saucepan, combine first 4 ingredients and stir. Bring to a boil over medium heat, stirring constantly, until thick (about 5 minutes). Remove from heat. Stir small amount of hot mixture into egg yolks. Return this to remaining mixture in pan. Bring to a boil, stirring constantly, for 1 minute. Remove from heat. Add lime peel, butter, and fresh lime juice. Cool. Sprinkle grated coconut on pie crust. Pour filling on top of coconut.

Meringue

3 egg whites
1 tsp fresh CALAVO Lime Juice
6 Tbsp sugar

Beat egg whites with lime juice until soft peaks form. Gradually add sugar, beating until stiff. Spread meringue over filling. Bake at 350°F 12–15 minutes or until meringue is golden brown. Cool thoroughly.

COURTESY CALAVO GROWERS OF CALIFORNIA.

Libby's Famous Pumpkin Pie

2 eggs, slightly beaten
1 can (16 oz) LIBBY'S Solid Pack Pumpkin
¾ cup sugar
½ tsp salt
1 tsp cinnamon
½ tsp ginger
¼ tsp cloves
1⅔ cups (13 fluid oz) evaporated milk or light cream
1 9-inch unbaked pie shell with high fluted edge
Crunchy Pecan Topping (below)

Preheat oven to 425°F. Mix filling ingredients in order given. Pour into pie shell. Bake at 425°F for 15 minutes. Reduce heat to 350°F and continue baking for 45 minutes or until knife inserted near center of pie filling comes out clean. Cool completely on wire rack. Before serving, add Crunchy Pecan Topping.

Topping

1 cup coarsely chopped pecans
⅔ cup firmly packed light brown sugar
3 Tbsp butter or margarine, melted
Whipped cream or dessert topping and pecan halves, for garnish

Mix pecans and brown sugar in a small bowl. Drizzle with butter; stir until mixture is uniformly moistened. Sprinkle mixture over cooled pumpkin pie. Broil about 5 inches from heat 1–2 minutes or until topping is bubbly. Serve while warm. Or let cool, then garnish with whipped cream or topping and extra pecan halves, if desired.

COURTESY, LIBBY'S.

PET®

Pet Sweet Potato Pie

3 to 4 large sweet potatoes (about 2¼ lb)
½ cup butter, softened
2 cups sugar
4 eggs
½ tsp nutmeg
½ tsp salt
1 tall can (13 fluid oz) PET Evaporated Milk
3 PET-RITZ Regular Pie Crust Shells or 2 PET-RITZ "Deep Dish" Pie Crust Shells

Cook sweet potatoes in boiling water until fork easily pierces potatoes. Remove from water. Cool slightly. Remove skins. Place hot cooked and peeled potatoes in large mixing bowl. Beat with electric mixer until smooth. There should be about 3½ cups of mashed sweet potatoes. Stir in butter and sugar. Beat in eggs, one at a time. Mix in nutmeg, salt, and evaporated milk. Pour into unbaked pie crusts. Place pans on cookie sheet. Bake in 425°F oven for 20 minutes. Lower heat to 325°F. Bake 30–45 minutes longer or until knife inserted near center comes out clean. Cool before serving. Makes two or three 9-inch pies.

PET, AN IC INDUSTRIES COMPANY, HOME ECONOMICS DEPT., P.O. BOX 392, ST. LOUIS, MO 63166.

Nestlé

Nestlé Chocolate Mousse Pie

1 11½-oz pkg (2 cups) NESTLÉ Milk Chocolate Morsels
¼ lb (16 large) marshmallows
½ cup milk
⅛ tsp salt
1 cup heavy cream
1 8-inch prepared graham cracker crumb crust

Combine over hot (not boiling) water, NESTLÉ Milk Chocolate Morsels, marshmallows, milk, and salt; heat until morsels and marshmallows melt and mixture is well blended. Cool thoroughly in refrigerator (about 1–1½ hours). In small bowl, beat heavy cream until stiff peaks form. Fold into cooled chocolate mixture. Pour into prepared graham cracker crumb crust. Chill in refrigerator at least 2 hours. Makes one 8-inch pie.

COURTESY THE NESTLE COMPANY, INC.

Pastel Party Pie

- *1 pkg (3 oz) JELL-O® Brand Gelatin, any flavor*
- *1¼ cups boiling water*
- *1 pint ice cream, any flavor*
- *1 baked 9-inch pie shell or graham cracker crumb crust, cooled**

*Or use unbaked 9-inch crumb crust or commercial crumb crust.

Dissolve gelatin in boiling water. Add ice cream by spoonfuls, stirring until melted and smooth. Chill until slightly thickened. Pour into pie shell. Chill until firm, about 2 hours. Garnish with prepared or thawed frozen whipped topping, if desired.

Suggested Combinations

Strawberry gelatin with vanilla, strawberry, or pineapple ice cream (or vanilla milk ice); lemon gelatin with vanilla or pineapple ice cream; orange gelatin with vanilla ice cream; raspberry gelatin with vanilla ice cream; lime gelatin with vanilla or pineapple ice cream; blackberry gelatin with vanilla ice cream; peach gelatin with vanilla ice cream.

REPRODUCED COURTESY OF GENERAL FOODS CORP., OWNER OF THE REGISTERED TRADEMARK JELL-O.

Colombo Yogurt Refrigerator Pie

- *1 9-inch baked graham cracker pie crust*
- *2 pkg (8 oz each) regular or imitation cream cheese, at room temperature*
- *⅓ cup honey*
- *¼ tsp salt*
- *1 tsp vanilla*
- *1 cup plain COLOMBO Whole-Milk Yogurt*
- *2 cups sweetened, sliced fresh or frozen strawberries*

In a large bowl, beat together cream cheese, honey, salt, and vanilla until smooth. Stir in yogurt. Pour into graham cracker crust and refrigerate overnight. Spoon strawberries over each serving. Yield: one 9-inch pie.

PERMISSION TO REPRODUCE GRANTED BY AMERICA'S ORIGINAL YOGURT COMPANY, COLOMBO, INC.

Heath Bits 'O Brickle Ice Cream Pie & Sauce*

Pie

- 1 *prepared 9-inch graham cracker pie shell*
- ½ *gal. vanilla ice cream, softened to spoon easily but not melted*
- ½ *bag BITS 'O BRICKLE*

Spoon ½ softened ice cream into prepared pie shell. Sprinkle ½ bag BITS 'O BRICKLE on top. Heap with remaining ice cream. Freeze.

Sauce

- 1½ *cups sugar*
- 1 *cup evaporated milk*
- *Remaining ½ bag BITS 'O BRICKLE*
- ¼ *cup butter or margarine*
- ¼ *cup light corn syrup*
- *Dash salt*

Combine sugar, milk, butter or margarine, syrup, and salt. Bring to boil over low heat; boil 1 minute. Remove from heat and stir in remaining BITS 'O BRICKLE. Cool, stirring occasionally. Chill. To serve, stir sauce well, then spoon over individual pie wedges. Remaining sauce may be refrigerated in a tightly covered container for use as a topping. Serves 8.

*May also be made with 6-oz chopped Heath Bars.
COURTESY L.S. HEATH & SONS, INC.

Hiram Walker Grasshopper Pie

- 2 *Tbsp butter*
- 14 *crushed Hydrox Cookies*
- 24 *marshmallows*
- ½ *cup milk*
- 4 *Tbsp HIRAM WALKER Creme de Menthe Green*
- 2 *Tbsp HIRAM WALKER Creme de Cacao White*
- 1 *cup whipped cream*

Melt butter, stir in crushed Hydrox cookies, use for crust (press into 8-inch pie plate). Melt marshmallows in milk. Cool. Stir in HIRAM WALKER liqueurs. Fold in whipped cream, pour into pie shell. Freeze, serve frozen; save few crumbs of crust mixture to sprinkle over top.

COURTESY HIRAM WALKER INCORPORATED.

Rold Gold® Brand Pretzels Chocolate Pie with Pretzel Crust

Crust

1 13-oz pkg ROLD GOLD® Brand Pretzels
3 Tbsp sugar
½ cup butter or margarine, melted

Crush pretzels very fine in blender or between waxed paper. Add sugar and butter or margarine. Mix thoroughly. Press ½ mixture in 9-inch pie plate. Bake at 350°F for 8 minutes. Cool. Pour in Chocolate Filling (recipe follows) and top with remaining pretzel mixture. Chill.

Filling

⅔ cup sugar
4 Tbsp cornstarch
2½ cups milk
3 3-oz squares unsweetened chocolate, cut in small pieces
3 egg yolks, slightly beaten
1 tsp vanilla extract

Combine sugar, cornstarch, milk, and chocolate in top of double boiler. Cook over boiling water until thickened, stirring constantly. Cover and cook 15 minutes. Stir part of hot chocolate mixture into egg yolks. Add to chocolate mixture. Mix thoroughly. Cool. Add vanilla extract and mix thoroughly.

Zagnut Crunchy Pie

9-inch pastry shell, baked and cooled
⅔ cup packed brown sugar
2 tsp unflavored gelatin
Dash salt
1¾ cups milk
2 eggs, separated
2 Tbsp butter
1 tsp vanilla
2 Tbsp granulated sugar
3 ZAGNUT Bars, coarsely chopped (about 1½ oz each)
½ cup unsweetened whipped cream
Sweetened whipped cream
Crushed ZAGNUT Bar

Combine brown sugar, gelatin, and salt. Stir in milk and beaten egg yolks. Cook over medium heat, stirring constantly, until gelatin is dissolved and mixture coats a spoon. Add butter and vanilla. Chill until partially set. Beat egg whites to soft peaks; gradually beat in granulated sugar, beating until stiff peaks form. Fold into gelatin mixture. Fold in candy and unsweetened whipped cream. Turn into prepared pie shell. Chill until firm. Garnish with sweetened whipped cream and chopped or crushed ZAGNUT Bar.

COURTESY OF D.L. CLARK COMPANY, DIVISION OF BEATRICE FOODS.

Dole® Pineapple Daisy Pie

- *1 cup flour*
- *½ cup whole wheat flour*
- *1 tsp salt*
- *¾ tsp allspice*
- *1 can (20 oz) DOLE® Pineapple Slices, in syrup*
- *½ cup oil*
- *2 eggs, separated*
- *1 Tbsp tapioca*
- *1 pkg (8 oz) cream cheese, softened*
- *8 oz vanilla yogurt*
- *1 tsp vanilla*
- *½ cup coconut, toasted*
- *¼ tsp cream of tartar*

Mix together flours, salt, and ½ tsp allspice. Drain pineapple, reserving syrup. Add 2 Tbsp syrup and oil to dry ingredients and mix well. Press dough into 9-inch pie plate. Flute edges and prick with fork. Bake at 350°F 15–18 minutes. Mix remaining syrup with egg yolks and tapioca in saucepan. Cook over low heat, stirring constantly until thick. Let cool. Beat cream cheese until smooth. Add yogurt, vanilla, ¼ tsp allspice, and tapioca mixture. Stir in coconut. Beat egg whites and cream of tartar until stiff peaks form. Fold into filling. Arrange 8 pineapple slices around sides of baked crust so that slices cover edge of crust. Pour in filling. Chill at least 2 hours. Garnish center with 2 remaining pineapple slices. Makes 6–8 servings.

COURTESY OF CASTLE & COOKE FOODS (DOLE®).

Johnston's® Ice Cream Sundae Pie

- *1 JOHNSTON'S® Chocolate Flavored Ready-Crust® Pie Crust*
- *2 pints ice cream**
- *2 pkg (5-oz size) JOHNSTON'S® Hot Fudge Ready-Topping*
- *¼ cup chopped nuts*
- *Whipped cream or topping for garnish*
- *Maraschino cherries*

Soften 2 pints ice cream in the refrigerator. Spoon into a mixing bowl, stirring until the ice cream is just pliable. Spoon it into pie crust, cover with inverted plastic lid, and place in freezer until hard. Serve pie with separate dishes of JOHNSTON'S® Hot Fudge Topping (heated), nuts, whipped topping, and cherries. Cut ice cream pie into wedges. Then pass the separate dishes and let everyone make their own ice cream sundae pie.

*Ice cream variations: 2 pints of the same flavor such as peppermint, pistachio nut, or fruit flavors or chocolate. Or use 2 flavors such as chocolate with peppermint, mint-chocolate chip, fruit, or nut ice creams.
COURTESY JOHNSTON'S® READY-CRUST® COMPANY.

Dole® Jamaican Cream Pie

Filling

1 pkg (4¾ oz) vanilla pudding mix (not instant)
½ tsp unflavored gelatin
1¾ cups milk
3 Tbsp dark Jamaican rum
1 cup whipping cream
3 DOLE® Bananas
Brown Butter Rum Crust (below)

Prepare and chill Brown Butter Rum Crust. Turn pudding mix into a 1-qt saucepan and mix in gelatin. Gradually stir in milk, mixing until smooth. Cook over moderate heat, stirring constantly, until mixture comes to a full boil. Remove from heat and cool slightly, then stir in rum. Cool completely, stirring occasionally to prevent crust forming on top. When cold, beat cream stiff and fold into pudding. Peel and slice bananas to measure 2 cups. Turn about ⅓ cooked mixture into pie shell and cover with ½ bananas. Repeat layers and top with remaining pudding. Chill thoroughly before cutting. Makes 6–8 servings.

Brown Butter Rum Crust

1¾ cups finely crushed packaged shortbread cookies
½ cup powdered sugar
6 Tbsp butter
1½ Tbsp dark rum

Mix cookie crumbs with powdered sugar. Melt butter in a small saucepan and heat until very lightly browned. Remove from heat and cool slightly. Stir in rum. Pour over crumb mixture and mix thoroughly. Press over bottom and sides of a buttered 9-inch pie pan. Chill.

COURTESY OF CASTLE & COOKE FOODS (DOLE®).

Keebler Nesselrode Pie

- *2 cups fine KEEBLER Deluxe Grahams cracker crumbs*
- *¼ cup butter or margarine, melted*
- *1½ tsp unflavored gelatin (½ packet)*
- *1 pkg (3 oz) vanilla pudding and pie filling mix*
- *2 cups whipped topping*
- *1 cup chopped, drained maraschino cherries*
- *½ cup chopped nuts*
- *6 maraschino cherries, halved*

In medium mixing bowl, combine crumbs and butter. Stir with a fork to blend. Press in bottom and up sides of 9-inch pie pan. Combine gelatin with dry pudding mix; prepare pudding according to package directions. Cool to room temperature. Fold in whipped topping, chopped cherries, and nuts. Spoon filling into pie crust and chill until firm, 3–4 hours. Decorate top with cherry halves. Refrigerate until ready to serve. Yield: one 9-inch pie.

RECIPE COURTESY OF KEEBLER COMPANY.

Kellogg's®

Kellogg's® Cherry Breeze

- *⅓ cup regular margarine or butter*
- *¼ cup sugar*
- *1 cup KELLOGG'S® CORN FLAKE CRUMBS*
- *1 pkg (8 oz) cream cheese, softened*
- *1 can (14 oz) sweetened condensed milk (not evaporated milk)*
- *½ cup lemon juice*
- *1 tsp vanilla flavoring*
- *1 can (1 lb 5 oz) cherry pie filling, chilled*

Measure margarine and sugar into small saucepan. Cook over low heat, stirring constantly, until mixture bubbles. Remove from heat. Add crumbs; mix well. With back of spoon, press crumb mixture evenly and firmly around sides and in bottom of 9-inch pie pan to form crust. Chill. Place cream cheese in large mixing bowl; beat until smooth. Add condensed milk gradually, beating until thoroughly combined. Stir in lemon juice and vanilla. Spread in chilled crumb crust. Refrigerate 3–4 hours, or until firm. Just before serving, spread cherry pie filling over top of pie. Cut into wedges to serve. Yield: 8 servings.

Note: to cut and remove pieces easily, place hot wet towel under bottom and around sides of pie pan; allow to stand a few minutes before cutting.

COURTESY OF KELLOGG COMPANY.

Quaker® Tempting Apple Crisp

- 4 *cups peeled and sliced cooking apples*
- 1 *Tbsp lemon juice*
- ⅓ *cup sifted all-purpose flour*
- 1 *cup QUAKER® Oats (quick or old fashioned, uncooked)*
- ½ *cup firmly packed brown sugar*
- ½ *tsp salt*
- 1 *tsp cinnamon*
- ⅓ *cup butter or margarine, melted*

Place apples in shallow baking dish. Sprinkle with lemon juice. Combine dry ingredients; add melted butter, mixing until crumbly. Sprinkle crumb mixture over apples. Bake in preheated moderate oven (350°F) 30 minutes or until apples are tender. Makes 6 servings.

RECIPE REPRODUCED WITH THE PERMISSION OF THE QUAKER OATS COMPANY.

Duncan Hines Blueberry Fruit Crunch

- 1 *pkg DUNCAN HINES Blueberry Muffin Mix*
- ¼ *cup (½ stick) butter or margarine*
- 1 *can (1 lb 5 oz) fruit-pie filling (cherry, peach, pineapple, apple, or blueberry)*
- ½ *tsp cinnamon*
- ½ *tsp almond extract, if desired*
- ¼ *cup chopped nuts*
- *Ice cream or whipped cream, if desired*

Preheat oven to 350°F. In a medium saucepan, melt butter; set aside to cool slightly. Empty blueberries into strainer and rinse under cold running water. Set aside to drain. Pour fruit-pie filling into an ungreased 8- or 9-inch-square pan. Sprinkle cinnamon and almond extract, if desired, and drained blueberries evenly over pie filling. Add dry muffin mix and nuts to cooled, melted butter; combine with a spoon or fork until crumbly. Distribute evenly over fruit in pan. Bake at 350°F for 30–40 minutes, until golden brown. If desired, serve with ice cream or whipped cream. Makes 8–10 servings.

COURTESY OF THE PROCTER & GAMBLE COMPANY.

Stokely's Plum Kuchen

- ½ cup butter or margarine, softened
- 1 cup sugar
- 1¼ cups flour
- ½ tsp salt
- ½ tsp cinnamon
- ¼ tsp baking powder
- 1 can (1 lb 14 oz) STOKELY'S Finest® Purple Plums, drained and pitted
- 1 egg, slightly beaten
- 1 cup whipping cream

Cream butter and sugar. Sift together next 4 ingredients. Blend flour and butter mixtures together until crumbly. Reserving ⅓ cup, press remaining crumbs into bottom and up sides (about 1 inch) of an ungreased 8 X 8 X 2-inch pan. Arrange STOKELY'S Plums on crust; sprinkle with remaining crumbs. Bake at 375°F for 15 minutes. Blend egg and cream; pour over plums. Bake 20–25 minutes longer or until custard is set. Cool completely. Makes 9 servings.

COURTESY STOKELY-VAN CAMP, INC.

Comstock Cherry Crisp

- 1 can (21 oz) COMSTOCK Cherry Pie Filling
- ¼ cup sifted all-purpose flour
- 2 Tbsp butter or margarine
- ¼ cup uncooked quick cooking oats
- ¼ cup firmly packed light brown sugar
- ½ tsp cinnamon
- ⅛ tsp nutmeg
- Whipped cream (optional)

Pour pie filling into 8-inch-square baking pan. In small bowl, combine flour and butter. With pastry blender or 2 knives, scissor-fashion, cut in butter. Add oats, brown sugar, cinnamon, and nutmeg; mix well. Sprinkle over cherries. Bake at 350°F for 30 minutes or until hot and bubbly. If desired, serve topped with whipped cream. Makes six ½-cup servings.

COURTESY COMSTOCK FOODS (A DIVISION OF CURTICE-BURNS, INC.).

Bisquick® Strawberry Squares Supreme

2 cups BISQUICK® Baking Mix
2 Tbsp sugar
¼ cup margarine or butter
2 egg yolks
1 cup dairy sour cream
⅓ cup sugar
4 cups sweetened cut-up strawberries

Heat oven to 375°F. Mix baking mix and 2 Tbsp sugar. Cut in margarine with pastry blender until mixture resembles fine crumbs. Pat evenly in bottom of ungreased baking pan, 9 X 9 X 2 inches. Bake 10 minutes. Beat egg yolks, sour cream, and ⅓ cup sugar until blended; spread over hot layer. Bake 20 minutes longer. Cool; cut into squares and top with strawberries. Garnish with whipped cream if desired. Yield: 9 servings.

COURTESY BETTY CROCKER FOOD & NUTRITION CENTER, GENERAL MILLS, INC. REGISTERED ® TRADEMARK OF GENERAL MILLS, INC.

Peter Pan Margaret's Peanut Butter Tarts

Pastry

⅓ cup PETER PAN Peanut Butter, Creamy
2⅔ cups flour
½ tsp salt
½ cup sugar
1 cup (2 sticks) butter or margarine, softened
2 eggs, well beaten

Sift flour, salt, and sugar together. Cut in butter and peanut butter until mixture resembles coarse crumbs and ingredients are well mixed. Stir in beaten eggs. Blend well. Knead dough slightly and shape into a ball. (Dough will be soft.) Wrap in wax paper or plastic wrap and refrigerate 20 minutes. Preheat oven to 350°F. For each tart, place 1 rounded Tbsp of dough into ungreased miniature muffin cups. Press and shape to form a pastry shell. Spoon 1 Tbsp Peanut Butter Filling (recipe below) into each tart. Bake 24–26 minutes or until filling is golden brown. Cool 5 minutes before removing from muffin pans.

Filling

½ cup PETER PAN Peanut Butter, Creamy
½ cup granulated sugar
½ cup packed brown sugar
1 tsp flour
2 eggs
2 Tbsp milk
1 tsp vanilla
Semisweet chocolate pieces
Jelly or preserves

Combine all ingredients except chocolate pieces and jelly and mix well. In half of the pastry-lined cups, drop 5 semisweet

chocolate pieces. In remaining cups, spoon ½ tsp of your favorite jelly or preserves. Top with enough Peanut Butter Filling to fill almost to the top. Yield: 45–48 tarts.
COURTESY SWIFT & COMPANY.

Smucker's Maids of Honor Tarts

- *1¼ cups unsifted flour, stirred before measuring*
- *1 tsp baking powder*
- *⅛ tsp salt*
- *6 Tbsp butter or margarine*
- *3 Tbsp sugar*
- *1 egg*
- *⅔ cup SMUCKER'S Strawberry Preserves*
- *⅓ cup chopped walnuts or pecans*
- *2 tsp lemon juice*
- *¼ tsp ground mace*

In small bowl, thoroughly stir together flour, baking powder, and salt. In medium bowl, cream together butter and sugar; beat in egg. Add flour mixture and stir until blended. Form pastry into 24 small balls, using 2 level tsp for each. Place each ball in small muffin-pan cup (1¼ X ¾ inches). Press pastry with fingers to evenly cover bottoms and sides of cups. Mix together preserves, nuts, lemon juice, and mace. Spoon 2 tsp of mixture into each tart shell. Bake in preheated 425°F oven 12 minutes or until pastry is lightly browned. Cool in pans on rack 5 minutes; remove from pans and cool thoroughly on racks. Serve plain or topped with whipped cream. Makes about 24 tarts.
COURTESY THE J.M. SMUCKER COMPANY.

Pepperidge Farm Napoleons

- *1 sheet PEPPERIDGE FARM Frozen "Bake It Fresh" Puff Pastry*
- *1 pkg (4⅛ oz) instant chocolate pudding*
- *1 cup sour cream*
- *½ cup milk*
- *1 cup confectioners' sugar*
- *1 Tbsp milk (approx.)*
- *2 squares (1 oz each) semisweet chocolate melted with 1 tsp vegetable shortening*

Thaw folded pastry sheet 20 minutes. Unfold gently and roll on floured surface to 18 X 11 inches. Cut crosswise to make

6 rectangles, about 3 X 11 inches each. Prick each sheet thoroughly with a fork and bake on ungreased baking sheet in preheated 350°F oven 18–22 minutes. Cool. Prepare pudding according to pkg directions, substituting 1 cup sour cream and ½ cup milk for the 2 cups milk, and mixing with an electric mixer. Make icing by blending sugar and milk to a smooth consistency. Spread on top of 2 pastry sheets. To decorate, drizzle chocolate in thin straight lines one inch apart crosswise and lengthwise over frosting. Evenly spread half of the pudding on 2 of the remaining pastry sheets. Cover each with a second pastry sheet and spread with remaining pudding. Top with decorated pastry sheets and chill at least 30 minutes. To serve, cut each assembled pastry with a serrated knife into 6 to 12 equal portions. Makes about 12 servings.

COURTESY PEPPERIDGE FARM, INC.

Cakes and Frostings

Hershey's Black Magic Cake

1¾ cups unsifted all-purpose flour
2 cups sugar
¾ cup HERSHEY'S Cocoa
2 tsp baking soda
1 tsp baking powder
1 tsp salt
2 eggs
1 cup strong black coffee (or 2 tsp instant coffee plus 1 cup boiling water)
1 cup buttermilk or sour milk (to sour milk, use 1 Tbsp vinegar, plus milk to equal 1 cup)
½ cup vegetable oil
1 tsp vanilla

Grease and dust with flour, one 13 X 9 X 2-inch pan or two 9-inch layer pans. Combine flour, sugar, HERSHEY'S Cocoa, baking soda, baking powder, and salt in large mixer bowl. Add eggs, coffee, buttermilk, oil, and vanilla. Beat on medium speed for 2 minutes (batter will be thin). Pour batter into pans. Bake at 350°F for 35–40 minutes for oblong pan, 30–35 minutes for layer pans, or until cake tester inserted in center comes out clean. Cool 10 minutes; remove from pans. Cool completely. Frost with your favorite vanilla frosting.

THIS RECIPE HAS BEEN DEVELOPED, TESTED AND APPROVED BY HERSHEY FOODS CORPORATION'S TEST KITCHEN.

M&M/Mars Milky Way Cake

- *2 Tbsp vegetable shortening*
- *¾ cup finely chopped nuts*
- *12 snack-size MILKY WAY Bars*
- *1 cup buttermilk, plain yogurt, or sour cream*
- *1 cup butter or margarine*
- *1½ cups sugar*
- *½ tsp vanilla*
- *4 eggs*
- *2½ cups flour*
- *1 tsp salt*
- *¾ tsp soda*

Generously grease 12-cup Bundt pan or 10-inch tube pan with shortening; coat pan with nuts. In heavy saucepan over low heat, melt MILKY WAY Bars with ¼ cup buttermilk, stirring frequently until smooth. Beat together butter and sugar until light and fluffy; blend in vanilla. Add eggs, one at a time, mixing well after each addition. Add combined flour, salt, and soda alternately with remaining ¾ cup buttermilk, mixing just until dry ingredients are moistened. Blend in MILKY WAY Bar mixture; spoon into prepared pan. Bake at 350°F 55–60 minutes or until wooden pick inserted in center comes out clean. Cool 10 minutes; invert onto wire rack. Cool completely. Makes one 12-cup Bundt or 10-inch tube pan cake.

Variation

Omit nuts; lightly flour greased pan.

COURTESY M&M/MARS.

Hellmann's Chocolate Mayonnaise Cake

- *2 cups unsifted flour*
- *⅔ cup unsweetened cocoa*
- *1¼ tsp baking soda*
- *¼ tsp baking powder*
- *1⅔ cups sugar*
- *3 eggs*
- *1 tsp vanilla*
- *1 cup HELLMANN'S or BEST FOODS Real Mayonnaise*
- *1⅓ cups water*

Grease and flour bottoms of two 9 X 1½-inch round baking pans. In medium bowl, stir together flour, cocoa, baking soda, and baking powder; set aside. In large bowl with mixer at high speed, beat sugar, eggs, and vanilla, occasionally scraping bowl, 3 minutes or until light and fluffy. Reduce speed to low; beat in HELLMANN'S Real Mayonnaise. Add flour mixture, in 4 additions, alternately with water, beginning and ending with flour. Pour into prepared pans. Bake in 350°F oven 30–35 minutes or until cake tester inserted in center comes out clean. Cool in pans 10 minutes. Remove; cool on wire racks. Frost as desired. Garnish with sliced almonds. Makes two 9-inch layers.

To prepare with cake mix: Use any chocolate cake mix that has pudding in the mix. Follow the pkg directions, eliminating the shortening and amount of water called for and instead use 1 cup real mayonnaise (not salad dressing) and 1 cup water.

COURTESY HELLMANN'S REAL MAYONNAISE.

Gold Medal® Black Midnight Cake

2¼ cups GOLD MEDAL® All-Purpose Flour or SOFTASILK® Cake Flour (do not use self-rising flour in this recipe)
1⅔ cups sugar
1¼ tsp baking soda
1 tsp salt
¼ tsp baking powder
1¼ cups water
¾ cup shortening
2 eggs
1 tsp vanilla
⅔ cup cocoa
Fudge Frosting (below)

Heat oven to 350°F. Grease and flour baking pan, 13 X 9 X 2 inches, or 3 baking pans, 8 X 1½ inches, or 2 baking pans, 9 X 1½ inches. Beat all ingredients except frosting in large mixer bowl on low speed, scraping bowl constantly, 30 seconds. Beat on high speed, scraping bowl occasionally, 3 minutes. Pour into pan(s). Bake until wooden pick inserted in center comes out clean, oblong 45 minutes, layers 30–35 minutes; cool. Frost with Fudge Frosting.

Fudge Frosting

½ cup shortening
2 cups sugar
3 squares (1 oz each) unsweetened chocolate or 3 envelopes (1 oz each) premelted chocolate
⅔ cup milk
½ tsp salt
2 tsp vanilla

Mix all ingredients except vanilla in 2½-qt saucepan. Heat to rolling boil, stirring occasionally. Boil 1 minute without stirring. Place pan in bowl of ice water. Beat until frosting is cold; stir in vanilla.

COURTESY BETTY CROCKER FOOD & NUTRITION CENTER, GENERAL MILLS, INC. REGISTERED® TRADEMARK OF GENERAL MILLS, INC.

Hershey's Chocolate Town Fudge Cake

4 blocks (4 oz) HERSHEY'S Baking Chocolate
½ cup hot water
½ cup sugar
½ cup butter or margarine
1¼ cups sugar
3 eggs
1 tsp vanilla
1⅓ cups all-purpose flour
1 tsp baking soda
1 tsp salt
⅔ cup milk

Grease and line with waxed paper, bottoms of two 9-inch layer pans. Grease waxed paper. Melt baking chocolate with hot water in top of double boiler over simmering water. Stir constantly until chocolate has melted and mixture is well blended. Add ½ cup sugar and stir until dissolved. Remove from heat and cool. Cream butter or margarine with 1¼ cups sugar until light and fluffy. Add eggs, one at a time, beating after each addition. Add vanilla. Combine flour, baking soda, and salt; add alternately with milk to creamed mixture. Beat after each addition until batter is smooth. Add chocolate mixture and blend well. Pour into prepared pans. Bake at 350°F 35–40 minutes. Cool 10 minutes before removing from pans. Frost as desired.

THIS RECIPE HAS BEEN DEVELOPED, TESTED AND APPROVED BY HERSHEY FOODS CORPORATION'S TEST KITCHEN.

Minute Maid®

Buttery Lemon Pound Cake

½ cup butter, softened
1 cup sugar
2 eggs, well beaten
1 Tbsp MINUTE MAID® 100% Pure Lemon Juice
½ tsp salt
1½ cups sifted flour
1 tsp baking powder
½ cup milk
⅓ cup MINUTE MAID® 100% Pure Lemon Juice
¼ cup sugar

Cream butter in 1 cup sugar. Add eggs and 1 Tbsp lemon juice. Mix well. Sift salt, flour, and baking powder together. Add alternately with milk to creamed mixture. Bake in a preheated 325°F oven, in a well-greased 8½ X 4½-inch loaf pan for 1 hour or until golden brown. Mix ⅓ cup lemon juice with remaining ¼ cup sugar. Use a toothpick to make holes in top of cake and drizzle lemon juice and sugar mixture over the top of the cake when removed from the oven. Delicious served warm.

MINUTE MAID IS A REGISTERED TRADEMARK OF THE COCA-COLA COMPANY. COURTESY THE COCA-COLA COMPANY FOODS DIVISION.

Marion-Kay® Sour Cream Nutmeg Cake

1 cup margarine
½ tsp Marion-Kay Butter Flavor
3 cups granulated sugar
6 eggs, separated
1 tsp Marion-Kay Pure Vanilla
3 cups sifted flour
¼ tsp baking soda
¼ tsp Marion-Kay Ground Nutmeg
1 cup commercial sour cream

Cream margarine, Marion-Kay Butter Flavor, and sugar in mixer about 3 minutes. Add egg yolks, one at a time, beating well after each addition. Stir in vanilla. Sift flour twice. Add baking soda and nutmeg, and sift again. Add sour cream alternately with the flour. Beat egg whites until stiff but not dry. Gently fold into cake batter. Bake this in 2 bread pans, greased and lined with waxed paper; or you may use a heavy tube pan. Bake 1 hour 15 minutes at 300°F. Allow cake 5–10 minutes to cool before removing from pans. This cake freezes well and does not need icing.
COURTESY MARION-KAY CO., INC.

Royal Boston Cream Pie

1 cup cold milk
1 pkg ROYAL® Instant Banana Cream Pudding
½ cup heavy cream, whipped
2 (9-inch) cake layers, baked and cooled
2 Tbsp BLUE BONNET® Margarine
1 square (1 oz) unsweetened chocolate
1 cup sifted confectioners' sugar
2 Tbsp boiling water

Pour cold milk into mixing bowl. Add ROYAL Instant Banana Cream Pudding and slowly beat with egg beater 2 minutes. Fold Pour cold milk into mixing bowl. Add ROYAL Instant Banana Cream Pudding and slowly beat with egg beater 2 minutes. Fold in whipped cream. Place 1 cake layer on serving dish; top with prepared banana filling. Let set 5 minutes, then top with remaining cake layer. Melt together BLUE BONNET Margarine and unsweetened chocolate. Stir in confectioners' sugar and boiling water. Beat until well blended. Pour over cake. Chill at least 1 hour before serving. Makes one 9-inch cake.
COURTESY OF STANDARD BRANDS INCORPORATED.

Swiss Miss Fudge Cupcakes

- *½ cup (1 stick) butter*
- *¾ cup sugar*
- *2 eggs*
- *1 tsp vanilla*
- *2 cups sifted all-purpose flour*
- *1 tsp soda*
- *¼ tsp salt*
- *4 envelopes (1 cup) SWISS MISS Hot Cocoa Mix*
- *1 cup water*

Beat butter and sugar until creamy and fluffy. Beat in eggs one at a time. Add vanilla. Add sifted dry ingredients alternately with water to creamed mixture. Line muffin pans with 2½-inch paper baking cups. Fill two-thirds full. Bake at 350°F for 20 minutes or until done. Cool on wire rack. Yield: 20 cupcakes.

COURTESY SANNA DIVISION, BEATRICE FOODS COMPANY.

Nabisco Party Cheese Cake

Crust

- *1 (6-oz) pkg NABISCO Zwieback, finely rolled (about 2 cups crumbs)*
- *2 Tbsp granulated sugar*
- *½ tsp ground cinnamon*
- *½ cup softened butter or margarine*

Thoroughly blend together NABISCO Zwieback crumbs, sugar, cinnamon, and butter or margarine. Press mixture firmly against bottom and sides of a 9-inch springform pan.

Filling

- *1 cup light cream*
- *2 (8-oz) pkg cream cheese, softened*
- *4 eggs*
- *1 cup granulated sugar*
- *1 tsp grated lemon rind*
- *4 Tbsp all-purpose flour*
- *¼ tsp salt*
- *2 Tbsp lemon juice*
- *Cherry pie filling (optional)*

Add cream gradually to cream cheese, beating until smooth. Beat eggs, sugar, and lemon rind until thick and light. Add flour and salt; add to cheese mixture; then stir in lemon juice. Pour into crust. Bake in a preheated slow oven (325°F) 1¼–1½ hours. Cool thoroughly before removing sides of pan. If desired, top with canned cherry pie filling. Makes 12 (2¼-inch) wedges.

COURTESY NABISCO, INC.

Nestlé Chocolate Swirl Cheesecake

1 6-oz pkg (1 cup) NESTLÉ Semi-Sweet Real Chocolate Morsels
½ cup sugar
1¼ cups graham cracker crumbs
2 Tbsp sugar
¼ cup butter, melted
2 8-oz pkg cream cheese, softened
¾ cup sugar
½ cup sour cream
1 tsp vanilla extract
4 eggs

Preheat oven to 325°F. Combine over hot (not boiling) water, NESTLÉ Semi-Sweet Real Chocolate Morsels and ½ cup sugar; heat until morsels melt and mixture is smooth. Remove from heat; set aside. In small bowl, combine graham cracker crumbs, 2 Tbsp sugar, and melted butter; mix well. Pat firmly into 9-inch springform pan, covering bottom and ½ to 1 inch up sides; set aside. In large bowl, beat cream cheese until light and creamy. Gradually beat in ¾ cup sugar. Mix in sour cream and vanilla extract. Add eggs, one at a time, beating well after each addition. Divide batter in half. Stir melted chocolate mixture into first half. Pour into crumb-lined pan; cover with plain batter. With a knife, swirl chocolate batter through plain batter to marbleize. Bake for 50 minutes or until only a 2–3 inch circle in center will shake. Cool at room temperature; refrigerate until ready to serve. Makes one 9-inch cake.

COURTESY THE NESTLE COMPANY, INC.

Friendship Low-Calorie Cheesecake

4 eggs
1 Tbsp lemon juice
1 tsp vanilla
2 tsp soft margarine
6 pkg Sweet and Low
1 lb FRIENDSHIP Pot Style Cottage Cheese
1 8-oz can sweetened crushed pineapple, well drained

Preheat oven to 350°F. In a blender, combine until smooth all ingredients except pineapple. Fold in drained pineapple. Pour into a springform pan and bake 45 minutes.

RECIPE COURTESY OF FRIENDSHIP FOODS' HOME ECONOMIST, HELEN SCHWARTZ.

Nabisco Famous Chocolate Refrigerator Roll

1 cup heavy cream
2 Tbsp granulated sugar
½ tsp vanilla extract
20 NABISCO Famous Chocolate Wafers
Red candied cherries (optional)

Whip cream with sugar and vanilla until stiff. Spread wafers with part of cream. Put together in stacks of 4 or 5. Chill 15 minutes. Stand stacks on edge on plate to make 1 long roll. Frost outside of roll with remaining cream. Refrigerate at least 3 hours. Garnish with red candied cherries, if desired. Cut diagonally at a 45-degree angle. Roll may be frozen, if desired. Remove from freezer to refrigerator about 1 hour before serving. Makes 8 (about ¾ inch) slices.
COURTESY NABISCO, INC.

Promise Carrot-Walnut Cake

1 cup (½ lb) PROMISE Margarine
2 cups sugar
1 tsp cinnamon
½ tsp nutmeg
1 Tbsp grated orange rind
1½ cups grated or finely shredded pared raw carrots
⅔ cup chopped walnuts
3 cups sifted all-purpose flour
3 tsp baking powder
½ tsp salt
⅔ cup orange juice
4 egg whites, stiffly beaten

In large bowl, cream margarine and sugar. Add cinnamon, nutmeg, orange rind, carrots, and walnuts. Sift together flour, baking powder, and salt; blend into carrot mixture alternately with orange juice. Fold in beaten egg whites. Turn into a 10-inch tube pan that has been coated with margarine and dusted with flour. Bake in 350°F oven 60–70 minutes, until cake tester inserted in cake comes out clean. Cool in pan 20 minutes, then turn out of pan and cool on wire rack. Cover top with Orange Glaze (see below). Yield: 12 servings.

Orange Glaze

1½ cups sifted confectioners' sugar
1 Tbsp PROMISE Margarine
½ tsp grated orange rind
2 Tbsp orange juice

Blend confectioners' sugar with margarine, orange rind, and orange juice in a small bowl.
COURTESY LEVER BROTHERS COMPANY.

Arm & Hammer® Applesauce Cake

2 cups sifted all-purpose flour
1 tsp ARM & HAMMER Baking Soda
¾ tsp salt
1 tsp ground cinnamon
⅛ tsp ground cloves
½ cup vegetable shortening
1 cup firmly packed light brown sugar
1 egg
1 cup sweetened applesauce
1½ tsp grated lemon peel
3 Tbsp vinegar
1 cup dark seedless raisins

Sift together flour, baking soda, salt, and spices. Using an electric mixer, cream shortening until soft in large bowl; add sugar gradually, creaming until light and fluffy. Beat in egg. Stir together applesauce, lemon peel, and vinegar; add alternately with dry ingredients to creamed mixture, beginning and ending with dry ingredients. Beat well after each addition. Stir in raisins. Turn into greased and floured 8-inch-square baking pan. Bake in 350°F oven 55 minutes or until toothpick inserted in center of cake comes out clean. Cool in pan 10 minutes; remove from pan and cool on rack. Serve with whipped cream if desired. Makes one 8-inch-square cake.

RECIPE COURTESY OF ARM & HAMMER DIVISION, CHURCH & DWIGHT CO., INC.

Helen Hiland's Wheatena Apple Cake

1 cup finely chopped pecans
½ cup sugar
1 tsp cinnamon
2 Tbsp WHEATENA, uncooked
1 cup grated apples, well packed
½ cup butter or margarine
1 cup sugar
3 eggs
3 cups sifted flour
3 tsp baking powder
1 tsp soda
¼ cup WHEATENA
¾ cup sour cream

Combine first 4 ingredients; set aside. Grate apples. Cream butter with sugar; add eggs, one at a time, and cream until light. Sift flour, baking powder, and soda together; add WHEATENA. Add dry ingredients to creamed mixture alternately with apples and sour cream. Spoon ½ the batter into well-greased, 10-inch tube pan. Sprinkle with ½ the nut mixture; cover with remaining batter and top with remaining nut mixture. Bake in preheated

375°F oven 50–55 minutes or until tests done. Cool slightly before removing from pan.

COURTESY STANDARD MILLING COMPANY.

Del Monte Mixed Fruit Upside-Down Cake

- *1 pkg (11 oz) DEL MONTE Mixed Dried Fruits, cooked and drained*
- *½ cup margarine or butter*
- *1 cup firmly packed brown sugar*
- *6 walnut halves*
- *1 pkg (18½ oz) lemon cake mix*

Pit prunes. Melt margarine in 13 X 9-inch pan or 12-inch skillet. Add sugar. Arrange fruits and nuts in sugar mixture. Prepare cake mix as package directs. Spread over fruit. Bake at 350°F, 45–50 minutes or until tests done. Cool 5 minutes, then invert onto large serving dish. Serve warm or cold with whipped cream, if desired. Yield: 12–16 servings.

COURTESY DEL MONTE KITCHENS, DEL MONTE CORPORATION, P.O. BOX 3575, SAN FRANCISCO, CA 94119.

Pillsbury Sweet Fruitcake

- *2 eggs*
- *2 pkg PILLSBURY Date or Nut Quick Bread Mix*
- *2 cups (12–13 oz) candied cherries**
- *2 cups water*
- *2 cups pecans (halved or chopped)*
- *2 cups raisins*
- *1 cup candied pineapple, cut in wedges**

Heat oven to 350°F. Grease and flour bottom and sides of 12-cup fluted tube pan or 10-inch tube pan. In large bowl, combine eggs and water. Add remaining ingredients; by hand, stir until combined. Pour into prepared pan. Bake at 350°F 65–75 minutes or until toothpick inserted in center comes out clean. Cool 30 minutes; loosen edges and remove from pan. Cool completely. Store tightly wrapped in refrigerator. If desired, glaze with warm corn syrup; decorate with candied fruits and nuts.

High Altitude

Above 3,500 feet, add 2 Tbsp flour to mix. Bake at 375°F 60–70 minutes.

*Note: if desired, substitute 2 lb (4 cups) candied fruit mixture for candied cherries and pineapple.

COURTESY OF THE PILLSBURY COMPANY.

PET®

Pet Holiday Fruitcake

1½ cups raisins
1½ cups golden raisins
1 cup sunflower seeds
2 cups PET Funsten Chopped Walnuts
1 cup PET Funsten Chopped Almonds
2 cups chopped dates
1 cup chopped dried apricots
3 tsp grated lemon peel
3 tsp grated orange peel
1 jar (16½ oz) MUSSELMAN'S Natural Style Apple Sauce
1 can (16 oz) MUSSELMAN'S Red Tart Pitted Cherries
8 medium eggs
1½ cups honey
1 cup oil
4 tsp baking soda
2 cups whole wheat flour
2 cups unbleached flour
Brandy

In a large bowl, mix together raisins, golden raisins, sunflower seeds, walnuts, almonds, dates, apricots, lemon peel, orange peel, and apple sauce. Drain cherries and pat dry with a paper towel. Add to the fruit and nut mixture and let stand 2–3 hours or overnight. Beat together eggs, honey, and oil. Add baking soda, whole wheat flour and unbleached flour, one-third at a time. Pour batter over fruit and nut mixture and mix well. Pour mixture into 3 greased, 9 X 5 X 3-inch loaf pans. Bake at 300°F for 1 hour 20 minutes. Cool. Remove from pans. Let stand on wire racks 3–4 hours. Seal tightly and store 2–3 weeks to enhance flavor.

Optional: soak cheesecloth in ½ cup brandy for each cake and wrap around cakes. Wrap in foil, seal, and store in a cool, dry place. Keep 2–3 weeks before serving. Drizzle cakes once a week with ¼ cup brandy each.

PET, AN IC INDUSTRIES COMPANY, HOME ECONOMICS DEPT., P.O. BOX 392, ST. LOUIS, MO 63166.

Grandma's Molasses Gingerbread

½ cup shortening
½ cup sugar
1 cup GRANDMA'S Molasses
2 eggs
2½ cups all-purpose flour
1 tsp salt
2 tsp baking powder
½ tsp baking soda
1 tsp ginger
2 tsp cinnamon
½ tsp ground cloves
1 cup hot water

Cream shortening with sugar; add molasses and eggs. Beat well. Sift dry ingredients; add alternately with water. Bake in greased 9-inch-square pan about 50 minutes at 350°F.

COURTESY GRANDMA'S UNSULPHURED MOLASSES, A REGISTERED TRADEMARK OF DUFFY-MOTT COMPANY, INC., NEW YORK 10017.

Wilderness Strawberry-Filled Jelly Roll

- 1 *can (21 oz) WILDERNESS Strawberry Fruit Filling*
- ¾ *cup sugar, sifted*
- 4 *eggs, separated*
- 1 *tsp vanilla*
- ¾ *cup cake flour, sift before measuring*
- ¾ *tsp baking powder*
- ¼ *tsp salt*
- *Confectioners' sugar*

Line jelly roll pan (15½ X 10½ X 1 inches) with waxed paper. Heavily grease and flour the waxed paper. Separate eggs and beat the yolks. Gradually add sifted sugar and vanilla to yolks, beating until creamy. Sift flour and baking powder together and gradually add to the egg mixture. Beat the batter until smooth. Whip the egg whites and salt until stiff but not dry. Fold them into the cake batter. Spread the dough into pan and bake at 375°F for about 13 minutes. Loosen cake from edges of pan. Invert cake onto towel sprinkled with confectioners' sugar. Trim off the hard edges of cake. While hot, roll cake and towel from narrow end. Cool on wire rack, unroll, remove towel, and spread cake with strawberry fruit filling. Reroll, sprinkle with confectioners' sugar.

COURTESY OF WILDERNESS FOODS.

Corn Chex® Peachy Pecan Cake

- 2 *cups sifted all-purpose flour*
- 3 *tsp baking powder*
- ½ *tsp baking soda*
- ½ *salt*
- ½ *cup plus 2 Tbsp butter or margarine*
- 1 *cup packed brown sugar*
- 3 *cups CORN CHEX® cereal, crushed to 1 cup*
- ⅔ *cup chopped pecans*
- 2 *eggs, beaten*
- 1 *cup milk*
- 1 *cup whipping cream*
- 1½ *to 2 cups sliced peaches, sweetened*

Preheat oven to 350°F. Grease three 8-inch, round cake pans. Sift together flour, baking powder, baking soda, and salt. Cut in butter and sugar until it resembles coarse crumbs. Stir in Chex and pecans. Add egg and milk. Mix just until all dry ingredients are moistened. Turn into pans. Bake 15–20 minutes or until tester inserted in center comes out clean. Let cool in pans

15 minutes. At serving time, whip cream. Spoon about a third of the peaches and cream between each 2 layers. Top with remaining cream. Garnish with peach slices. Good with sliced bananas, too. Makes one 3-layer cake.

CREATED AND TESTED AT CHECKERBOARD KITCHENS. REPRINTED COURTESY OF RALSTON PURINA COMPANY.

Pillsbury Strawberry Shortcake

- *1 10-oz can HUNGRY JACK® Refrigerated Big Flaky Biscuits*
- *2 Tbsp margarine or butter, melted*
- *2 to 4 Tbsp sugar*
- *1 pint (2 cups) fresh strawberries, sliced and sweetened (or 1 pint frozen strawberries)*
- *Whipped cream*

Heat oven to 400°F. Grease a cookie sheet. Separate dough into 10 biscuits. Gently press 2 biscuits together for each shortcake. Dip top and sides of each in melted margarine, then in sugar. Place on prepared cookie sheet. Bake at 400°F 14–17 minutes or until golden brown. Cool slightly; split and fill with strawberries and whipped cream. Top with additional strawberries and whipped cream. Yield: 5 shortcakes.

COURTESY OF THE PILLSBURY COMPANY.

Dromedary Petit Fours

- *1 (17-oz) pkg DROMEDARY Pound Cake Mix*
- *¾ cup milk*
- *2 eggs*
- *1 cup granulated sugar*
- *¼ cup butter or margarine*
- *¼ cup shortening*
- *½ cup milk*
- *½ tsp salt*
- *3 cups sifted confectioners' sugar*
- *½ tsp vanilla extract*
- *Food coloring*
- *Chuckles Flower Buds (see below)*

Prepare DROMEDARY Pound Cake Mix according to label directions, using ¾ cup milk and 2 eggs. Pour into greased 9 X 9 X 2-inch baking pan. Bake in preheated slow oven (325°F) 45–50 minutes or until done. Cool in pan 15 minutes. Loosen edges with spatula; remove from pan. Cool. Cut cake with serrated-edge knife into 20 pieces 2 inches by 1¾ inches. Combine next 5 ingredients in saucepan. Bring to a boil over moderate heat, stirring constantly. Boil vigorously 1 minute. Remove from heat; stir in confectioners' sugar and vanilla, beating until smooth. Tint with food coloring as desired. Cool 2–3 minutes or until frosting is a good consistency for dipping. Dip each piece of cake into frosting, using fork to hold cake, covering top and sides with frosting. Reheat frosting if necessary. Place on wire rack until set. Decorate with Chuckles Flower Buds. Makes 20 (2 X1¾-inch) petit fours.

Flower Buds

Flatten small Chuckles Spice Drops into thin ovals with rolling pin on sugared surface. Cut in half crosswise. Roll on half at angle to form center of bud; add second leaf, overlapping to form petal. Snip green spice drops for leaves.

COURTESY NABISCO, INC.

Domino® No-Cook Fluffy Frosting

⅓ cup butter or margarine, softened
1 tsp vanilla extract
¼ tsp salt
2 unbeaten egg whites
1 lb DOMINO® Confectioners 10-X Powdered Sugar
Milk

Cream butter or margarine with vanilla and salt until fluffy. Add egg whites and sugar alternately, a little at a time, beating well after each addition. Add 1 Tbsp milk and beat. If necessary, add more milk to make of desired spreading consistency. Yield: about 2 cups, enough for two 9-inch, round layers.

Variations

Orange fluffy frosting: add 2 Tbsp grated orange rind when creaming butter, etc.

Chocolate fluffy frosting: add 3 squares unsweetened baking chocolate, melted and cooled to mixture, before adding milk.

Mocha fluffy frosting: add 2 tsp instant coffee powder to chocolate variation when adding chocolate.

COURTESY AMSTAR CORPORATION, AMERICAN SUGAR DIVISION.

Marshmallow Fluff Seven-Minute Frosting

2 egg whites
1 cup sugar
¼ tsp cream of tartar
⅛ tsp salt
¼ cup water
1 cup (½ jar) MARSHMALLOW FLUFF
1 tsp vanilla extract

Combine all ingredients except vanilla in top of double boiler. Place over boiling water; beat with rotary beater until mixture holds soft peaks. Remove top of double boiler from lower part; beat until mixture holds stiff peaks. Beat in vanilla. Yield: frosting for two 8- or 9-inch layers.

COURTESY DURKEE-MOWER, INC.

Hershey's Chocolate Buttercream Frosting

¾ cup HERSHEY'S Cocoa
2⅔ cups unsifted confectioners' sugar
6 Tbsp butter or margarine
4–5 Tbsp milk
1 tsp vanilla

Combine cocoa and confectioners' sugar in a bowl. Cream butter with ½ cup HERSHEY'S Cocoa mixture in small mixer bowl. Add remaining cocoa mixture alternately with milk, beating to spreading consistency. Blend in vanilla. Makes 2 cups of frosting.

THIS RECIPE HAS BEEN DEVELOPED, TESTED AND APPROVED BY HERSHEY FOODS CORPORATION'S TEST KITCHEN.

"Philly" Chocolate Frosting

1 8-oz pkg PHILADELPHIA BRAND Cream Cheese
1 Tbsp milk
1 tsp vanilla
Dash of salt
5 cups sifted confectioners' sugar
3 1-oz squares unsweetened chocolate, melted

Combine softened cream cheese, milk, vanilla and salt, mixing until well blended. Gradually add sugar, mixing well after each

addition. Stir in chocolate. Fills and frosts two 8- or 9-inch cake layers.
COURTESY OF KRAFT, INC.

Blue Diamond® Broiled-On Cake Topping

½ cup BLUE DIAMOND® Sliced Natural Almonds
¼ cup packed brown sugar
3 Tbsp honey
1½ Tbsp butter or margarine, melted

Combine all ingredients and spread over one 8- or 9-inch round or square cake layer. Place under preheated broiler for about 1 minute, watching carefully, until bubbly and lightly browned.
COURTESY CALIFORNIA ALMOND GROWERS EXCHANGE.

Custards and Other Desserts

Uncle Ben's® Old-Fashioned Rice Pudding

1¾ cups water
½ cup UNCLE BEN'S® CONVERTED® Brand Rice
½ tsp salt
2 cups milk
2 eggs, beaten
⅓ cup sugar
1 tsp vanilla
¼ cup raisins, steamed in water and drained (optional)
Nutmeg or cinnamon (optional)

Heat oven to 350°F. Bring water to boil. Stir in rice and salt. Cover and simmer until all water is absorbed, about 30 minutes. Add milk and boil gently, stirring occasionally, until mixture thickens slightly, about 5 minutes. Combine eggs, sugar, and vanilla in bowl. Gradually stir in rice mixture; mix well. Pour into a greased 1½-qt casserole. If desired, stir in raisins and sprinkle nutmeg or cinnamon over top. Place casserole in a pan containing about 1 inch hot water. Bake, uncovered, in 350°F oven 45–50 minutes or until knife inserted near center comes out clean. Serve warm or chilled. Makes 5–6 servings.
COURTESY UNCLE BEN'S FOODS.

Arnold Indian Pudding

- 4 cups ARNOLD Cornbread Stuffin'
- 3 cups milk
- ½ cup dark molasses
- 1 tsp salt
- ¼ cup sugar
- 1 tsp cinnamon
- 1 tsp nutmeg
- 4 Tbsp butter
- 2 eggs, well beaten

Scald milk in top of double boiler. Add molasses, salt, sugar, cinnamon, nutmeg, and butter. Stir until well blended. In mixing bowl, combine ARNOLD Stuffin', milk mixture, and beaten eggs. Mix well. Pour into a greased 2-qt casserole and bake at 350°F for 1 hour.

COURTESY ARNOLD BAKERS, INC. (OROWEAT FOODS COMPANY).

Pet Pumpkin Custard

- 1 can (16 oz) pumpkin
- 1 egg
- 3 Tbsp flour
- 1 tsp salt
- 1 tsp cinnamon
- ½ tsp allspice
- ½ tsp cloves
- ¼ tsp ginger
- 1 can (1⅔ cups) PET Evaporated Skimmed Milk
- 2 tsp liquid artificial sweetener or 1 cup sugar

Beat together pumpkin and egg. Mix in flour, salt, cinnamon, allspice, cloves, and ginger. Gradually stir in evaporated skimmed milk and sweetener. Pour into 8 individual custard cups. Place cups in large baking pan. Pour hot water around cups to 1-inch deep. Bake in 350°F oven for 1 hour or until knife inserted near the center comes out clean. Serve topped with whipped topping, if desired. Makes 8 servings.

PET, AN IC INDUSTRIES COMPANY, HOME ECONOMICS DEPT., P.O. BOX 392, ST. LOUIS, MO 63166.

All-Time Favorite Puff Pudding

- ¼ cup butter or margarine
- ½ cup sugar or honey
- 1 tsp grated lemon rind
- 2 egg yolks
- 3 Tbsp lemon juice
- 2 Tbsp all-purpose flour
- ¼ cup POST® GRAPE-NUTS® Brand Cereal
- 1 cup milk
- 2 egg whites, stiffly beaten

Thoroughly cream butter with sugar and lemon rind. Add egg yolks; beat until light and fluffy. Blend in lemon juice, flour, cereal, and milk. (Mixture will look curdled, but this will not affect finished product.) Fold in beaten egg whites. Pour into greased 1-qt baking dish; place the dish in pan of hot water. Bake at 325°F for 1 hour 15 minutes or until top springs back when lightly touched. When done, pudding has a cakelike layer on top with custard below. Serve warm or cold with cream or prepared whipped topping, if desired. Makes 6 servings. *For individual puddings*, pour mixture into five 5-oz or four 6-oz custard cups or souffle cups. Bake for about 40 minutes.

REPRODUCED COURTESY OF GENERAL FOODS CORP., OWNER OF THE REGISTERED TRADEMARKS POST AND GRAPE-NUTS.

Swiss Miss Chocolate Pudding

2 envelopes (½ cup) SWISS MISS Hot Cocoa Mix
1½ cups water
2 Tbsp cornstarch
¼ cup sugar
1 tsp vanilla

In saucepan, combine cocoa mix and water; heat to boiling and reduce heat. Combine cornstarch and sugar. Slowly stir into cocoa mixture; cook over medium heat until slightly thickened, stirring constantly. Stir in vanilla. Cool slightly. Spoon into dessert dishes. Cover tightly with plastic wrap, and chill. Yield: 3 servings.

COURTESY SANNA DIVISION, BEATRICE FOODS COMPANY.

Maillard Mocha Mousse

1 4-oz bar MAILLARD Eagle Sweet Chocolate
¼ tsp instant coffee powder
2 Tbsp sugar
2 Tbsp hot water
2 large eggs, separated (or 3 small eggs)
½ tsp vanilla extract
¼ pint whipping cream, chilled

In the top of a double boiler, melt 11 squares of chocolate. Dissolve instant coffee and sugar in water. Stir into melted chocolate. Allow to cool slightly. Add egg yolks one at a time, mixing well after each addition. Add vanilla and fold in stiffly beaten egg whites. Spoon into 4 individual dishes and refrigerate several hours. Serve topped with freshly whipped cream and garnish by grating 1 square of MAILLARD Eagle Sweet Chocolate.

COURTESY OF THE MAILLARD CORPORATION, BETHLEHEM, PENNSYLVANIA.

Eagle® Brand Easy Homemade Chocolate Ice Cream

1 (14 oz) can EAGLE® Brand Sweetened Condensed Milk (not evaporated milk)
⅔ cup chocolate-flavored syrup
2 cups (1 pint) BORDEN® Whipping Cream, whipped

In large bowl, stir together sweetened condensed milk and syrup. Fold in whipped cream. Pour into aluminum foil-lined 9 X 5-inch loaf pan; cover. Freeze 6 hours or until firm. Scoop ice cream from pan or remove from pan, peel off foil, and slice. Return leftovers to freezer. Makes about 1½ qt.

A TESTED RECIPE DEVELOPED IN THE BORDEN KITCHENS. EAGLE BRAND IS A REGISTERED TRADEMARK OF BORDEN, INC.

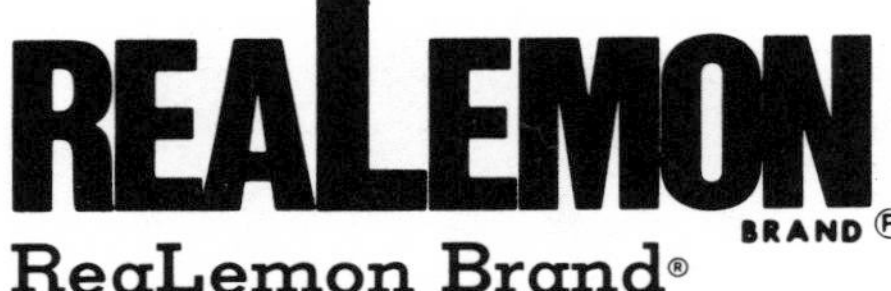

ReaLemon Brand® Creamy Lemon Sherbet

1 cup sugar
2 cups (1 pint) BORDEN® Whipping Cream (unwhipped)
½ cup REALEMON® Reconstituted Lemon Juice
Few drops yellow food coloring

In medium bowl, combine sugar and cream, stirring until dissolved. Stir in REALEMON® Reconstituted Lemon Juice and food coloring. Pour into 8-inch square pan or directly into sherbet dishes. Freeze 3 hours or until firm. Remove from freezer 5 minutes before serving. Return leftovers to freezer. Makes about 3 cups.

A TESTED RECIPE DEVELOPED IN THE BORDEN KITCHENS. REALEMON IS A REGISTERED TRADEMARK OF BORDEN, INC.

Sunkist® Lemon Cake Top Pudding

- 4 eggs, separated
- 1 cup sugar
- 3 Tbsp butter or margarine, softened
- 3 Tbsp flour
- ¼ tsp salt
- ⅓ cup juice of fresh-squeezed SUNKIST® Lemons
- 1 cup milk
- 2 tsp fresh grated SUNKIST® Lemon peel
- ¼ cup sliced almonds

In small bowl of electric mixer, beat egg whites until foamy; gradually add ¼ cup sugar, beating until soft peaks form. Set aside. In large bowl, using same beaters, beat egg yolks and butter well. Gradually add remaining ¾ cup sugar, beating until well blended (about 5 minutes). Add flour, salt and lemon juice; mix well. Blend in milk and lemon peel. Gently fold in beaten egg whites. Sprinkle almonds over bottom of buttered 1½-qt casserole; pour in batter. Set casserole in shallow pan filled with ½ inch hot water. Bake at 325°F 55–60 minutes or until lightly browned. Serve warm or chilled. Makes 6 servings.

COURTESY SUNKIST GROWERS, INC.

Stokely's Easy Cherry Pudding

- ½ cup butter or margarine
- 1 cup sugar
- 1 cup flour
- 2 tsp baking powder
- ¾ cup milk
- 1 can (1 lb) STOKELY'S Finest® Red Sour Pitted Cherries
- ½ cup sugar

In 9-inch-square pan, melt butter or margarine. In bowl, combine next 4 ingredients. Mix until well blended. Pour over melted butter; do not stir. Pour undrained STOKELY'S Cherries over batter; do not stir. Sprinkle ½ cup sugar over cherries; do not stir. Bake at 325°F for 1 hour. Makes 9 servings.

COURTESY STOKELY-VAN CAMP, INC.

Comstock Grandfather's Blueberry Mold

- 1 cup boiling water
- 1 pkg (3 oz) lemon-flavored gelatin
- ½ cup cold water
- 1 can (21 oz) COMSTOCK Blueberry Pie Filling
- 1 cup (½ pint) sour cream
- 1 Tbsp ReaLemon Reconstituted Lemon Juice

In large bowl, pour boiling water over gelatin; stir to dissolve. Add cold water. Chill until gelatin is about the consistency of unbeaten egg white. In medium bowl, blend pie filling, sour cream, and lemon juice; fold into gelatin. Turn into lightly oiled 1-qt mold. Chill about 4 hours or until set. Unmold. Makes eight ½-cup servings.

COURTESY COMSTOCK FOODS (A DIVISION OF CURTICE-BURNS, INC.).

Heublein Bread Pudding Deluxe

Pudding

- *1 cup HEUBLEIN Brandy Alexander*
- *3 cups milk*
- *¼ cup butter (or margarine), softened*
- *5 slices day-old white bread*
- *⅓ cup brown sugar*
- *2 eggs, slightly beaten*
- *½ tsp salt*
- *1 tsp vanilla*

In medium saucepan, heat HEUBLEIN Brandy Alexander and milk to boiling point. Spread butter on bread slices. Cut into small cubes. Combine all ingredients and pour into buttered 2-qt casserole. Bake in preheated 325°F oven 1 hour. Spoon into serving dishes and top with Golden Foamy Sauce (recipe follows). Serves 6–8.

Sauce

- *2 eggs, separated*
- *2 Tbsp HEUBLEIN Brandy Alexander*
- *½ cup sugar*

In medium mixing bowl, beat egg whites until soft peaks form. Gradually add ¼ cup sugar, beating until stiff but not dry. In small mixing bowl, beat egg yolks, remaining sugar, and HEUBLEIN Brandy Alexander until thickened. Fold into egg-white mixture.

COURTESY HEUBLEIN BRANDY ALEXANDER.

Wilderness Mock Plum Pudding

- *1 can (21 oz) WILDERNESS French Apple Fruit Filling*
- *1 pkg (14½ oz) gingerbread mix*
- *2 Tbsp butter or margarine*
- *⅓ cup brown sugar*

Pour can of WILDERNESS French Apple Fruit Filling in lightly buttered 9 X 9-inch pan. Dot with butter and sprinkle on brown sugar. Prepare gingerbread according to directions on package. Spread over filling. Bake at 350°F 35–45 minutes. Serve warm, plain or with whipped cream.

COURTESY OF WILDERNESS FOODS.

Comstock Peach Smoothee

- *1 can (21 oz) COMSTOCK Peach Pie Filling*
- *1 can (14 oz) Eagle Brand Sweetened Condensed Milk*
- *1 Tbsp ReaLemon Reconstituted Lemon Juice*
- *½ cup chopped pecans*
- *2 Tbsp chopped candied ginger*
- *1½ cups heavy cream, whipped*

In large mixer bowl, beat pie filling and sweetened condensed milk together until peaches are crushed. Mix in lemon juice, pecans, and candied ginger. Fold in whipped cream. Pour into shallow metal pans and freeze until firm. Makes 1½ qt.

COURTESY COMSTOCK FOODS (A DIVISION OF CURTICE-BURNS, INC.).

Dole® Doubly Delicious Crêpes

Crêpes

- *2 eggs*
- *⅔ cup milk*
- *⅔ cup sifted flour*
- *3 Tbsp melted butter*
- *2 Tbsp sugar*
- *1 small DOLE® Banana, mashed*
- *¼ tsp salt*
- *Melted butter*

In blender jar, combine all ingredients except melted butter; blend smooth. Refrigerate about 1 hour. Heat a small crêpe pan, brush lightly with melted butter, and add 2 Tbsp batter. Tilt pan quickly to spread. Cook over moderate heat until browned. Turn and brown second side. Turn out and repeat until all of batter is baked. Makes 12–14 (6-inch) crêpes.

Filling

- *2 Tbsp butter*
- *3 DOLE® Bananas, sliced*
- *¾ cup brown sugar, packed*
- *¼ cup water*
- *2 tsp cornstarch*
- *2 tsp lemon juice*
- *1 cup whipping cream*
- *1 tsp vanilla*
- *Dash salt*

Melt butter in large heavy skillet over medium high heat. Add bananas, 1 cup at a time, and sauté until lightly browned, turning occasionally. Remove to warm platter and repeat with remaining bananas. Reduce heat, add sugar and 2 Tbsp water to skillet. Cook until syrupy. Mix cornstarch with remaining 2 Tbsp water. Stir into syrup and simmer, stirring until mixture boils and thickens. Remove from heat, stir in lemon juice and add bananas. Beat cream with vanilla and salt until stiff. Spread each crepe with 2 level Tbsp whipped cream and fold in half, then make second fold to form a triangle. Place 2 crepes, slightly overlapping, on each serving plate. Top with 2 Tbsp bananas and syrup and serve at once. Makes 6 servings.

COURTESY OF CASTLE & COOKE FOODS (DOLE®)

Ocean Spray's Cranberries Jubilee Recipe

1 cup sugar
1½ cups water
2 cups OCEAN SPRAY® Fresh or Frozen Cranberries
¼ cup brandy
Vanilla ice cream

Combine sugar and water in saucepan, stirring to dissolve sugar. Bring to boiling; boil 5 minutes. Add cranberries and bring to boiling again; cook 5 minutes. Turn into heat-proof bowl or blazer pan of chafing dish. Heat brandy. Ignite brandy and pour over cranberry mixture. Blend into sauce and serve immediately over ice cream. Makes 2½ cups sauce.

COURTESY OCEAN SPRAY CRANBERRIES, INC.

No-Cal Baked Apples

4 Rome Beauty apples
½ cup NO-CAL Black Cherry Flavoring
½ cup water
Cinnamon

Core apples and place in baking dish. Mix flavoring with water. Pour half over apples. Sprinkle with cinnamon. Spoon remaining syrup over apples as they bake. Bake until soft. (You may substitute ½ bottle of NO-CAL Black Cherry Soda in place of the flavoring-and-water combination.)

COURTESY OF NO-CAL COMPANY, INC.

Dole® Special Bananas Foster

3 large firm-ripe DOLE® Bananas
1½ Tbsp lemon juice
½ cup brown sugar, packed
¼ cup butter
Cinnamon
2 Tbsp crême de banana
3 Tbsp light rum
Vanilla, coffee, or banana ice cream

Peel bananas. Cut fruit in half lengthwise, then crosswise into quarters. Drizzle with lemon juice. Heat brown sugar and butter together in a 10-inch skillet until sugar is melted and caramelized. Add bananas and cook slowly a minute or two until heated and glazed. Sprinkle lightly with cinnamon. Add crême de banana and rum. Ignite and continue to spoon liquid over bananas until flames die out. Serve over firm vanilla, coffee, or banana ice cream. Makes 6 servings.

COURTESY OF CASTLE & COOKE FOODS (DOLE®).

Del Monte Individual Baked Alaskas

8 sponge-cake circles or leftover cake cut in circles
1 can (15¼ oz) DEL MONTE Sliced Pineapple, drained
1 qt strawberry ice cream
8 egg whites
¾ tsp cream of tartar
¾ cup sugar
1 tsp vanilla

Cut 8 heavy brown paper circles larger than cake circles. Place cake circles on paper. Top each with a pineapple slice and scoop of ice cream. Place in freezer. Beat egg whites and cream of tartar until frothy. Gradually add sugar and vanilla, beating until glossy and stiff. Remove alaskas from freezer, one at a time. Spread meringue over ice cream, pineapple, and cake, sealing to edges of cake all around. Return to freezer. Repeat until all are covered with meringue. Just before serving, bake at 500°F, 3–5 minutes. Serve immediately. Yield: 8 servings.

COURTESY DEL MONTE KITCHENS, DEL MONTE CORPORATION, P.O. BOX 3575, SAN FRANCISCO, CA 94119.

Milk Dud Caramel Rum Sauce

1⅓ cups Milk Duds
3 Tbsp milk
1 tsp rum flavoring

Melt Milk Duds with milk in top of a double boiler over boiling water. Cool to lukewarm. Stir in rum flavoring. Serve over ice cream. Yield: ½ cup.

COURTESY OF D.L. CLARK COMPANY, DIVISION OF BEATRICE FOODS.

Nestlé

Nestlé Creamy Milk Chocolate Fondue

½ cup heavy cream
2 Tbsp corn syrup
1 11½-oz pkg (2 cups) NESTLÉ Milk Chocolate Morsels
2 tsp vanilla extract

In fondue pot or saucepan, combine cream and corn syrup; heat, stirring constantly until blended. Add package NESTLÉ'S Milk Chocolate Morsels; stir until morsels melt and mixture is smooth. Stir in vanilla extract. Serve with assorted fruits, cake cubes, or as sauce over ice cream. Makes 2 cups.
COURTESY THE NESTLE COMPANY, INC.

Cookies and Candies

Nestlé Toll House Cookies

2¼ cups unsifted *flour*
1 tsp baking soda
1 tsp salt
1 cup butter, softened
¾ cup sugar
¾ cup firmly packed brown sugar
1 tsp vanilla extract
2 eggs
1 12-oz pkg (2 cups) NESTLÉ Semi-Sweet Real Chocolate Morsels
1 cup chopped nuts

Preheat oven to 375°F. In small bowl, combine flour, baking soda, and salt; set aside. In large bowl, combine butter, sugar, brown sugar, and vanilla extract; beat until creamy. Beat in eggs. Gradually add flour mixture; mix well. Stir in NESTLÉ Semi-Sweet Real Chocolate Morsels and nuts. Drop by rounded teaspoon onto ungreased cookie sheets. Bake 8–10 minutes. Makes one hundred 2-inch cookies.
COURTESY THE NESTLE COMPANY, INC.

Land O'Lakes Old Fashioned Butter Cookies

1 cup LAND O LAKES® Sweet Cream Butter, softened
1 cup sugar
1 egg
2½ cups all-purpose flour
1 tsp baking powder
2 Tbsp orange juice
1 tsp vanilla

In 3-qt mixer bowl, cream butter, sugar, and egg until light and fluffy. Beat in flour, baking powder, orange juice, and vanilla until smooth and well combined. Chill 2–3 hours or until firm enough to be rolled. Preheat oven to 400°F. Roll out dough, half at a time, on well-floured surface to ⅛- to ¼-inch thickness. Cut out with cookie cutters. Place on ungreased cookie sheet. Bake near center of 400°F oven 6–10 minutes or until golden brown on edges. Cool on wire rack. Frost. Yield: 6 dozen 2-inch cookies.

For a crispier cookie, roll to ⅛-inch thickness; for a softer cookie, roll to ¼ inch.

Butter Cream Frosting

3 cups confectioners' sugar
⅓ cup LAND O LAKES® Sweet Cream Butter, softened
1 to 2 Tbsp milk
1 tsp vanilla

In 1½-qt mixer bowl, cream sugar and butter at low speed until combined. Add milk and vanilla. Beat at high speed until fluffy (about 1½ minutes).

COURTESY OF THE LAND O'LAKES KITCHENS, MINNEAPOLIS, MN.

Domino® Grandma's Sugar Cookies

4 cups sifted all-purpose flour
¾ tsp cream of tartar
1 tsp cinnamon
1 tsp salt
1 cup (½ lb) soft butter or margarine
2 cups firmly packed DOMINO® Light Brown Sugar
3 eggs
½ cup DOMINO® Granulated Sugar
Food coloring

Sift flour, cream of tartar, cinnamon, and salt together. Cream butter and brown sugar thoroughly. Add 2 eggs and 1 egg yolk (reserve 1 egg white), beating until light. Gradually add flour mixture, beating thoroughly after each addition. Wrap dough in wax paper and chill several hours. Roll out part of dough at a time, ⅛ inch thick, on lightly floured board. Cut with fancy cutters. Brush tops of cookies with slightly beaten reserved egg white. Sprinkle with colored sugar (add a few drops of food coloring to tint granulated sugar; mix well). Bake on greased baking sheets in hot oven 400°F 8–10 minutes. Yield: 3–4 dozen cookies.

COURTESY AMSTAR CORPORATION, AMERICAN SUGAR DIVISION.

Quaker® Chewy Oatmeal Cookies

1 cup sifted all-purpose flour
¾ tsp soda
½ tsp salt
1 tsp cinnamon
¼ tsp nutmeg
¾ cup shortening, soft
1⅓ cups firmly packed brown sugar
2 eggs
1 tsp vanilla
2 cups QUAKER® Oats (quick or old fashioned, uncooked)
1 cup raisins

Sift together flour, soda, salt, cinnamon, and nutmeg into bowl. Add shortening, sugar, eggs, and vanilla; beat until smooth, about 2 minutes. Stir in oats and raisins. Drop by heaping teaspoonfuls onto greased cookie sheets. Bake in preheated moderate oven (350°F) 12–15 minutes. Makes about 3½ dozen.

RECIPE REPRODUCED WITH THE PERMISSION OF THE QUAKER OATS COMPANY.

Nestlé

Nestlé Oatmeal Scotchies

2 cups unsifted flour
2 tsp baking powder
1 tsp baking soda
1 tsp salt
1 cup butter, softened
1½ cups firmly packed brown sugar
2 eggs
1 Tbsp water
1½ cups quick oats, uncooked
1 12-oz pkg (2 cups) NESTLÉ Butterscotch Morsels
½ tsp orange extract

Preheat oven to 375°F. In small bowl, combine flour, baking powder, baking soda, and salt; set aside. In large bowl, combine butter, brown sugar, eggs, and water; beat until creamy. Gradually add flour mixture. Stir in oats, NESTLÉ Butterscotch Morsels, and orange extract. Drop by slightly rounded tablespoon onto greased cookie sheets. Bake 10–12 minutes. Makes 4 dozen 3-inch cookies.

Variations

Omit ½ tsp orange extract and substitute one of the following:

½ tsp orange rind
½ tsp lemon rind
½ tsp allspice
½ tsp mace
½ tsp cloves
½ tsp nutmeg
1 tsp ginger
1 tsp cinnamon
2 Tbsp molasses

COURTESY THE NESTLE COMPANY, INC.

Maypo Barbara Uhlmann's Oatmeal Cookies

¾ cup soft shortening
1 cup brown sugar, firmly packed
½ cup granulated sugar
1 egg
¼ cup water
1 tsp vanilla
1 cup sifted flour
1 tsp salt
½ tsp soda
3 cups MAYPO 30-Second Oatmeal
1 cup raisins
1 cup chopped nuts

Cream shortening and sugars. Add egg, water, and vanilla; mix well. Sift dry ingredients together; add to creamed mixture and blend well. Stir in MAYPO Oatmeal, raisins, and nuts; mix thoroughly. Drop by teaspoon onto lightly greased cookie sheet. Bake in preheated 350°F oven 12–15 minutes, or until tests done. Remove from pan; cool on rack. Makes about 5 dozen.

COURTESY STANDARD MILLING COMPANY.

"M&M's" Chocolate Crunch Cookies

1 cup butter or margarine
1½ cups firmly packed light brown sugar
2 eggs
1½ tsp vanilla
2½ cups flour
1 tsp salt
¾ tsp soda

1½ cups "M&M's" Plain Chocolate Candies
½ cup chopped nuts, if desired

Beat together butter and sugar until light and fluffy; blend in eggs with vanilla. Add combined dry ingredients; mix well. Add candies and nuts; mix well. Drop by rounded teaspoon onto greased cookie sheet. Bake at 375°F 9–11 minutes or until golden brown. Immediately press about 3 additional candies firmly into top of each cookie. Cool thoroughly. Makes about 5 dozen cookies.

COURTESY M&M/MARS.

Diamond Walnuts Rocky Road Walnut Drops

- *½ cup butter*
- *⅔ cup brown sugar, packed*
- *1 tsp vanilla*
- *1 egg, beaten*
- *½ cup (3 oz) semisweet real chocolate pieces, melted*
- *½ cup chopped DIAMOND Walnuts*
- *1½ cups sifted all-purpose flour*
- *½ tsp soda*
- *¾ tsp salt*
- *1 tsp instant coffee powder*
- *⅓ cup milk*
- *12 to 14 marshmallows*
- *36 to 40 DIAMOND Walnuts halves or large pieces*
- *Chocolate Frosting*

Cream butter, sugar, and vanilla until light and fluffy. Beat in egg. Add melted chocolate and walnuts, mixing well. Resift flour with soda, salt, and coffee powder. Add to creamed mixture, along with milk; stir until well blended. Drop by rounded tsp onto greased cookie sheets. Bake at 350°F 10 minutes or just until cookies test done. (Be careful not to overbake, as cookies should be moist.) Cut marshmallows crosswise into thirds. As soon as cookies are baked, top each one with a marshmallow slice and return to oven 1 minute to set marshmallows. Remove cookies to wire racks; top each marshmallow with a walnut half or piece, pressing down lightly to make it stick. When cookies are nearly cool, place racks over waxed paper and carefully spoon or ladle warm Chocolate Frosting (see below) over each top. Let stand until set. Frosting that drips on waxed paper may be scraped up and reheated to use again. Makes 3–3¼ dozen cookies.

Chocolate Frosting

- *¼ cup butter or margarine*
- *⅓ cup milk or light cream*
- *½ cup (3 oz) semisweet real chocolate pieces*
- *¼ tsp salt*
- *1 tsp vanilla*
- *2½ cups sifted powdered sugar*

Combine butter, milk, and chocolate in top of double boiler. Place over hot (not boiling) water until melted and smooth, stirring occasionally. Add vanilla and beat in powdered sugar until smooth. Spoon warm frosting over baked cookies. *Note*: If a doubly thick frosting is desired, just double the frosting recipe. This heavy coating will make an almost candylike cookie.

COURTESY DIAMOND WALNUT GROWERS, INC., STOCKTON, CALIFORNIA.

Skippy Peanut Butter Cookies

2½ cups unsifted flour
1 tsp baking powder
1 tsp baking soda
1 tsp salt
1 cup corn oil margarine
1 cup SKIPPY Creamy or Super Chunk Peanut Butter
1 cup sugar
1 cup firmly packed brown sugar
2 eggs, beaten
1 tsp vanilla

Stir together flour, baking powder, baking soda, and salt. In large bowl, with mixer at medium speed, beat margarine and peanut butter until smooth. Beat in sugars until blended. Beat in eggs and vanilla. Add flour mixture and beat well. If necessary, chill dough. Shape into 1-inch balls. Place on ungreased cookie sheet, 2 inches apart. Flatten with floured fork, making crisscross pattern. Bake in 350°F oven 12 minutes or until lightly browned. Cool on wire rack. Makes 6 dozen 2-inch cookies.

Variations

Orange peanut butter cookies: Follow basic recipe. Add 2 Tbsp grated orange rind with eggs. Makes 6 dozen.

Coconut balls: Follow basic recipe. Roll in flaked coconut before baking. Makes 6 dozen.

Peanut butter sandwich cookies: Follow basic recipe. Spread bottoms of half of the cookies with peanut butter; top with remaining cookies. Makes about 3 dozen.

Jelly thumbprint cookies: Follow basic recipe. Instead of flattening with thumb, press small indentation in each with thumb. While the cookies are still warm, press again with thumb. Cool. Fill indentation with jelly or jam.

Peanut butter spritz cookies: Follow basic recipe. Put through cookie press. Bake as directed. If desired, dip ends in melted chocolate. Makes 8 dozen.

Peanut butter refrigerator cookies: Follow basic recipe. Shape into 2 rolls 1½ inches in diameter. Wrap in plastic wrap and refrigerate. Slice into ¼-inch-thick slices. Bake as directed. Makes about 8 dozen.

Peanut butter crackles: Follow basic recipe. Roll in sugar before placing on cookie sheet; do not flatten. Bake as directed 15–18 minutes. Immediately press chocolate candy kiss firmly into top of each cookie (cookie will crack around the edge).

COURTESY SKIPPY PEANUT BUTTER.

Peter Pan Peanutty Chocolate Surprises

- *1 cup PETER PAN Peanut Butter, Creamy or Crunchy*
- *1 stick (½ cup) butter or margarine*
- *1 cup packed brown sugar*
- *2 eggs*
- *1 cup flour*
- *1 tsp baking powder*
- *1 tsp cinnamon*
- *2 milk chocolate candy bars (8 oz each) or 1-lb bag chocolate kisses or stars*
- *Powdered sugar (optional)*

Cream peanut butter, butter, and sugar. Beat in eggs. Combine flour, baking powder, and cinnamon. Add gradually until well blended. Chill dough. Break chocolate bars, if used, into pieces. Wrap about 1 tsp dough around each chocolate piece. Place on cooky sheet and bake in 350°F oven 10–12 minutes. Remove and cool slightly. Roll in powdered sugar, if desired, and let cool completely. Yield: about 72 cookies.

COURTESY SWIFT & COMPANY.

Blue Diamond® Chinese Almond Cookies

- *½ cup BLUE DIAMOND® Whole Natural Almonds*
- *1 cup sifted all-purpose flour*
- *½ tsp baking powder*
- *¼ tsp salt*
- *½ cup butter or margarine*
- *⅓ cup granulated sugar*
- *½ tsp almond extract*
- *1 Tbsp gin, vodka, or water*

Reserve 36 whole almonds; finely chop or grind remainder. Sift flour with baking powder and salt. Thoroughly cream butter and sugar. Stir in all remaining ingredients except whole almonds. Form dough into 36 balls. Place on greased cookie sheets. Press 1 whole almond in center of each ball. Bake in 350°F oven 20 minutes or until lightly browned. Makes 3 dozen.

COURTESY CALIFORNIA ALMOND GROWERS EXCHANGE.

Smucker's Thimble Cookies

- ½ *cup butter or margarine*
- ⅓ *cup confectioners' sugar*
- 1 *egg, separated*
- ½ *tsp vanilla extract*
- 1 *cup unsifted flour, stirred before measuring*
- ⅛ *tsp salt*
- ¾ *cup finely chopped pecans*
- ½ *cup SMUCKER'S Red Raspberry Jelly*

Cream together butter and sugar. Add egg yolk and vanilla extract; beat well. Stir in flour and salt. If necessary, chill dough until firm enough to handle. Working with half the dough at a time, measure level teaspoon of dough onto waxed paper. Shape into ¾-inch balls. Using a fork, dip balls, one at a time, into slightly beaten egg white, then roll in nuts. Place 2 inches apart on ungreased baking sheets. With thimble or thumb, make a depression in center of each. Bake in 350°F oven 5 minutes. Remove from oven. Make depression again. Bake an additional 5–7 minutes or until set. Cool on racks. At serving time, fill centers with red raspberry jelly. Makes about 3½ dozen 1½-inch cookies.

COURTESY THE J. M. SMUCKER COMPANY.

Roman Meal Cereal Spice Drops

- ½ *cup shortening*
- 1½ *cups brown sugar, packed*
- 3 *eggs, slightly beaten*
- ¼ *cup milk*
- 1 *tsp vanilla*
- 1⅔ *cups sifted flour*
- 1½ *tsp baking powder*
- ½ *tsp salt*
- 1 *tsp cinnamon*
- 1 *tsp nutmeg*
- 1 *tsp cloves*
- 2 *cups ROMAN MEAL Cereal*
- 1 *cup raisins*
- 1 *cup chopped nuts (optional)*

Cream shortening and sugar. Blend in eggs, milk, and vanilla. Add flour sifted with baking powder, spices, and salt; mix thoroughly. Add cereal, raisins, and nuts. Drop from teaspoon about 2 inches apart onto cookie sheet. Bake 10–12 minutes at 375°F. Makes 4–5 dozen cookies.

COURTESY ROMAN MEAL COMPANY.

Friendship Rugelach (Crescent Cookies)

Friendship®

Dough

½ lb butter
1 cup FRIENDSHIP Cottage Cheese
2 cups flour
¼ tsp salt

Filling

½ cup chopped walnuts
½ cup chopped dates
½ cup sugar
½ cup milk

Mix all dough ingredients until smooth. Refrigerate 1 hour or more until firm. Combine all filling ingredients and simmer over low flame until tender and thick. Chill. Roll out dough so it's approximately ⅛-inch thick. Cut into 3-inch triangles. Place ½ tsp cold filling on each triangle and roll into crescent. (Sprinkle with cinnamon and sugar, if desired.) Place crescents on cookie sheet and bake at 400°F about 15–20 minutes, until brown. Brush with powdered sugar.

RECIPE COURTESY OF FRIENDSHIP FOODS' HOME ECONOMIST, HELEN SCHWARTZ.

None Such® Prize Cookies

1 cup shortening
1½ cups sugar
3 eggs
3 cups unsifted flour
1 tsp baking soda
½ tsp salt
1⅓ cups (½ 28-oz jar) NONE SUCH® Ready-to-Use Mince Meat

Preheat oven to 375°F. In large mixer bowl, cream together shortening and sugar. Add eggs, beating until smooth. Combine dry ingredients; gradually add to creamed mixture. Stir in mince meat. Drop by rounded teaspoon, 2 inches apart, onto greased baking sheets. Bake 8–10 minutes or until lightly browned. *For a less moist and more crisp cookie*, substitute one 9-oz pkg NONE SUCH® Condensed Mince Meat, crumbled, in place of ready-to-use mince meat. Makes about 6½ dozen cookies.

A TESTED RECIPE DEVELOPED IN THE BORDEN KITCHENS. NONE SUCH IS A REGISTERED TRADEMARK OF BORDEN, INC.

Coconut Macaroons

Baker's Coconuts

1⅓ cups (about) BAKER'S® ANGEL FLAKE® Coconut
⅓ cup sugar
2 Tbsp all-purpose flour
⅛ tsp salt
2 egg whites
½ tsp almond extract

Combine coconut, sugar, flour, and salt in mixing bowl. Stir in egg whites and almond extract; mix well. Drop from teaspoon onto lightly greased baking sheets. Garnish with candied cherry halves, if desired. Bake at 325°F 20–25 minutes, or until edges of cookies are golden brown. Remove from baking sheets immediately. Makes about 1½ dozen.

REPRODUCED COURTESY OF GENERAL FOODS CORP., OWNER OF THE REGISTERED TRADEMARKS BAKER'S AND ANGEL FLAKE.

Sun-Maid® Storybook Gingerbread Men

½ cup shortening
½ cup brown sugar (packed)
3¼ cups sifted all-purpose flour
1 tsp salt
1 tsp soda
½ tsp cinnamon
½ tsp ginger
⅛ tsp cloves
¾ cup molasses
¼ cup water
Frosting (see below)
SUN-MAID® Zante Currants (orange box)

Cream shortening and sugar together. Resift flour with salt, soda, and spices. Blend into creamed mixture alternately with molasses and water. Chill about 1 hour. Roll half the dough at a time, ¼ inch thick. Cut with floured gingerbread-man cutter. Lift onto lightly greased baking sheets, using broad spatula. Return scraps of dough to refrigerator while rolling second portion. Bake above oven center in moderate oven (350°F) about 12 minutes, until cookies spring back when touched lightly in center. Do not allow cookies to brown. Cool 1 minute on baking sheet, then remove to wire racks. When cold, decorate with Frosting (see below) and currants. Makes 20 men, each 4 inches tall.

Frosting

1 cup sifted powdered sugar
1 tsp light corn syrup
2½ tsp warm water
¼ tsp vanilla

Stir together sugar, corn syrup, water, and vanilla.

COURTESY SUN-MAID GROWERS OF CALIFORNIA, KINGSBURG, CALIFORNIA.

Kellogg's®

Kellogg's® Cherry Winks

- 2¼ *cups regular all-purpose flour*
- 2 *tsp baking powder*
- ½ *tsp salt*
- ¾ *cup regular margarine or butter, softened*
- 1 *cup sugar*
- 2 *eggs*
- 2 *Tbsp milk*
- 1 *tsp vanilla flavoring*
- 1 *cup chopped nuts*
- 1 *cup finely cut, pitted dates*
- ⅓ *cup finely chopped maraschino cherries*
- 2⅔ *cups KELLOGG'S CORN FLAKES® cereal, crushed to measure 1⅓ cups*
- 15 *maraschino cherries, cut into quarters*

Stir together flour, baking powder, and salt. Set aside. In large mixing bowl, beat margarine and sugar until light and fluffy. Add eggs. Beat well. Stir in milk and vanilla. Add flour mixture. Mix until well combined. Stir in nuts, dates, and chopped cherries. Portion dough, using level tablespoon. Shape into balls. Roll in crushed cereal. Place about 2 inches apart on greased baking sheets. Top each with cherry quarter. Bake in oven at 375°F about 10 minutes or until lightly browned. Remove immediately from baking sheets. Cool on wire racks. Yield: about 5 dozen.

COURTESY OF KELLOGG COMPANY.

HERSHEY'S®

Hershey's Honey Brownies
(formerly Honeybear Brownies)

- ⅓ *cup butter or margarine*
- ¾ *cup sugar*
- ⅓ *cup honey*
- 2 *tsp vanilla*
- 2 *eggs*
- ½ *cup unsifted all-purpose flour*
- ⅓ *cup HERSHEY'S Cocoa*
- ½ *tsp salt*
- 1 *cup chopped nuts*

Grease one 9-inch-square pan. Cream butter and sugar in small mixer bowl; blend in honey and vanilla. Add eggs, one at a time, beating well after each addition. Combine flour, HERSHEY'S Cocoa, and salt; gradually add to creamed mixture. Stir in nuts. Pour into pan. Bake at 350°F 25–30 minutes or until brownies begin to pull away from edge of pan. Cool in pan. Frost with Creamy Brownie Frosting (recipe follows) and cut. Makes 16 brownies.

Creamy Brownie Frosting

3 Tbsp butter
3 Tbsp HERSHEY'S Cocoa
1 Tbsp honey
½ tsp vanilla
1 cup confectioners' sugar
1 to 2 Tbsp milk

Cream butter, HERSHEY'S Cocoa, honey, and vanilla in small mixer bowl; add confectioners' sugar and milk, beating until of spreading consistency. Yield: about 1 cup frosting.

THESE RECIPES HAVE BEEN DEVELOPED, TESTED AND APPROVED BY HERSHEY FOODS CORPORATION'S TEST KITCHEN.

Brownies

2 squares BAKER'S® Unsweetened Chocolate
⅓ cup soft butter or other shortening
⅔ cup unsifted all-purpose flour or ¾ cup sifted SWANS DOWN® Cake Flour
½ tsp CALUMET® Baking Powder
¼ tsp salt
2 eggs

1 cup sugar
1 tsp vanilla
½ cup chopped nuts or ¾ cup BAKER'S ANGEL FLAKE® Coconut

Melt chocolate with butter over low heat. Mix flour with baking powder and salt. Beat eggs well; then gradually beat in sugar. Blend in chocolate mixture and vanilla. Add flour mixture and mix well. Stir in nuts. Spread in greased 8-inch-square pan. Bake at 350°F for 25 minutes (for moist chewy brownies) or about 30 minutes or until cake tester inserted in center comes out clean (for cakelike brownies). Cool in pan; then cut into squares or rectangles. Makes about 20 brownies. *Note*: Recipe may be doubled; bake in greased 13 X 9-inch pan at 350°F 25–30 minutes as directed. Makes about 40 brownies.

JIF Layered Peanut Butter Brownies

2 cups JIF Creamy Peanut Butter
1 cup sugar
2 eggs
1 family-size pkg brownie mix

Preheat oven to 350°F. Combine JIF Creamy Peanut Butter, sugar, and eggs. Spread in greased 13 X 9 X 2-inch baking pan. Prepare brownie mix according to package directions for cake-like brownies. Spread over layer in pan. Bake in 350°F oven for 40 minutes. Cool; cut into triangles or bars. Makes about 2 dozen.
COURTESY OF THE PROCTER & GAMBLE COMPANY.

Diamond Walnuts Chewy Walnut Squares

1 cup brown sugar, firmly packed
1 tsp vanilla
1 large egg
½ cup all-purpose flour
¼ tsp soda
¼ tsp salt
1 cup coarsely chopped DIAMOND Walnuts

Measure brown sugar and vanilla into mixing bowl and add egg. Stir until smooth and well blended. Sift flour with soda and salt. Add to first mixture and stir until all of flour is moistened. Fold in walnuts. Turn into 8-inch-square prepared, lined pan and spread with spoon or spatula. Bake at 350°F 18–20 minutes. Cookies will be soft in center when baked. Cool in pan. Lift from pan by paper (instructions follow) and place on cutting board. Peel off paper and cut into squares with sharp knife. Makes 16 squares, each about 1¾ inches.

Paper Pan Liner

Center 8-inch-square pan on 12-inch square of brown paper. Outline base of pan with a pencil. Continue lines to edge of paper. Fold along marked lines and cut from edge of paper to line marking pan's edge along 2 opposite sides. Grease pan. Fit paper liner in pan and grease paper. This easy way to line a pan can be used for all bar cookies, and helps prevent broken edges and corners.
COURTESY DIAMOND WALNUT GROWERS, INC., STOCKTON, CALIFORNIA.

Eagle® Brand Magic Cookie Bars

½ *cup margarine or butter*
1½ *cups graham cracker crumbs*
1 *14-oz can EAGLE® Brand Sweetened Condensed Milk (not evaporated milk)*
1 *6-oz pkg semisweet chocolate morsels*
1 *3½-oz can flaked coconut (1⅓ cups)*
1 *cup chopped nuts*

Preheat oven to 350°F (325°F for glass dish). In 13 X 9-inch baking pan, melt margarine in oven. Sprinkle crumbs over margarine; pour sweetened condensed milk evenly over crumbs. Top evenly with remaining ingredients; press down gently. Bake 25–30 minutes or until lightly browned. Cool thoroughly before cutting. Store, loosely covered, at room temperature. Makes 24 bars.

A TESTED RECIPE DEVELOPED IN THE BORDEN KITCHENS. EAGLE BRAND IS A REGISTERED TRADEMARK OF BORDEN, INC.

Jack Frost Lemon Squares

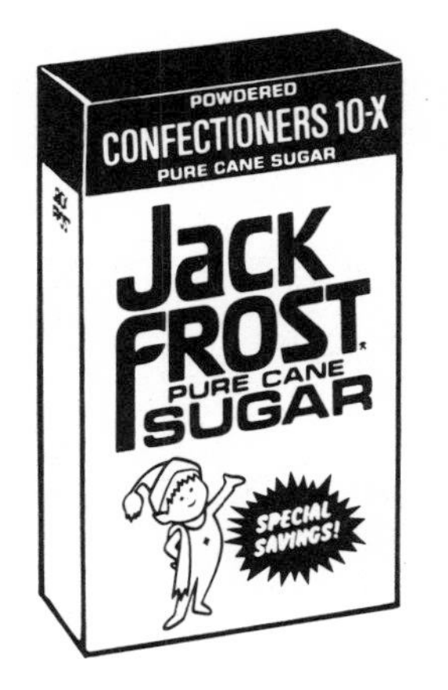

Bottom Layer

½ *cup butter or margarine*
1 *cup sifted flour*
¼ *cup JACK FROST 10X Confectioners Sugar*

Top Layer

1 *cup JACK FROST Granulated Sugar*
2 *Tbsp flour*
½ *tsp baking powder*
2 *eggs, beaten*
3 *Tbsp lemon juice*

Preheat oven to 350°F. Cream butter with sugar, and add flour slowly. Pat into 8-inch-square pan. Bake 15 minutes. Combine ingredients for top layer; pour over baked bottom layer. Bake 25 minutes. Sprinkle with JACK FROST 10X Confectioners Sugar while hot. Cut into squares. Yields 2 dozen.

COURTESY JACK FROST SUGAR.

Quaker® 100% Natural Granola Bars

3 cups QUAKER® 100% Natural Cereal
½ cup raisins
⅓ cup wheat germ
⅓ cup firmly packed brown sugar
¼ cup butter or margarine
3 Tbsp honey

Combine cereal, raisins, and wheat germ in large bowl. Combine sugar, butter, and honey. Cook over low heat, stirring occasionally, until smooth. Pour over cereal mixture; mix well. Firmly press into a foil-lined 9-inch square baking pan. Bake in preheated moderate oven (350°F) 12–14 minutes or until golden brown. Cool completely. Remove pan and foil; cut into bars. Makes 9-inch square. *Variation*: Substitute ⅔ cup finely chopped nuts for wheat germ.

RECIPE REPRODUCED WITH THE PERMISSION OF THE QUAKER OATS COMPANY.

Princeton Farms Caramel Popcorn Crunch

½-lb pkg dairy-fresh caramels (28 caramels)
2 Tbsp water
2 qt PRINCETON FARMS Popped Corn, salted

Add water to caramels and melt in top of double boiler. Toss mixture with popcorn till every kernel is coated. Spread and dry on greased surface. Break apart.

COURTESY PRINCETON FARMS.

Tootsie Roll Polka Dot Popcorn Treats

2 cups miniature (1¢) TOOTSIE ROLLS, cut into ½-inch pieces (about 50 rolls)
6 qt popped corn
1 cup chopped walnuts
2 cups sugar

⅔ cup light corn syrup
⅔ cup water
½ cup (1 stick) butter

Mix together TOOTSIE ROLL pieces, popped corn, and nuts in a large bowl. Cook sugar, syrup, water, and butter to a hard crack stage (240°F). Pour over corn mixture and toss to coat. With buttered hands, shape mixture into about 12–15 balls. Let cool.

COURTESY TOOTSIE ROLL INDUSTRIES, INC.

Argo Melting Moments

1 cup unsifted flour
½ cup ARGO or KINGSFORD'S Corn Starch
½ cup confectioners' sugar
¾ cup corn oil margarine

In medium bowl, stir flour, corn starch, and confectioners' sugar. In large bowl with mixer at medium speed, beat margarine until smooth. Add flour mixture and beat until combined. Refrigerate 1 hour. Shape into 1-inch balls. Place about 1½ inches apart on ungreased cookie sheet; flatten with lightly floured fork. Bake in 300°F oven 20 minutes or until edges are lightly browned. Makes about 3 dozen cookies.

Melting Moments with Nuts: Follow recipe for Melting Moments. Shape dough into 1-inch balls or into logs ½ inch thick and 3 inches long. Roll in finely chopped nuts. Bake. *Or*: Scatter nuts on waxed paper, place balls of dough on nuts, and flatten with bottom of glass dipped in flour. With spatula, place cookies nut-side-up on ungreased cookie sheet. Bake.

Chocolate Melting Moments: Follow recipe for Melting Moments. Stir ¼ cup cocoa and ¼ tsp salt with dry ingredients. If desired, place a nut on top of each cookie before baking.

Rich Chocolate Melting Moments: Follow recipe for Melting Moments. Stir 1 square (1 oz) semisweet chocolate, melted and cooled into margarine.

Coconut Melting Moments: Follow recipe for Melting Moments. Add 1 cup finely chopped flaked coconut to flour mixture.

Melting Moments Amandine: Follow recipe for Melting Moments. Add 1 cup finely chopped almonds to flour mixture.

COURTESY ARGO CORN STARCH.

Kellogg's

Kellogg's® Rice Krispies® Marshmallow Treats

¼ cup regular margarine or butter
1 pkg (10 oz, about 40) regular marshmallows, or
4 cups miniature marshmallows*
5 cups KELLOGG'S® RICE KRISPIES® cereal

Melt margarine in large saucepan over low heat. Add marshmallows and stir until completely melted. Cook over low heat 3 minutes longer, stirring constantly. Remove from heat. Add cereal. Stir until well coated. Using buttered spatula or waxed paper, press mixture evenly into buttered 13 X 9 X 2-inch pan. Cut into 2-inch squares when cool. Yield: 24 squares, 2 X 2 inches.

Variations

To make thicker squares, press warm mixture into buttered 9 X 9 X 2-inch pan.

Marshmallow Creme Treats: About 2 cups marshmallow creme may be substituted for marshmallows. Add to melted margarine and stir until well blended. Cook over low heat about 5 minutes longer, stirring constantly. Remove from heat. Add cereal and proceed as directed above.

Peanut Treats: Add 1 cup salted cocktail peanuts to the cereal.

Peanut Butter Treats: Stir ¼ cup peanut butter into marshmallow mixture just before adding the cereal.

Raisin Treats: Add 1 cup seedless raisins to the cereal.

COCOA KRISPIES® Cereal Treats: 6 cups COCOA KRISPIES cereal may be substituted for the 5 cups RICE KRISPIES cereal.

*Best results are obtained when using fresh marshmallows.
COURTESY OF KELLOGG COMPANY.

Nestlé

Nestlé Scotch Crispies

- 1 12-oz pkg (2 cups) NESTLÉ Butterscotch Morsels
- 1 cup peanut butter
- 6 cups oven-toasted rice cereal

Melt over hot (not boiling) water, NESTLÉ Butterscotch Morsels and peanut butter; stir until morsels melt and mixture is smooth. Transfer butterscotch mixture to large bowl. Add rice cereal; mix well. Press mixture into aluminum foil-lined 13 X 9 X 2-inch baking pan. Chill in refrigerator until firm (about 1 hour). Cut into 1½-inch squares. Makes 48 1½-inch squares.

COURTESY THE NESTLE COMPANY, INC.

Domino® Creamy New Orleans Pralines

1½ cups firmly packed DOMINO® Light or Dark Brown Sugar
1½ cups DOMINO® Granulated Sugar
1 cup evaporated milk
3 Tbsp butter
½ tsp vanilla extract
2 cups pecan halves

Combine sugars and milk. Place over low heat and stir until dissolved. Bring to boil; lower heat and cook to 234°F. Remove from heat; add butter, extract; cool to 200°F without stirring. Add pecans. Beat until creamy and candy holds shape. Drop by large spoonfuls on buttered surface or waxed paper. Yield: 12–18 pralines.

COURTESY AMSTAR CORPORATION, AMERICAN SUGAR DIVISION.

Blue Diamond® Choco-Almond Confections

1¼ cup BLUE DIAMOND® Chopped Natural Almonds, toasted
3 squares (1 oz each) milk chocolate
½ cup orange juice
½ cup granulated sugar
3 cups crushed lemon, orange, or vanilla wafers
2 Tbsp Curaçao or orange juice

In blender or food processor, finely grind ¼ cup almonds; set aside. Combine chocolate with orange juice and sugar in saucepan. Cook over medium heat, stirring constantly until sugar is dissolved and chocolate is melted. Remove from heat and mix in crushed wafers, Curaçao, and chopped almonds. Chill mixture at least 1 hour. Form into small balls; roll in the ground almonds. Refrigerate in airtight container for several days, for best flavor to develop. Makes about 3 dozen.

COURTESY CALIFORNIA ALMOND GROWERS EXCHANGE.

Kraft Caramel Apples

49 (14-oz bag) KRAFT Caramels
2 Tbsp water
4 or 5 medium-size apples, washed and dried
Wooden sticks

Melt caramels with water in covered double boiler or in saucepan over low heat. Stir occasionally until sauce is smooth. Insert a wooden stick into stem end of each apple. Dip into hot caramel sauce; turn until coated. Scrape off excess sauce from bottom of apples. Place on greased waxed paper; chill until firm. Keep in cool place.

COURTESY OF KRAFT, INC.

Nabisco "Some Mores" Sandwiches

4 (1.2-oz) milk chocolate candy bars
24 NABISCO Graham Crackers squares
12 large marshmallows

Divide each chocolate bar into 3 (about 2-inch) squares. Top 12 NABISCO Graham Crackers with a square of chocolate and a marshmallow. Place on a cookie sheet and bake in a preheated moderate oven (350°F) about 5–7 minutes, or until marshmallows are lightly browned. Then top with remaining crackers; press together lighty to make sandwiches. Makes 12 (about 2½ X 2½-inch) sandwiches.

COURTESY NABISCO, INC.

Diamond Walnuts White Fudge

2 cups granulated sugar
½ cup dairy sour cream
⅓ cup white corn syrup
2 Tbsp butter
¼ tsp salt
2 tsp vanilla, rum, or brandy flavoring
¼ cup quartered candied cherries
1 cup coarsely chopped DIAMOND Walnuts

Combine first 5 ingredients in saucepan; bring to a boil slowly, stirring until sugar dissolves. Boil, without stirring, over medium heat to 236°F on candy thermometer, or until a little mixture dropped in cold water forms a soft ball. Remove from heat and

let stand 15 minutes; do not stir. Add flavoring; beat until mixture starts to lose its gloss (about 8 minutes). Stir in cherries and walnuts and quickly pour into a greased shallow pan. Cool and cut into squares. Makes about 1½ lb fudge.
COURTESY DIAMOND WALNUT GROWERS, INC., STOCKTON, CALIFORNIA.

Hershey's Old-Fashioned Creamy Fudge

2 cups sugar
¾ cup milk
2½ blocks (2½ oz) HERSHEY'S Baking Chocolate
2 Tbsp light corn syrup
¼ tsp salt
2 Tbsp butter
1 tsp vanilla

Combine sugar, milk, baking chocolate, corn syrup, and salt in a heavy 2-qt saucepan. Cook over medium heat, stirring constantly, until mixture boils. Cook, stirring occasionally, to 234°F (or until small amount dropped into cold water forms a soft ball). Remove from heat. Add butter and vanilla. Do not stir. Allow fudge to cool at room temperature without stirring until it reaches 110°F. Beat until fudge thickens and loses some of its gloss. Quickly pour fudge into a lightly buttered 8-inch-square pan. Yield: about 1½ lb fudge.
THIS RECIPE HAS BEEN DEVELOPED, TESTED AND APPROVED BY HERSHEY FOODS CORPORATION'S TEST KITCHEN.

Ovaltine Fudge Candy

2 cups brown sugar
2 1-oz envelopes OVALTINE Hot Cocoa Mix
4 Tbsp milk
1 tsp vanilla
¼ lb butter
1 cup chopped nut meats (optional)
1 tsp baking powder

Mix all ingredients. Place in an open pan. Let cook for 5 minutes after mixture comes to a boil. Stir constantly. Remove from heat and add baking powder. Stir until mixture starts to thicken. Pour into buttered pan. Yield: 12 servings.

Marshmallow Fluff Never Fail Fudge

5 cups sugar
1 large (13-oz) can evaporated milk
¼ lb butter or margarine
¾ lb (12 oz) MARSHMALLOW FLUFF
1 tsp salt
1 tsp vanilla
1 cup walnut meats (optional)
2 large (12-oz) pkg semisweet chocolate pieces

Combine first 5 ingredients in 4-qt saucepan. Stir over medium heat until blended. Bring to a boil over medium high heat and continue boiling for 5 minutes. (Do not mistake escaping air bubbles for boiling. Overcook rather than undercook.) Remove from heat. Stir in chocolate and vanilla (and nuts if used) until chocolate is melted. Pour into 2 buttered 9 X 9-inch pans and cool. Yield: approx. 5 lb.

COURTESY DURKEE-MOWER, INC.

Index

PASTE YOUR FAVORITE RECIPES HERE

PASTE YOUR FAVORITE RECIPES HERE

PASTE YOUR FAVORITE RECIPES HERE

PASTE YOUR FAVORITE RECIPES HERE

PASTE YOUR FAVORITE RECIPES HERE

PASTE YOUR FAVORITE RECIPES HERE

PASTE YOUR FAVORITE RECIPES HERE

PASTE YOUR FAVORITE RECIPES HERE